YANKEE BEACON OF BUDDHIST LIGHT

This man touched the heart of Asia as no other white man before him had ever done, and had he not lived, it would be safe to hazard a dogmatic statement that the history of Asia would have been written differently and America would have been faced with a problem of cosmic proportions.

Kewal Motwani, *Col. H. S. Olcott, A Forgotten Page of American History*

Colonel Olcott in days of military service, about 1861

YANKEE BEACON
OF BUDDHIST LIGHT
Life of Col. Henry S. Olcott

(formerly published as Hammer on the Mountain)

by Howard Murphet

*This publication made possible with
the assistance of the Kern Foundation*

 The Theosophical Publishing House
Wheaton, Ill. U.S.A.
Madras, India / London, England

The Theosophical Publishing House
306 West Geneva Road
Wheaton, IL 60187

A publication of the Theosophical Publishing House, a
department of the Theosophical Society in America.

Library of Congress Cataloging-in-Publication Data

Murphet, Howard.
  Yankee beacon of Buddhist light.

  (A Quest book)
  Originally published as: Hammer on the mountain,
1972.
  "H.S. Olcott's works": p.
  Bibliography: p.
  1. Olcott, Henry Steel, 1832-1907. 2. Theosophists—
Biography. 3. Buddhists—Biography. I. Title.
[BP585.04M8 1988]   299'.934'0924   [B]   88-40133
ISBN 0-8356-0638-4 (pbk.)

Printed in the United States of America

Cover design by MADHU

CONTENTS

LIST OF ILLUSTRATIONS

ACKNOWLEDGMENTS

In connection with his research for this biography, the author wishes to acknowledge gratefully the help given by Miss Helen V. Zahara, and other members of The Theosophical Society in America, in obtaining historical documents from the National Archives, and other centers in the U.S.A. Thanks are also due to Mr. Boris de Zirkoff for his ready assistance in supplying certain biographical data, and to Mr. Victor A. Endersby for a timely lead regarding Colonel H. S. Olcott's private life.

In the main the material for the biography was gathered from the archives of The Theosophical Society's international headquarters at Adyar, Madras, India: Olcott's handwritten diaries, kept without a break from 1874 until his death, correspondence (public and private), reports, lectures, certificates, pamphlets, H. P. Blavatsky's scrapbooks, and other documents.

In addition the following are the most important of the books and journals found of interest and value.

Old Diary Leaves (6 vols.), by Henry Steel Olcott, The Theosophical Publishing House, Madras, India, 1928-1935 (2nd edition).

People from the Other World, by Henry S. Olcott, American Publishing Co., Hartford, Conn., 1875.

Hints on Esoteric Theosophy, compiled by A. O. Hume, 1882.

Isis Unveiled, by H. P. Blavatsky, J. W. Bouton, New York, 1877 (original edition); part of *H. P. Blavatsky Collected Writings,* The Theosophical Publishing House, Wheaton, Illinois, 1972 (revised edition).

The Theosophical Movement (1875-1925), by members of the United Lodge of Theosophists, Los Angeles, E. P. Dutton & Co., New York, 1925.

A Short History of The Theosophical Society, by Josephine Ransom, The Theosophical Publishing House, Madras, India, 1938.

Theosophy, by Alvin Boyd Kuhn, Henry Holt & Co., New York, 1930.

The Occult World, by A. P. Sinnett, The Theosophical Publishing House, London, 1969 (9th edition).

Esoteric Buddhism, by A. P. Sinnett, Houghton Mifflin Co., 1884.

Damodar, by Sven Eek, The Theosophical Publishing House, Madras, India, 1965.

William Quan Judge: A Theosophical Pioneer, compiled by Sven Eek and Boris de Zirkoff, The Theosophical Publishing House, Wheaton, Illinois, 1969.

The Mahatma Letters to A. P. Sinnett, transcribed and compiled by A. T. Barker, The Theosophical Publishing House, Madras, India, 1962 (3rd edition).

Letters from the Masters of the Wisdom (First and Second Series), compiled by C. Jinarajadasa, The Theosophical Publishing House, Madras, India, 1919.

The Real H. P. Blavatsky, by William Kingsland, John M. Watkins, London, 1928.

Some Account of My Intercourse With Madame Blavatsky, by Madame Coulomb, 1885.

Defense of Madame Blavatsky (2 vols.), by Beatrice Hastings, privately published in England, 1937.

Obituary: The Hodgson Report on Madame Blavatsky, by Adlai E. Waterman, The Theosophical Publishing House, Madras, India, 1963.

Proceedings of The Society for Psychical Research, December 1885, London.

The Hall of Magic Mirrors, by Victor A. Endersby, Carlton Press, New York, 1969.

The Fall of the British Empire, by Colin Cross, Coward-McCann, Inc., New York, 1969.

The Web of Conspiracy, by Theodore Roscoe, Prentice-Hall, New York, 1969.

"The War's Carnival of Fraud," by Henry S. Olcott, published in *The Annals of War,* The Times Publishing Co., Philadelphia, 1879.

The Theosophist (early issues), journal of The Theosophical Society, Adyar, Madras, India.

"How We Hanged John Brown," from *New India,* November 17, 1928.

HOWARD MURPHET

PROLOGUE

In the middle years of the last century an Indian poet, saint, and alchemist, known as Ramalingar Pillay, roamed southern India, teaching, preaching, composing and singing the praises of God. He is credited with having had a number of supernormal, yogic powers, the most unusual one being his power to fool the camera. No photographer ever succeeded in getting a true picture of the saint; always his face, hands, and feet had vanished leaving a blob of white.

The theme he preached most forcefully was the universal brotherhood of man. He formed a society to put the principles of such brotherhood into practice and to propagate the true Vedic doctrines. But though people flocked around him to witness his miracles and to gain what benefits they could from his powers, they did not really want to practice his tenets of brotherhood; these called for too much sacrifice of personal wealth.

Pained and disappointed by his failure, the saint told his listeners that they were not fit to be members of his society. Yet he assured them that a true Brotherhood did exist. It was in the far north of India, and its teachings would, in time, be spread throughout India and abroad. The saint prophesied that, a few years after his own passing, a person from Russia and another from America would come to India and launch a movement for the recognition and understanding of the universal brotherhood of man. Other foreigners would join them and help to make known the great truths which he, himself, had failed to propagate. The movement would be inspired and spurred on by the great Brotherhood of the far north. Many wonders would be worked in

India, and the doctrines would be spread throughout the world.

Ramalingar Pillay, like a "Voice crying in the wilderness," spoke prophecies to that effect on many occasions. The first of several of his followers to put them on record was a Tamil pundit of the Presidency College in Madras who wrote an article on Saint Ramalingar Pillay for *The Theosophist* of July 1882.

As interesting as his prophecy was the manner of the saint's death. He had for a year or two been announcing his intention of going into permanent *samadhi*. In 1874 — the year when the Russian and American, destined to fulfill his prediction, first met—he carried out his intention.

"On the 30th of that month (January), at Metucupam, we saw our master for the last time," writes the Tamil pundit. "Selecting a small building he entered its solitary room after taking an affectionate farewell of his *chelas,* stretched himself on the carpet, and then, by his orders the door was locked and the only opening walled-up."

In accordance with the saint's instructions, none of his followers attempted to open the room. But after about a year the door was forced open by order of the British authorities. Nothing was to be seen but a vacant room.

The British Collector of the area, Mr. J. H. Garstin, I.C.S., suspecting foul play, ordered a thorough search of the place. But no traces of the devout old poet-saint were ever found. "The components of his body were given back to the original elements," said his followers.

This must have been a hard story to swallow for the two British officials of the area—Mr. Garstin and the District Medical Officer. But perhaps they had learned that in India scientific law and common sense are often confounded. So they decided officially that he was a very great saint, and the records of the district tell that the two British officials contributed money for a function in which a crowd of poor people were fed to honor his memory.

Chapter 1

OF PURITAN STOCK

"What can ennoble fools or cowards? Alas, not all the blood of all the Howards!" quoted Henry Steel* Olcott when, in 1874, he edited a book on his ancestry. Henry was proud of the Puritan stock from which he had sprung, considering it "a better heritage than even a share of the blood royal."

The book went back to the first Olcott to settle in America, and once, when visiting England, Henry tried to trace the deeper roots of his family tree. He formed the opinion that he had probably descended from Bishop Dr. John Alcock, a favorite of Henry VII, who in 1496 founded Jesus College, Cambridge. But this descent was not properly established, and Henry wrote that some other member of the family should continue the research.

Someone did, but failed to get back as far as Dr. John Alcock. *The Olcotts and Their Kindred,* by Mary L. B. Olcott, was published in 1956. It traces the Olcott tree back through recorded father-to-son line of descent to Randle Alcock who was born in about 1580. The book says, however, that the name Olcott evolved from the Norman place name, Olcotes. It is found in the old London records under various weird spellings. In the Pipe Rolls of John (1199-1216) it is rendered as Ulecote, Ulcote, Ulecott, Hullcote and other variations. Sometimes it became Alcock, Alcocke, Allcox, and so on. The cock must have been important somewhere along the line because one stands vigilantly at the crest of the Olcott family's coat-of-arms. The motto written beneath is "Vigilate" (Be watchful).

---

* In many publications this is incorrectly spelled "Steele."

Four generations after Randle Alcock, his descendant Thomas Olcott (at times written Thomas Alcock) set off for the wilds of America. He did not go with the Pilgrim Fathers in the *Mayflower* but some ten years later. The records of those who sailed in this period (between 1632 and 1636) were burned, but it was in one of those years that young Thomas Olcott crossed to the New World—whether for adventure, for gain, or for conscience' sake history does not tell.

In 1638 his name appears in the records of Hartford, Connecticut, as a landowner and trader. His trading enterprises took him as far south as Virginia, and on one of these trips he died. He had only been some twenty years in the Colony, but in that time had established a sound commercial enterprise which his widow and sons carried on for many years at Hartford. Among the goods listed in the will of this pioneer Olcott were seven books, two of which were Bibles.

Tracing the line down through Thomas's second son, Samuel, we come, after six generations, to Henry Wyckoff Olcott, living in the year 1832 in Orange, New Jersey, and engaged in business.

On August 2nd of that year, the seventh generation of the line, after pioneer Thomas, was ushered in with the birth of the first child to Henry Wyckoff and his wife Emily (nee Steel). They called the child Henry Steel, following the custom of giving the mother's maiden name to the first son.

Three years later came the second child, Isabella; then two more daughters—Anna and Emily. Henry Steel was fourteen years old before his first brother, Emmett Robinson, was born. Then four years afterwards, the youngest of the family, George Potts, appeared.

After bearing this family of six, spaced out from 1832 to 1850, Emily Olcott died. She was forty-four years old at the time, and her youngest son, George, was only six. Presumably Isabella (known as Belle), then twenty-one, took over the role of mother and housekeeper.

Henry Wyckoff survived his widow for many years. He was apparently still alive when Henry Steel revised and brought up-to-date the book on the Olcott ancestry in 1874. It records his mother's death as in 1856, but not that of his father, Henry Wyckoff.

The parents were typical New World Puritans—religious, God-fearing, devout. The mother had a reputation for great piety in the family circles, and Henry Steel writes lovingly of his "noble and revered parents."

But little is known of the boy's home life and childhood. At some time the family moved from Orange to New York City and Henry attended one of the public schools there. He must have done very well at the school for, at the age of fifteen, he entered New York University. But after a year there his formal education was brought to an abrupt end.

Some misfortune struck Henry senior's business interests, and funds were not available for Henry junior to continue at college. So at the age of sixteen, his education incomplete, untrained for any profession, and with no opening for him in his father's business, young Henry had to get out and carve some career for himself.

Chapter 2

YEARS OF PREPARATION
1848 - 1874

We next hear of Henry following a plough in the fields of Ohio, near Elyria, share-farming a 50-acre plot. Why he jumped from a university in New York and a commercial family background to such an occupation is hard to say. But he seems by disposition to have needed at times to make a clean break with the old and launch out on the completely new. He enjoyed a challenge. The pioneer blood ran strongly in his veins. But what was the practical link between the old life and the new? We get a hint of that from his own writings later in his life.

At about this time—to be precise, in the year 1848 when Henry left home—modern spiritualism made its debut before the world. It began in a humble way at Rochester, N.Y., in the home of John Fox whose daughters heard knockings and rappings on walls and furniture. No physical cause of the noises could be found. Tests were made, questions were asked. Answers came from whatever agencies lay behind the rappings. This was done according to a prearranged code, such as one knock for "yes," two for "no," and three for "maybe."

The phenomena developed much beyond this, and began in other centers, both in America and Europe. The attention of the whole western world was soon drawn to the flood of fantastic phenomena—levitations, materializations, apports, direct voice communications, and so forth.

The majority of people scoffed, but many did not. Home circles for trial and investigation were formed in all classes of society, from the humble log cabin to the fashionable drawing rooms of New York, Paris, London. Some leading

men of the time became interested, while many turned their
heads aside, afraid to look. The press generally was hostile,
though some leading newspapers treated the occurrences
without prejudice. And the movement soon had its own
press supporting it. Spiritualism, with all its psychical and
physical phenomena, was one of the most startling and significant developments of the latter half of the nineteenth
century.

Under different names, and perhaps in milder forms, this
same force has been known since the beginning of recorded
history. Its strong appearance in the nineteenth century was
not at first a public one. During the decade before 1848,
when the Fox sisters heard the rappings that echoed round
the world, communications with beings of some invisible
sphere had been practiced quietly and secretly by the Society
of Shakers, and perhaps others.

But by the mid-century everybody was hearing about spiritualism, and naturally many were curious. The curiosity
and interest were heightened by the fact that the invisible
entities claimed to be souls of those who had lived on earth,
while at the same time the philosophers of modern science—
custodians of the new learning—were stating emphatically
that man was entirely mortal, that he had no soul to live on
after his death.

Henry, brought up by strictly orthodox Presbyterian parents, was introduced to spiritualism by his mother's brothers,
Edgar, Isaac, and George Steel. These men with their families were apparently landowners and farmers in Ohio within
easy reach of Henry's 50-acre plot. Writing in his *Old Diary
Leaves* toward the end of his life, Olcott mentions having
contacted these Steel brothers again at a later period in Cali-
fornia, where they had moved and become owners of large
ranches. He says, "I may almost regard them as my greatest
benefactors in this incarnation, since it was from them, and
the other bright minds and noble souls connected with them
in a spiritualistic group, that I first learned to think and
aspire along the lines which led me ultimately to H.P.B.*
and the Theosophical movement."

So it seems possible, and likely, that as well as introducing

---
* H. P. Blavatsky

him to spiritualism, the Steel brothers were the link that brought him as a lad to farming life in Ohio.

Another study that helped feed the mind of a youth, starved by the dull routine and heavy physical labor of farming, was mesmerism. This had become fashionable and popular a little before spiritualism. Its discoverer, Dr. F. A. Mesmer of Austria, had postulated that a vital magnetic current or fluid—called Od—could be made to flow from an operator to his patient with powerful and obvious effects. Mesmer was hounded out of Vienna and Paris by the conservative medical interests, and died in obscurity in Switzerland. But many people read his books and tried to practice the mesmeric system on compliant friends. One of these amateur mesmerists was young Henry who, with a good fund of vitality in his constitution, found himself getting tangible results.

Then the opportunity came to put the system and his own powers to a practical test. The daughter of a neighboring farmer had to undergo a difficult dental operation. Those were the days before chemical anaesthetics were readily available, especially in country districts. With the permission of her parents, Henry accompanied the girl to the dentist, and just before the operation performed his mesmeric passes, willing the flow of Od, the vital current, to the appropriate part of the girl's anatomy to act as a local anaesthetic. Then Henry waited anxiously to see what good, if any, his mesmeric art had achieved.

The operation, it is reported, was successful, the patient feeling none of the terrible pain she must have suffered but for Dr. Mesmer and the young farmer.

These realistic years close to nature, the smell of the soil in his nostrils, the handle of the plough or pitchfork in his hands, were perhaps better for character formation than college education. But the obscure life of an Ohio farmer was not to be his destiny. His brain was too active, his ambitions too strong for that. After four or five years of country life, he returned East to study agricultural chemistry and other aspects of scientific farming.

We are not told where the money came from for these studies; most likely Henry had saved it from his farming profits. The course of study took place at the model farm of Professor J. J. Mapes, near Newark, New Jersey. Mapes, too, was interested in spiritualism.

So under his influence Henry was led further away from the strict Puritan fold in which he had been reared. Also he became assistant editor of the professor's magazine, *The Working Farmer,* and discovered his talent for journalism.

After about two years of training in scientific agriculture, a stroke of luck took Henry another step onward toward his destiny. A relative left him a legacy. This was sufficient for him to join forces with a fellow student of Newark and start his own school of agricultural science. Situated near Mount Vernon, New York, it was called the Westchester Farm School. It was based on Swiss models, and was one of the pioneers of scientific agricultural education in America. From here the American public began to hear the name of Henry Steel Olcott for the first time.

Tensions between the slave states of the South and the free states of the North, and talk by the South of secession from the Union, were at this time being felt and heard. War seemed imminent, and the North wanted to be independent of the South for its vital supply of sugar. Many people thought that a Chinese sugar, called sorgho, might be grown in the North, and provide the answer. Seeds of sorgho were brought from France, where it had been cultivated, and several plantation owners experimented with trying to grow it there.

Henry Olcott planted some of the seeds at Westchester, and with typical thoroughness, went wholeheartedly into the culture and refinement of both sorgho and an African sugar plant called imphee. He became an authority on this politically important matter, and was asked to lecture in 1856 before the legislatures of Ohio, Massachusetts, and New York. These lectures he expanded into a book published in 1857, entitled: *Sorgho and Imphee, The Chinese and African Sugar Canes: A Treatise on Origin, Varieties and Culture.* It went through seven editions, and was placed by the State of Illinois in its libraries and recommended as a school text.

Henry's second book, *Yale Agricultural Lectures,* followed in 1858, and in the same year, at the age of 26, he made his first trip abroad. He visited various European countries to study and report on agricultural schools there. We are not told who sponsored—and paid expenses for—this European tour, but Henry's report on the schools appeared in the first edition of *Appleton's American Cyclopedia, 1859.*

Then the promising career he was building for himself in this field of activity crashed. Despite the name he was making in agricultural and educational circles, his Westchester Farm School had to close for want of support. Perhaps this pioneer work was a little ahead of the times. Whatever the reason, the project failed and his small capital was lost. As when his father's financial difficulties had interrupted his education, Henry found himself back at base, with nothing.

But the truth of the saying among Buddhists—"When one door closes, another opens"—was demonstrated. Several doors opened to young Olcott, according to a biographical sketch written by his friend Alexander Fullerton. Two of these were: the directorship of the Agricultural Bureau in Washington, and the Chair of Agriculture at the University of Athens in Greece. Fullerton does not say why neither of these offers was accepted. It seems that this independent young man had no taste for officialdom, and no doubt he felt that his destiny lay in other directions. It was, unknown to himself, leading him toward new experiences which would be of value to the main work he had to do in life.

*   *   *

After the farm school closed, he went to live at the New York family home run by his sister Isabella ("Belle"). His mother had died a couple of years earlier—"praying till the last," according to one of her nephews, "that her wayward son, Henry, would return to the Christian fold." This prayer must have been inspired by his deviation into spiritualism, as his work for Theosophy and his adoption of the Buddhist religion did not come until long after her death.

Olcott's experience in teaching, writing, and lecturing on scientific agriculture helped him to obtain a post as Associate Agricultural Editor on one of the leading dailies—the *New York Tribune.* At the same time he became the American correspondent of the *Mark Lane Express,* the great British organ of the corn trade.

So began Henry's two-year period as a full-time newspaper man. Though his columns concerned the man on the land, he was happy to turn his hand to anything that called for initiative or promised adventure. This led him into one hair-raising assignment where he nearly found himself hanged along with John Brown of popular song fame.

Descendant of Peter Brown of the *Mayflower,* John Brown was trained for the Congregational ministry, but instead turned to surveying and farming. He fathered twenty children and became deeply involved in the bitter conflict between those for and those against the spread of slavery. Brown believed that he had a divine commission to destroy slavery in America—not by "the milk-and-water methods" of his contemporaries, but by violent means.

The plucky, but not very wise, old fire-eater conceived the plan of setting up a stronghold in the mountains of Virginia where runaway slaves could take refuge from their pursuers. For this stronghold Brown needed arms and ammunition, and to obtain them he decided to attack the Federal arsenal at Harper's Ferry. With only 18 men (5 of them Negroes) he assaulted the arsenal. In the fighting two of his own sons were among the killed, and John Brown himself was wounded. But he captured the arsenal.

The authorities could not, of course, condone such action. Colonel Robert E. Lee, later of Civil War fame, led a force of marines against Brown's tiny private army, overpowered it, and captured the wounded leader. John was tried and sentenced to be hanged at Charlestown, Virginia (now West Virginia), on December 2nd, 1859—less than two months after his successful raid on the Federal arsenal.

Henry's paper, the *New York Tribune,* was Abolitionist and had constantly voiced the principles that John Brown held so dear. The paper was, of course, more than unpopular in Virginia. Olcott writes:

"One after another three gentlemen had been driven out of Charlestown and Harper's Ferry on the suspicion that they were the correspondents who supplied the *Tribune* with its vivid accounts of local occurrences; and when, in spite of this, the letters still continued to appear, they gave out that they would hang the mysterious unknown to the nearest tree on sight. . . .

"The fatal 2nd of December was now fast approaching, and it seemed as if the paper [the *Tribune*] would be forced to let the day pass without having a correspondent on the ground, to tell John Brown's friends how he met his doom. . . . I went to the Managing Editor and volunteered to undertake the job, if he would allow me to do it in my own way. With some remonstrance about the risks I would run, he at last consented, and gave me *carte blanche* to go and come and do as I chose."

Henry had no illusions about the danger of entering the slave areas on this particular mission. He remembered that earlier, when he was on a visit to South Carolina in the interests of scientific farming, a southern newspaper had recommended that he be thrown in jail solely on the grounds that he was on the staff of the *New York Tribune,* albeit his job at that time had nothing to do with politics. Now with mob emotions aflame over the John Brown affair, if he were caught in Charlestown as the *Tribune* man to report on the hanging, it might be a lynching instead of a jail cell for him this time.

Charlestown was known to be a veritable camp, filled with infantry, cavalry, and artillery. This was because a band of men was expected from over the mountains in a bid to rescue John Brown. Sentries were said to be posted in the streets of Charlestown to stop anyone at will, and a provost-guard boarded every train entering the city. Also it came to Henry's ears that a sum of money had been offered privately for the capture of any *Tribune* man who managed to get into the town.

He had to think hard about his plan of campaign. Eventually, while waiting at Petersburg, he heard of a party of reinforcements leaving next day to join a unit of the Petersburg Grays which was on duty at Charlestown. Through the help of an old influential friend—who had no idea of his present mission—Olcott managed to join this party as a special volunteer, eager to serve the cause of the South.

On the train going to the scene of action, being in civilian clothes while his companions were in uniform, Henry was very conspicuous and had some bad moments. Once, for instance, as he was leaving the train at Charlestown, he saw a rabid secessionist of the South who knew him well, plus the fact that he was on the staff of the hated *Tribune*. In the flurry of dodging this and other dangers, he left his trunk behind at the station. This, he was told, would be taken to the provost-marshal's office until claimed. But it was marked: "New York," which in this situation was enough to lead to awkward questions. Yet it would be equally dangerous to leave the trunk unclaimed as its owner could be easily hunted down.

It was a very serious predicament—probably a matter of life and death. Henry cudgeled his brains for an hour and finally decided to try what Masonry would do for him.

"I picked out a fine, brave young fellow of the Staff, a perfect gentleman, and, under the seal of Masonic confidence, told him who I was, and directed him to go to the Court House, and claim and bring away my trunk." The plan worked. But life at Charlestown was still precarious with the constant peril of meeting someone who knew him.

Apart from his report to the *Tribune* on the hanging, Olcott wrote a long article entitled "How we hanged John Brown" which was published many years later. The vivid descriptive writing in this brings back that far-off winter's morning which, in a way, heralded the storm of bloodshed and terror that was soon to break over the country as civil war.

He writes: "All eyes were turned to the jail, a scant half-mile away down the road; but nothing could be seen, but the glint of bayonets and gilt buttons and straps, in the bright sunshine, until, of a sudden, the mass opened right and left, and a wagon drawn by two white horses came into view. In it, seated on a long box of fresh-cut deal, was an old man of erect figure, clad in a black suit, with a black slouch hat on his head, and blood-red worsted slippers on his feet. . . .

"Now, isn't that pitiful? Isn't it enough to make a stone image blush, to think of all this great army, with its flying flags, and its brass guns, and its videttes and patrols all the way up to the foot of the Blue Ridge Mountains hailing one wounded Kansas farmer to execution? I couldn't help thinking of all this as the head of the column filed into the field, between the loaded howitzers, and I looked upon the majestic face of the Man of Destiny. For an instant our eyes met. Whether he read anything in mine of the thoughts that crowded my mind, I cannot say, but an expression of intense enquiry came into his, and he gave me a glance I shall never forget. As his wagon turned in from the dusty road, and the whole array of military was presented to his view, the old man straightened himself up on his coffin, and proudly surveyed the scene. . . . He fully appreciated the effect of all this display of military upon public opinion, for you will recollect he said one day in prison: 'I am not sure but the object I have in view will be better served by my dying than by my living; I must think of that'. . . .

"John Brown descended, with self-possession and dignity, and mounted the gallows-steps. He looked about at earth and sky and people, and remarked to Captain Avis, his jailer, upon the beauty of the scene. . . . It seemed to me he longed for a glimpse of one friendly face; then with another glance at the sky and the far-away Blue Ridge, he turned to the sheriff, and signified that he was ready. His slouch hat was removed, his elbows and ankles pinioned, and a white hood was drawn over his head. The world was gone from his sight forever . . ."

To the Abolitionists of the North, John Brown was a martyr, and so the well-known song was composed:

> John Brown's body lies a-mouldering in the grave,
> But his soul goes marching on. . . . .

Olcott got safely back to New York where there were more pleasant things to contemplate than the violence and fear he had just witnessed down in Virginia. There was, for example, Mary Eplee Morgan whom he was courting. Seeming to be firmly established as a journalist-editor, and with his finances in good shape, he married Mary about four months after the Charlestown assignment—that is, on April 26th, 1860.

Mary was the daughter of the Reverend Richard Morgan D.D., Rector of the Episcopal Church in Huguenot Street, New Rochelle. The fact that she was a strictly orthodox churchwoman, and he a dabbler in such questionable practices as spiritualism and psychic investigation, did not loom very large to the young couple. They were in love, they thought, and the future seemed bright.

The year 1861 began happily enough for Mr. and Mrs. Henry Olcott. In January of that year their first child was born—a son. He was named Richard Morgan after his maternal grandfather.

But the clouds of national conflict were darkening heavily, and in April, 1861, the Civil War began. As men do in war, Henry forgot his dislike of officialdom and authoritarianism. Suddenly it seemed that the things for which the North was fighting—the abolition of slavery, industrial progress, the solidarity of the nation through the continuance of the Union—were the most important in life. Agricultural journalism sank into insignificance.

Henry volunteered for action in the field, and we next hear of him as a signals officer. Writing of this period himself, he says: "I passed at the front the first year of the war, joining the Burnside expedition at Annapolis, participating in the capture of Roanoke Island, the battle of Newbern, the siege and capture of Fort Macon, the battles on the Rappahannock during Pope's retreat and other military operations."*

What his actual rank was at this time we do not know, but he was apparently in a position that enabled him to talk personally with General Burnside. Describing the attack on Roanoke Island in vessels of the wrong draught, hired for the army by agents at exorbitant prices, Olcott writes: "Conversing with Burnside as the vessel we were on stuck fast half-way over the swash, I offered to send an account of this infamy to the Northern press and denounce the responsible parties by name."*

The General felt, however, that he must take the responsibility himself, and did not accept Olcott's offer. But he probably made a mental note of it.

One day in the fall of 1862, when Henry was in Washington with his horse "ready saddled for a start next morning with General Burnside to join Hooker with the Ninth

_____
* From *The Annals of War*, the Times Publishing Co., Philadelphia, 1879.

Corps," he found himself instead taken off to a military hospital. He was one of the many casualties of those wartime enemies—malaria and dysentery.

Two months later, while he was still convalescing, he received an order that both surprised and dismayed him. He was detailed to carry out special investigations into the operations of one Solomon Kohnstamm, a big army contractor who was suspected of fraud. Henry was puzzled as to why he, a signals officer, should have been chosen for this job. Agricultural science and journalism could scarcely be considered a training for such detective work. Had Burnside remembered the conversation at Roanoke Island and, feeling that Olcott's hatred of dishonest practices was sufficient qualification, recommended him? Or was it just one of those unaccountable things that happen in wartime?

The job was supposed to be a brief one. It should, they said, not take more than a fortnight to determine if Kohnstamm had been robbing Uncle Sam to the tune of some $25,000, as suspected. After that, Olcott would be free to rejoin his unit in the field.

So in November 1862, he started on the investigation. For the work he was stationed in New York and able to live at home. This was a compensation. Four months earlier, in June, his second son, William Topping, had been born. Richard Morgan Olcott was nearly two now. Dr. the Rev. Morgan preached the righteousness of the Northern cause from his pulpit, and Mary was proud of her hero from the battlefield. The hero himself reveled in the domestic felicity as a respite from the horrors, ugliness, and discomfort of the front.

But he was discovering a worse ugliness in the machinations of the "enemy" behind the lines. Corruption was on a much wider scale than had at first been suspected, and Kohnstamm was by no means the only villain. More and more cases of suspected fraud, corruption, and misconduct, came onto Olcott's desk at 93 Franklin Street, New York. The work increased; his staff of detectives and stenographers was enlarged; eventually he had to take an office in Washington as well as New York. The job, which was supposed to take a fortnight, went on and on.

Henry was given the rank of Colonel for this important, and frequently dangerous, task of bringing to book the racketeers or agents—some of them powerful and ruthless—who were either trying to make quick fortunes out of the war, or giving undercover help to the enemy. Olcott's correspondence with top officials at the War Department, written in the copperplate handwriting of the clerks of those days, reveals the variety and extent of his activities as Special Commissioner.

Among the matters into which he probed were: the sailing of vessels from New York with arms destined for the enemy, the corrupt complicity of high officers of both the services and the Government in trying to make personal profits out of the war, the issuing of passports in Washington to enemy agents to get through the lines, and the apprehension and arrest of spies and other southern agents in New York, who were, among other things, carrying dispatches to their allies, or potential allies, in Europe.

In one of his reports the Colonel says: "The Government has been in the habit of paying ruinous prices for the charter of vessels, some of which have been perfectly unseaworthy. The precious lives of officers and men, and public property of the value of millions of dollars, have been entrusted to rotten steamboat hulks, and greedy speculators and middlemen have been paid, for their use, prices of the most extortionate nature."

On one of hundreds of cases investigated, he reports that "by a corrupt conspiracy between a government purchasing agent, an inspector, a Cincinnati contractor, an Indianapolis horse dealer, and Republican politician, the United States had been systematically robbed of one million dollars in the purchase of horses and mules, at the Cincinnati corral, during the preceding year."

But perhaps the star performer in what Henry called "The War's Carnival of Fraud" was the one who first triggered official suspicion—Solomon Kohnstamm. This man's main crime consisted "in his procuring from landlords—generally German saloon-keepers—their signatures to blank vouchers (bills for the board and lodging of recruits for volunteer regiments). These blank vouchers he would have filled in by his clerks for, say, one or two thousand dollars each, and then either get unprincipled commissioned officers to append their certificates for an agreed price, or, cheaper still, forge them. By this device he drew over three hundred thousand dollars from the Mustering and Disbursing Office in New York, of which sum the greater proportion was in due time ascertained by me to be fraud."

But bringing this racketeer to heel was by no means easy. He had for years been a big businessman in the city of New York. He entertained lavishly and bribed liberally. He had many influential friends, some of whom were quite respectable and not aware of his crimes. To make matters worse, through an official blunder, Kohnstamm had been arrested prematurely, before the Colonel could gather all the necessary evidence. Loud voices of protest were raised among the public, and pressures from the contractor's friends and certain political groups were brought to bear. Before long it came to Henry's ears from a reliable source that he, the United States Marshal, and even the Secretary of War were to be "indicted for resisting the writ of habeas corpus under the alleged unconstitutional act of Congress suspending the same."

It was a situation that called for bold action without delay. Olcott took the initiative and went before a grand jury with his papers, answering any questions they cared to ask. "The result was a vote of commendation for what had been done, and all danger of indictment was removed." Then, with his newspaper experience standing him in good stead, he made a bid for better public and press relations. He invited the journalists to a conference, and gave them an outline of the facts that had so far been revealed by his investigations. The newspaper stories next day caused a sensation. Public sympathy was immediately enlisted for the work he was doing. Never afterwards, he said, did the press interfere with the discharge of his official labors, so that he was able to carry out his duties with the efficiency and secrecy required.

Finally, forty-eight bills of indictment were brought against Kohnstamm. Political pressures were overcome, the contractor was brought to trial, and in May 1864, he was sentenced to ten years with hard labor at Sing Sing prison. The outcome so pleased the Secretary of War that he sent the following telegram to his Special Investigator:

WAR DEPARTMENT, May 21st., 1864
To: Colonel H. S. Olcott, New York:

I heartily congratulate you upon the result of today's trial. It is as important to the Government as the winning of a battle.

Edwin M. Stanton, Secretary of War.

Henry's Herculean labors in what he called "cleaning out the Augean stables" of the Army were so successful and so gratifying to the authorities that, after about fifteen months as Special Commissioner for the War Department, he was asked by Secretary of the Navy Welles to perform similar services for that department. Stanton agreed to loan the Colonel temporarily. So he was officially commissioned as Special Investigator for the Navy.

He found the same abuses, the same corruption, the same systematic robbery of the Navy Department, as he had uncovered in connection with the Army. He set himself to clean out this Augean stable, too—"without fear or favor." The rank, position, or power of the wrongdoer meant nothing whatever to Henry Olcott. And so the flow of anonymous threatening letters increased. Indeed, his life was frequently in danger from those whose rackets he was bent on exposing.

At the same time tragedy entered his domestic life. A third son, named Henry Steel, died at the age of four months while the Colonel was busy fighting his grim battle against the ring of rogues who were fleecing the Navy of hundreds of thousands of dollars. Some of them were the same crooked contractors whose scent he had caught behind the scenes in Army affairs. With untiring energy he traveled from state to state as required. (In one semi-annual report he states that during the preceding six months he had traveled over 19,000 miles and examined, with the help of his assistants, 817 witnesses.)

* * *

On the evening of April 14, 1865, while the Colonel was working late at his office in New York, a tragic event that staggered the North took place in Ford's Theatre, Washington. As the audience quietly watched the drama, *Our American Cousin,* John Wilkes Booth, well-known as an actor (though not in this cast) leaped from a box above onto the stage. He faced the audience and cried, *"Sic semper tyrannis."* Then dashing through the stage door he mounted a waiting horse and rode off into the darkness.

In the box from which he had jumped, Abraham Lincoln, the wartime President of the United States, lay in his blood, with one of Booth's bullets buried in his brain. This great man and statesman, whose hands had once, like Henry's, held a plough, died that April night as the Civil War, which he had steered to victory, drew toward its close.

The next day Colonel Olcott sent the following telegram to Stanton in Washington:

> Hon. E. M. Stanton, Secretary of War,
> If Lieutenant-Colonel Morgan or I or any of my employees can serve you and the country in any way, no matter what, or anywhere, we are ready.
> H. S. Olcott.

The reply came within a couple of hours:

> H. S. Olcott, New York.
> I desire your services. Come to Washington at once, and bring your force of detectives with you. Answer.
> Edwin M. Stanton, Secretary of War.

The Colonel replied promptly that he would be leaving New York by midnight with such of his men as lived in town. The rest would follow next day.

At Washington Olcott, who had now proved himself to the authorities as a highly efficient and incorruptible investigator, was appointed as one of a three-man commission whose job it was to gather all the evidence that could be found concerning any conspiracy behind the assassination, and to flush out the conspirators. The actual killer, John Booth, was on the run from police and army, like a fox before the hounds. There was little doubt that he would be taken, but none of those in the murder plot must be allowed to escape the net.

During the next fortnight all information about the case, from whatever source, was laid before this committee of investigation, consisting of Olcott and two other colonels. In his book, *The Web of Conspiracy*, Theodore Roscoe, an official historian for the U.S. Government, describes some of Olcott's activities during this hectic fortnight of national crisis.

On the day following his arrival in Washington, for instance, the Colonel made the first arrest of a major conspirator, Ned Spangler. He also spent many hours interrogating Mary Suratt who conducted the boardinghouse at which the plotters had held their meetings. Her son, John H. Suratt, was thought to be John Booth's chief accomplice. By this time Henry Olcott had had a great deal of experience in the art of interrogation. A verbatim report of the exchange between him and Mary Suratt is to be found in the United States of America's National Archives, and Theodore Roscoe calls it "an exemplary illustration of 1865 police interrogation technique." That busy first day ended at 11 p.m. when General Augur, Commander of the District of Columbia, "ordered Colonel H. S. Olcott to mount the raid" on the Suratt boardinghouse.

Meantime the "fox" was still on the run. Although General Robert E. Lee of the Confederacy had officially surrendered to General Ulysses Grant of the Union army on April 9th, the armies of the South were still in the field, and John Booth was doing his best to reach them. But he was hampered by damage to his leg, caused apparently in that dramatic jump from the President's box to the stage. Twelve days after the assassination, on April 26th, the "hounds" surrounded the "fox" in a hideout on a farm, and the kill was made. Though why Booth was not taken alive for trial—which may have revealed much that will now remain forever hidden—is one of the strange question marks of history. Soon after this event Colonel Olcott was able to return to his pressing duties in New York.

Mary Suratt was subsequently tried before a military tribunal. The chief witness for the prosecution was a drunken innkeeper named Lloyd, and the case against Mrs. Suratt as an accomplice was very weak. If the Colonel's report on his interrogation of her had been brought forward, the case might have been too weak for a conviction. Anyway the report was not produced at the trial, and the lawyers for the defense did not even know of its existence. For some reason the swift dispatch of Mary Suratt was more important than considerations of justice, let alone mercy. At all events she was convicted and hanged.

After the end of the war Olcott still carried on his special work. There was much unfinished business in bringing miscreants to punishment, also he wanted to devise new methods of procedure to ensure against future abuses in the services. In the Navy Department, for instance, he introduced a new system of bookkeeping calculated to prevent the kind of "carnival of corruption" that he had found during the war. The system was eventually introduced in all the Navy yards on the Atlantic seaboard.

Toward the end of 1865, three years after the beginning of his "fortnight's job," Olcott resigned his commission. His chiefs, in letters of farewell, thanked him for the good work done, and their letters provide many testimonials to the Colonel's honesty, integrity, and moral courage.

Olcott had been given unlimited authority "because he made no mistakes that called for correction and had not committed one single act of dishonesty," stated the Secretary of War.

He had, wrote the Judge-Advocate General of the Army, "been the means of rescuing vast sums of public money from peculators and swindlers for whom the vigor and skillfulness of [his] investigations had been a continual terror." He had done his work with thoroughness, "zeal, ability, and uncompromising faithfulness to duty despite the clamors and calumnies" with which he had been assailed in the interests of crime. The Assistant Secretaries of War and the Navy wrote of him in similar vein.

The Special Counsel and Solicitor of the Navy Department, Mr. W. E. Chandler wrote: "I have never met with a gentleman entrusted with important duties of more capacity, rapidity and reliability." He bore testimony to the Colonel's "entire uprightness and integrity of character . . .," saying that he may well be proud of the fact that he had come through without any assault on his reputation when one considered the "corruption, audacity and power of many villains in high position whom you [Olcott] had prosecuted and punished. . . ."

These yellowing letters in the archives of The Theosophical Society prove to all who care to read them that, after three years down in the mud of fraud and corruption, Henry Olcott, like the mudfish, had come out clean; none of it had stuck to him.

His high reputation and many contacts could undoubtedly have secured him a good government post after his work as a Special Commissioner was over, but perhaps he had had enough of official circles. At any rate he decided to start on an entirely new career.

*   *   *

There can be no doubt that during his three years as an investigator Henry had gained some insights into the criminal mentality and the workings of the law. He had evidently also developed an interest in the legal profession, and he decided to start at the bottom and train for it. Thus in 1866 he obtained a job in a law office.

Working and studying hard, he completed his training in two years and was admitted to the Bar in New York in 1868. In his law practice he specialized in customs, internal revenue and insurance cases. He was appointed Secretary and Director of the National Insurance Convention which was attempting to codify and simplify laws affecting insurance in the various States. Officials met from many areas for conferences, and their resolutions were compiled and published by Olcott in two large volumes. This became a standard work on insurance matters.

The Colonel (as he was still called) built up a thriving law practice, with many important clients, including the United States Treasury, the New York Stock Exchange, the Corporation of New York City, the Panama Railway, and the United Steel Manufacturers of Sheffield, England.

In 1870 business took Henry on his second journey abroad —to London. Here, showing that his old interest in the occult was by no means dead, he took the opportunity of visiting some famous British mediums. Soon after his return to New York another old interest became active. He began to relieve

the monotony of legal practice with occasional stints in journalism. One was a three-months part-time job as dramatic
critic for the *New York Sun*. This was mainly evening work
and did not interfere with his profession. He covered an interesting variety of stage shows for the *Sun*—from a sword-
swallowing performance to Johann Strauss' first concert in
America in July 1872.

Another free-lance journalistic venture, two years later,
was to open the doorway to an entirely new way of life. But
meantime, Henry writes much later on, he was enjoying the
fleshpots. Though from a long line of Puritans, he was no
"puritan" in the accepted sense of today. Describing himself
as he was at that time, he writes that he was "a man absorbed
in all sorts of worldly public and private undertakings and
speculation".*

He was, in fact, a typical man of the world, successful pro-
fessionally and popular socially. But he was meeting with
real trouble on the domestic front.

None of the records tell us what actually went wrong with
his marriage. We can only make guesses. There had been
two domestic tragedies: a boy and a girl had been lost in early
childhood, leaving the Olcotts only two of the four children
born to them. But such things were fairly common in families of the Victorian age. It is hardly likely to have caused
the growing rift between Henry and Mary. More likely the
cause was a slow canker from the germs of disruption already
there at the beginning—inherent in the contrast and clash
between their deepest, strongly-held spiritual interests and
attitudes.

Mary Eplee Olcott was a conservative, narrow, orthodox
church-goer. She feared and hated the new heresies, such as
spiritualism and free-thought. She clung to ideas, beliefs and
rituals that were long-established and safe.

Henry, on the other hand, was a blown-in-the-glass pioneer, a scientist at heart, anxious to attack the enigma of life
from fundamentals, deeply involved in the new thought, the
few liberalizing influences of the day. He could not accept
the creed of his forefathers, of his father-in-law, of the established Church generally. Mary could accept nothing else.

* See a letter written in *Hints on Esoteric Theosophy, No. 1.*

Whatever the complex of causes, the differences were powerful enough to bring about a divorce in those days when divorces were frowned upon and rare.

Official records, showing the actual date of the divorce, have not been discovered. But William Quan Judge, in a letter to a Mr. C. L. Robertson of Minneapolis, says: "It is true he was divorced from his wife, but that was before he had even heard of Madame Blavatsky" (he met her in 1874). In the same letter Judge writes: "it has always been well-known that he [Olcott] permitted the divorce in order to satisfy Mrs. Olcott who did not care for him, and who has always been blamed, even by her own relatives".*

Judge was a close acquaintance of the Olcott family (Henry, Mary, and the sons), and his statement concerning the period when the divorce took place is probably correct. If so, Henry was already divorced when, on a July morning in 1874, a thought went blowing through his brain which was to lead him, in course of time, onto a strange trail to far-off horizons. This is how he describes the event:

> I was sitting in my law office thinking over a heavy case in which I had been retained by the Corporation of the City of New York, when it occurred to me that for years I had paid no attention to the Spiritualist movement. I do not know what association of ideas made my mind pass from the mechanical construction of water-meters to Modern Spiritualism, but, at all events, I went around the corner to a dealers and bought a copy of the *Banner of Light*. In it I read an account of certain incredible phenomena, viz., the solidification of phantom forms, which were said to be occurring at a farm-house in the township of Chittenden, in the State of Vermont, several hundred miles distant from New York. I saw at once that, if it were true that visitors could see, even touch and converse with, deceased relatives who had found means to reconstruct their bodies and clothing so as to be temporarily solid, visible and tangible, this was the most important fact in modern physical science. I determined to go and see for myself.

---

* In August 1881 W. Q. Judge reported by letter to the Colonel in India that his ex-wife, Mary E. Olcott, had married "a Southern man named Cannon. I suppose we may call it a cannon-shot. He is poor. They are gone away somewhere."

Chapter 3

AMONG THE SPOOKS
1874

Colonel Olcott halted at the doorway of the dining-room and, clutching the arm of his companion, Alfred Kappes, gasped:

"Good Gracious! look at *that* specimen, will you."

Over the last month Olcott's articles in the New York *Daily Graphic* had been bringing a mixed bag to the Eddy farmhouse, at Chittenden, Vermont, but even so, the lady now at the table rocked the boat of his equanimity. Her scarlet Garibaldi shirt brought such a note of vivid contrast to the dun room and the drab clothing of the other diners. A lively mop of red-brown hair stood out from her head, "silken-soft and crinkled to the roots like the fleece of a Cotswold ewe." And there was something about her bearing and features—something imperious and at the same time sympathetic. . .

The place opposite to her at the long table was empty, so the Colonel hurried across and sat there. He wanted to examine the "specimen" more closely. Reading character from faces was one of his hobbies; this was what he called a "massive Calmuck face," a masterful face, full of power, yet there was a suggestion of refinement and culture in it.

The lady was speaking French to her female companion, also a newcomer. Henry decided from her accent and fluency that she was probably Parisian; all sorts of odd things came out of Paris.

The midday meal over, the two new arrivals rose and went outside. Henry followed them. It was a glorious noon, with the sun glinting on the emerald pastures and lighting up the autumnal tints of the trees. The peaks of the Green Moun-

Helena Petrovna Blavatsky (1831-1891). This sketch was drawn by the artist James Montgomery Flagg from an 1875 portrait

tains stood sentinel to the peaceful Chittenden valley; even the spooky old farmhouse looked cheerful for once.

Garibaldi shirt rolled a cigarette and searched for her matches. This was Henry's chance.

"*Permettez-moi, Madame,*" he said, stepping forward with a lighted match.

Then he lit his pipe and they began to converse in French. She told him that she had come to the Eddy Homestead because she was deeply interested in the phenomena described in the *Daily Graphic.* In fact, she said, all New York was interested, and there was such a demand for the paper that she had been forced to pay a dollar a copy for it.

"Even so, I hesitated about coming," she smiled enigmatically. "I was afraid that Colonel Olcott might drag me into one of his articles."

"You need have no fear on that score, Madame. He won't mention you unless you permit it. I can assure you of that, because *I* am Henry Olcott—at your service!"

She laughed without any trace of embarrassment; perhaps she had known it all along. She introduced her friend who was a French-Canadian, and told him that her own name was Helena Petrovna Blavatsky. She had indeed lived in Paris, but was very much a Russian. The name, first heard on that sunny noonday of October 14, 1874, was to become a very potent factor in his life—though he little suspected it at the time.

Now forty-two years of age, Olcott was a fine looking man with a firm jaw, high, confident nose, and fashionable mutton-chop side-whiskers. Blue, kindly eyes looked through pince-nez glasses, and he seemed to emanate a warm, friendly, magnetic aura. He and Helena Blavatsky became friends immediately.

This was the Colonel's second visit to the home of the Eddy family. After the first, a short one, he had written an account of his experience for the *Sun,* which was, he states, "copied pretty much throughout the whole world," and so the Chittenden "ghost-farm" moved into the domain of world-wide interest—and controversy.

Another of the big New York papers, the *Daily Graphic,* proposed to Olcott that he should return to Chittenden and

make a fuller investigation, sending regular reports, in the
form of letters, to the paper. Here was something that appealed strongly to the born seeker after occult knowledge.
Besides, it would be good to get away into fresh fields from
the routine of law practice. So he writes, "I made the necessary disposition of office arrangements, and on September
17th was back at the Eddy Homestead." With him was sent
the artist Alfred Kappes to make sketches of the phantoms,
or whatever they were, for illustrating the newspaper stories.

The Colonel had felt pretty sure on his first visit that
the ghostly figures appearing each night were indeed from
beyond the mortal veil, but he had to eliminate from his
mind any doubt on that score.

He must, therefore, create test conditions and amass evidence that would not only remove those doubts, but at the
same time throw a spanner into the arguments of the skeptics——of which there were many. The Eddy house was of
timber, L-shaped and two-storied. The séance room, known
as the "circle room", or the "ghost shop", was on the upper
floor stretching above the dining room, kitchen, and small
pantry. At one end of this long room was a platform on
which the specters paraded. At the rear of the platform
was the closet, or cabinet, for the trance medium, William
Eddy. Running his measuring tape over this cabinet, Olcott
found that it was seven feet by two feet, seven inches.
Its wall and floor were quite solid and he could find no
loose boards or panels that might permit entry from below.

Apart from the curtained doorway to the platform, through
which the phantoms came and went, there was only one
other opening in the cabinet; that was a small window to
the open air nearly fourteen feet above the ground. So any
accomplice entering this way must somehow scale the sheer
outer wall, and then climb through a window about two
feet, two inches square. To eliminate any possibility of
this unlikely contingency, particularly as no ladder could
be found on the premises, the window was watched from
outside during séances. And to make doubly sure, the
Colonel tacked a fine mosquito net over the window, sealing
the edging with wax, stamped with his signet ring. If anyone opened and re-sealed the net, he would know.

Eddy Farmhouse, Chittenden, Vermont, as it appeared in 1874

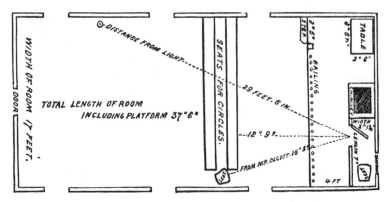

Ground Plan of Circle Room at Eddy Farmhouse. Sketch by Alfred Kappes, reproduced from *People from the Other World* by Henry S. Olcott.

This eliminated the window, and by thorough checking and rechecking—helped by a mechanical engineer—he established to his entire satisfaction that the only entry to the cabinet was through the door in full view of the audience. Moreover, the small cabinet contained no cupboards in which people or props could be hidden.

The question was then: could William Eddy, unhelped by confederates or props, such as costumes, wigs and masks, step from the cabinet and impersonate the great variety of characters who played in the ghostly drama? Having witnessed such sights as "babies being carried out from the cabinet by women; young girls with lithe forms, yellow hair and short stature, old men and women standing in full sight and speaking, half grown children seen, two at a time simultaneously with another form; costumes of different makes; bald heads, gray hair, heads of black shocky hair, curly hair," figures instantly recognized as deceased friends, and solid-looking apparitions, speaking audibly in a foreign language, the Colonel felt that fraud was an impossibility especially when one considered the figure and style of the simple farmer who acted as medium. William Eddy was 5 feet 9 inches in height, thick in build (he weighed 179 pounds), stiff-jointed, heavy and rather clumsy in movement. No one could imagine him executing the dances performed by the squaw, Honto, and some other characters. He was poorly educated, spoke with a strong New England accent, and was scarcely actor enough to produce the good English, let alone the foreign languages, sometimes spoken from the platform.

William's brother, Horatio, was of similar type and style, though slighter in build. He too was a medium, though of a different kind. Both brothers had inherited the *psi* faculty from their mother, and a long line of "psychics," extending back to an ancestor who was sentenced to death at Salem for witchcraft in the dark days of 1692.

In their childhood the Eddy boys, like their mother, seemed unable to prevent weird things going on around them; but the father, Zephaniah Eddy, had been violently opposed to all psychism. In the words of the Colonel, he had been "a narrow-minded man, strong in his prejudices, a

bigoted religionist and very little educated." Like his puri-
tanical neighbors, he regarded all psychic phenomena as the
work of the devil. He tried to beat and burn and scald the
evil one out of the members of his family. When all such
exorcism failed, he decided to make money out of the devil
by hiring out his mediumistic children to a traveling show-
man. Thus, for many years the Eddy children suffered from
superstitious mobs, and from the cruel, painful "tests" of
heartless "investigators."

If they were cheating now at the farmhouse—by some
means undetected—what was their motive? They did not
charge an entry fee to the "show," so it could not be money
they wanted, thought the Colonel. The board and lodging
charged for those who stayed at the farmhouse was quite
moderate, and many sponged on the Eddys, paying nothing
at all. So there was not much profit from the boarders.
Besides, though these farmers were rough and rude, often
at feud with their neighbors, they were generous, "giving
to the poor every spare dollar they earned."

The Eddy brothers did not act like people seeking publicity and notoriety, either. They were unfriendly and un-
cooperative toward any reporters, and even suspicious of the
Colonel, even though his reports in the press were fair and
favorable.

Some people maintained that the brothers were impelled
to give these semipublic performances by the manifesting
"spirits," or the Powers *behind* whatever entities were showing themselves. Much later on Henry came to think, through
what Madame Blavatsky told him, that this was the true
explanation.

The audience in the ghost shop—usually some twenty or
thirty in number—sat on rows of forms in front of the platform. With them on most occasions were the other living
members of the Eddy family, apart from the medium. Olcott
does not say how many family members there were, but there
appear to have been several sisters. The mother had been
dead for nearly two years, and the father, Zephaniah, for
fourteen.

For William's séances an oil lamp, turned low, burned
toward the rear of the room, so that the light was dim. Some

mediums demand Stygian darkness, most others need the light to be dim; very few get results in full light.

At about seven in the evening, after helping wash up the supper dishes, William would plod heavily up the stairs to the séance room, climb onto the platform and enter the cabinet before the sitting spectators. After a few minutes the curtain would stir and one of the "people from the other world" would glide onto the platform. The first one the Colonel saw on his first evening there was the American Indian woman known to all as Honto. He describes her thus: "young, dark-complexioned . . . lithe and springy in movement, full of fun . . . and inquisitiveness. She measures 5 feet and 3 inches in height against a painted scale I had placed beside the cabinet door." So if it was really the medium, he had suddenly become supple, and lopped six inches off his height.

Honto was one of the regulars, and the Colonel saw her about thirty times during his sojourn at the farm. After a time sitting in the dim séance room, his eyes would grow accustomed to the light, and he could distinguish features, read the measuring scale, make notes, and do other things. Alfred Kappes was able to see well enough to make rough sketches. Concerning Honto, the Colonel goes on to say that she had long black hair about a yard down her back, she changed her dress often and danced a lot in a light graceful manner. None of these things spelled "William"—even if he could have carried the costumes and wig into the cabinet, undetected by the search that Olcott, the trained detective, sometimes made of him.

There were other interesting members of the regular phantom cast. Santum, the Indian chief, was 6 feet and three inches in height—six inches taller than William. He was dressed in buckskin, with a feather on his head, and a powder horn slung across his shoulders. Mrs. Eaton was a little wrinkled old phantom with a piping voice. She was always attired in shawl and bonnet, was said to have lived in New York State, and had been appearing on the stage since the beginning of the series. Though the majority of the constant visitors were American Indians, many different white folk appeared during the sessions. These often purported to be the relations, or friends, of one or another of the sitters, and were usually recognized and greeted as such. Other white visitors gave their names, former addresses and times of death. One evening often produced many different picturesque characters of varying colors, sizes and heights, wearing different clothes and ornaments. The intervals between the exit of one character and the entrance of the next were timed by the Colonel; they ranged from half a minute to five minutes. Sometimes two adults, or an adult and two children, would appear together—something of a magical feat, it would seem, for a cheating medium, under the circumstances. And what a huge stock of props the imposter must have had! Olcott states that during his stay at the homestead more than four hundred of these manifestations paraded before him.

But of all who took part in the fantastic nightly drama, the most bizarre and amazing of the characters made their debut after the arrival of Madame Blavatsky. At the séance on the evening of October 14th, after the regular American Indian characters had greeted the spectators, done their acts, and bowed out, there was a pause, then the curtain was thrust aside and out stepped a picturesque character in baggy trousers, yellow leggings and white fez. Madame Blavatsky recognized him at once in his Caucasian costume. He was from the city of Kutais, and had waited on her when she stayed there with her aunt, Madame Witte. His name was Michalko Guegidze. Seeing that he carried a guitar, Madame asked him, in his own Georgian dialect, to render several Caucasian national songs. This he did.

Others of Madame Blavatsky's spectacular connections, coming from far-off places to the ghost shop in the old farmhouse on subsequent evenings were:

(1) Hassan Agha, a wealthy Persian merchant of Tiflis; "dressed," said Madame Blavatsky "as Persian merchants generally are. . . . Everything in its right place. . . ." She and her family had known this man for twenty years at Tiflis. He spoke "half in Georgian and half in Persian," and made three appearances on the platform.

(2) Marya, an old servant of the family, a nurse of Madame Blavatsky's sister. Her attire was that of a Russian peasant,

and she spoke a few words in Russian, calling Madame by an endearing name which she had used in the latter's childhood.

(3) Gustave A. Hahn, late President of the Criminal Court at Grogno, Russia, and Madame Blavatsky's uncle. He was portly, with an aristocratic air, and was dressed in a conventional black evening suit. The Russian decoration of St. Anne was suspended from his neck by the correct red and black ribbon. At first sight the lady thought the phantom was her father—not long dead—but as he drew closer and greeted her in Russian, she recognized him as her father's brother. The two, she said, had been strikingly similar in appearance.

Later the same evening she found that her uncle had "apported" something of great interest from Russia. It was delivered during what was known as the "dark circle" when the oil light was extinguished. Horatio Eddy was the medium for these often exuberant séances, when American Indians danced wildly in the darkness, weird noises were heard, the furniture flung about and often turned upside down. The room usually looked like the aftermath of a riot when the lamp was lit. Horatio did not go into the cabinet, but he was securely bound to a chair during the whole séance. The most energetic and psychokinetically powerful performer in these dark circles was George Dix, who claimed to be a deceased sailor.

On this particular evening his well-known voice was heard saying to the Russian lady: "Madame, I am about to give you a test of the genuineness of the manifestations in the circle. . . . I shall place in your hands the buckle of a medal of honor worn in life by your brave father, and buried with his body in Russia. This has been brought to you by your uncle, whom you have seen materialized this evening."

When the light was put on, Madame recognized the buckle in her hand as the one belonging to a medal presented by the Czar to her late father, Colonel Hahn, after the Turkish campaign of 1828. The buckle had certain peculiarities, such as a broken point to the pin, which made her feel sure it was indeed her father's—the one she had sometimes handled as a child.

"Apports" were, of course, not uncommon in the dark circle where PK power seemed to reach a tremendous height. Some of the objects found in the room immediately afterwards were from foreign parts; some were out of the way items, such as rare mineral specimens; some were very heavy and cumbersome—a big stone weighing 60 pounds and a cartwheel, evidently from some farmyard.

The three foreign-speaking visitors for Madame Blavatsky, with their outlandish yet quite authentic clothes, should have been enough to shake the doubters who blamed it all on William's trickery. And there were others, too, who would present even more formidable difficulties to the resources and ingenuity of a poor, simple farmer.

At one séance, when Madame Blavatsky was playing the parlor organ close to the edge of the platform, a fantastic figure came out of the cabinet, and stood a few feet from her. No one knew who or what he was, but the Colonel learned afterwards that he was a Kurdish warrior. All could see that he wore a unique uniform, with daggers and a curved sword in his belt. He greeted Madame Blavatsky with a strange gesture of respect, which—she said later—was peculiar to the tribes of the Kurdistan. Then the warrior's right hand, which had previously been empty, suddenly held "the most curious-looking weapon that I ever saw," said the Colonel. "It was a spear that might have been a dozen feet in length, with a long steel head of peculiar shape, the base of which was surrounded with a ring of ostrich plumes. This weapon, Mde. B. tells me, is always carried by the Khourdish (sic) horsemen." But it was hardly the kind of thing that could have been carried, unseen, into the cabinet by the medium, or stored there, without the Colonel's finding it.

Madame Blavatsky knew the warrior well. She had spent the summer of 1851 at a resort named Daratschi-Tchag (The Valley of Flowers) in the plain of Mount Ararat. Her husband, who was Vice-Governor of Erivan, had a bodyguard of fifty of these Kurdish warriors. The Chief, one named Saffar Ali Bek, was detailed by the Vice-Governor to be her personal escort. He rode after her everywhere on her equestrian excursions and she came to know him well— a man of great skill as a cavalier, but rather fond of showing-off that skill. She certainly had no difficulty, she said, in recognizing Ali Bek when his apparition stood within arm's length of her at the old farmhouse.

Another weird-looking character from the past of the much-traveled Russian lady was a black-as-ink juggler from Africa. He wore a curious costume, and a headgear of four high, bent horns, with a gilt ball hanging from each horn tip. Madame Blavatsky did not at first remember this man. But when he drew closer to her, she recognized the chief of a party of African super-jugglers whom she had encountered in Upper Egypt at a Ramazan feast. She had seen them perform a version of the incredible Indian rope trick. A full account of this "trick" is given in the Colonel's book, *People from the Other World.*

For William Eddy to be familiar with the apparel of such bizarre characters, let alone impersonate them under the restricted conditions, seemed well-nigh impossible to Henry Olcott. Whatever the apparitions were, they were not the medium, or flesh-and-blood confederates.

Among the tests devised by Olcott to demonstrate the genuineness, or otherwise, of the phenomena was the weighing of the "spirits." He procured from a nearby town one of Howes Standard Platform Scales. This was placed on the stage, and some of the phantoms were invited to step onto it. A number of them did so. The test revealed two interesting things: one, that the characters weighed less than would be expected from their appearance—but being materialized, they *did* have weight; and secondly, that they could change their weights as they wished, presumably by changing the degree of their materialization. To take one example, Honto looked like a woman of about 140 pounds, but the scales registered only 88 pounds. When she was asked by Henry to make herself lighter if possible, the reading dropped to only 58 pounds.

But to Olcott's mind the most satisfactory test was when one evening just before the usual time for the séance, he suggested that it be held downstairs in the reception room. William, being that night in a friendly, cooperative mood, agreed to the suggestion. A small closet, with no window or extra door, was improvised as a cabinet for the medium.

The Colonel assured himself that this closet was completely empty, and searched the medium just before he entered the closet to begin the séance.

After a few minutes, out from the new cabinet skipped Honto as lively as ever. She danced about the room among the sitters and then performed her well-known and most spectacular act—taking large shawls out of the empty air, swishing them about and throwing them around her shoulders. Other visitors who stepped that evening from the new closet—in which there had been no time or chance for an imposter to prepare anything in advance—included a woman carrying a child, a silver-haired old gentleman, and a child of about fourteen, recognized by her mother who was seated beside the Colonel.

Despite such events, convincing to those who saw them, Olcott was weighed down by the difficulty of giving adequate proof to the materialists who read the *Daily Graphic,* and the scoffers among his colleagues at the Lotos Club in New York. One reason for the difficulty was what he termed "pseudo-investigators" who popped into the Eddy Homestead for a night or two only, and then dashed off to write articles exposing the whole thing as a gigantic fraud. They had no concern about the truth of the matter, merely wanting to cash in on the public interest. One of these, a doctor named George Beard, declared that he could produce all the Eddy phantoms with "three dollars worth of second-hand drapery."

This was too much for those who had spent time studying the phenomena closely. Madame Blavatsky wrote a reply in the *Daily Graphic,* challenging Beard to make good his boast, and offering a reward of $500 if he succeeded. She knew that he couldn't, and Beard did not accept the challenge.

Such superficial exposés in the press were among the reasons why the Eddy mediums were not particularly friendly and helpful to reporters. Another reason was suggested to the Colonel by Mr. Frederick W. Evans of the Shakers who had had decades of experience of spiritualistic phenomena. Olcott could not see, for instance, why he was not allowed to go into the cabinet and see William Eddy sitting there in trance while one or more of the phantoms were outside walking about the stage. The mediums, and others, had said that his positive, powerful aura would have an adverse effect on the phenomena, weaken them and perhaps inhibit them. This, he understood, could be so. But why was William so suspicious of him? Could not the man see that he was an impartial investigator?

Mr. Evans, who had spent time at the Eddy farmhouse, wrote: "If you go there seeking with all your heart to see some dearly loved lost one . . . you will have no difficulty. But if you go, as evidently you have done, deeply exercised upon principles, prying into the source, the philosophy, the religion of the manifestations, the Eddys will wish the Old Harry had you—and the spirits will help them to send you to him."

In the same letter Evans offered an interesting suggestion as to why American Indians were so much in evidence at most spiritist séances. "While in the body they (the Indians) lived much in the lower spirit world. When out of the body they go not far from the physical world. . . . They are part and parcel of the earth, and are attracted and attached to the matter of which earthly human beings are compounded."

Regarding the riddle of the powerful Eddy materializations, Mr. Evans made an observation which the Colonel was to hear confirmed later from another source. After giving his verdict that the manifestations were quite genuine, Evans said:

"I think the *immediate* materializing spirits are influenced—controlled—by other spirits, in and out of the body. They who *plan* the labor on a farm, do not always *perform* the labor." He went on to say that it is when the mediums are *not* too intellectual or spiritual-minded, that materializations are most possible and likely. But the planners and controllers behind the scenes will be intellectual and highly spiritual.

With the ghost parades taking place in the evening only, Henry found enough time for writing and conversation during the golden days of that fateful fall. Before the departure of the Russian lady, nearly a fortnight after she had first startled his eyes in the dining room, the two had become well acquainted. He found her vital, witty, cosmopolitan, with interests like his own. She had evidently traveled in many lands and seen strange things. She spoke of being acquainted with adepts in the higher magic. Modern spiritualism, she said, was too materialistic, and it lacked a sound basic philosophy.

Henry was inclined to agree with her. He had, himself, already arrived at the conclusion that there was something wrong. His experience and careful investigations convinced him beyond doubt that a proportion of the phenomena of spiritualism was quite genuine. It was not just trickery by mediums. But some element was missing that made it unsatisfactory. The particular individuals one hoped and prayed to contact from beyond the veil did not, in general, appear. And those who did come had nothing important to say; they seemed unable to teach anything worthwhile. Séances became nothing more than social parties with the dead, so to speak. Certainly the spirits, if they were what they said they were, gave proof of one most important fact: life after death. But it led no further. The yearnings for more light on the riddles and problems of "life, death and the vast forever" were left unsatisfied.

The Colonel felt that his Russian friend had more knowledge of these deep matters than she had so far revealed. There was a sphinx-like quality about her. And she had a titanic inner strength. In fact she seemed more like a strong male companion than a female friend. He was soon calling her "Jack," and she obviously liked it. Before she left for her residence in New York, they had agreed to meet there after his return.

Meantime he had plenty to do at the Eddy homestead. In addition to the *Daily Graphic* articles, he was busy preparing a book manuscript, based largely on the same material. This was for a publishing firm in Hartford, Connecticut, the city of his earliest American ancestors.

With spiritualism now making the columns of several leading American newspapers, Henry had hopes that his book would be a good seller. But apart from material profits— welcome though they were—he had high hopes that his book would help to break the complacency of the two enemies of that elusive maiden, Truth. Now, as in the days of jesting

Pilate, and as ever, one of her enemies was the established religion. This seemed always to become the toady of political power and the *status quo*. But now, in the nineteenth century, another powerful enemy was arising—atheistic philosophy, born of the young, half-baked, but self-assured, physical sciences.

About the middle of November 1874, after some two months among the Chittenden spooks, the Colonel returned to New York.

Chapter 4

MYSTERIOUS BROTHERHOOD
1875

Before the Colonel's book was ready for the publishers, a heavy blow fell on spiritualism. Through two professional mediums, Mr. and Mrs. Nelson Holmes, a spirit figure, calling herself "Katie King," was appearing as a fully materialized attractive young woman. Her fame was being spread in journals, such as *Galaxy* and *Atlantic Monthly,* by two well-known writers on spiritualism—social reformer Robert Dale Owen and General Francis J. Lippitt of the American Army.

Then one day Eliza White, a woman of real flesh and blood, confessed that *she* was "Katie King," a paid confederate of the Holmes couple. Eliza's confession was made public by Robert Owen; and one Dr. Henry T. Child, who had been manager and promoter of Mr. and Mrs. Holmes, joined lustily in the public condemnation of the "mediums."

The great majority of "borderline believers" concluded that spiritualism was wholly a fake. Spiritualist journals lost heavily in subscribers and popular books on the subject lay unsold on the publishers' shelves. All this greatly alarmed the Colonel's prospective publishers, and it began to look as though the book on which he had set such high hopes would not even reach print.

Henry felt that there was something wrong in the general conclusion that was being drawn from the Eliza White confession. It may, indeed, be that the Holmes couple were guilty of cheating, but reports of the Katie King manifestations, and the circumstances surrounding them, suggested strongly that they were not all fakes.

A letter from Mr. Robert Owen showed that that fine old gentleman held the same view: "I believe they (the Holmes mediums) have been latterly playing us false, which *may* be only supplementing the genuine with the spurious; but it does cast a doubt . . . so I shall probably not use them in my next book. . . . It is a loss; but you and Mr. Crookes have amply made it up." This referred to Olcott's recent articles in the *Daily Graphic* and to Sir William Crookes' pamphlets on his experimental work in psychic research.

After thinking it over, the Colonel, with the agreement of Robert Owen and the Holmes couple, went to Philadelphia with the express purpose of investigating the Holmes mediums, and their claim that Katie King was genuine, in a series of test séances. The conditions of the tests were as rigid as Olcott's ingenuity and imagination could devise. For example, he put the medium being employed for the materializations into a cloth bag, tightened the drawstring of the bag around the medium's neck so that the arms were trapped inside, knotted the string behind, and sealed the knot with sealing wax on a silver coin, stamping the seal with his own signet ring. Finally, he pinned the sides of the bag to the medium's sleeves, which were inside.

The medium, thus bagged-up and immobilized, was left in the cabinet. The latter was shaped something like a triangular wardrobe, the only entrance being a door in front facing the committee of investigation. On each side of the door were small glassless windows. The Colonel made sure that there were no secret panels and, in case such had eluded him, tacked mosquito netting on the outside of the cabinet, to cover all but the front which was in plain view of all. Before a séance the Colonel would move the cabinet to any position in the room he chose as a further insurance against cheating. Usually the séances were conducted at the house of the mediums, but sometimes at Olcott's hotel in Girard Street.

One of the committee assisting the Colonel was Madame Blavatsky who was also on a visit to Philadelphia. Sometimes as many as fifteen people—including members of the committee—gathered to watch the test phenomena. The usual procedure was that Henry would secure the medium in the cabinet, as described, make absolutely certain that there was no one else hidden in the small cabinet, and walk out, closing the door behind him. Immediately he would hear the bolt on the *inside* of the cabinet door pushed home so that the door was locked.

This startling and instant demonstration of power within the cabinet must be psychic, he felt, or as it is called today psychokinetic (PK). It was followed by what appeared to be definite materializations. Faces—nothing like that of the medium inside—appeared at the glassless windows. Could these be masks held up by the "armless" medium? To test this unlikely hypothesis the Colonel would put his arm through the window and sweep it all around and behind the materialized head. It was never attached to anything—not even a body. Furthermore the eyes and lips would move in what seemed a natural manner, and a voice would often be heard. Sometimes not faces but arms would appear, waving through the windows.

But the crux of the investigations concerned the controversial figure, Katie King. Several times her face appeared at one of the windows, yet Henry hoped for something more. He wanted her, under these controlled test conditions, to walk out of the cabinet as a full-length figure. This she was supposed to have done frequently at non-controlled séances, particularly for Robert Dale Owen. At some of these—or perhaps at all of them—she may have been the self-confessed confederate, Eliza White. But Eliza could not possibly gain entrance to this well-sealed cabinet.

Time was growing short, and the last test of the series was approaching. A dramatic demonstration was essential if interest in the great spiritualistic movement was to be revived. Would it come? Madame Blavatsky, of whose supernormal powers Henry had already seen many signs, assured him that it would. She had, she said, issued "orders" to that effect. The "orders" had been given to "John King," an astral figure who was often with Madame, like a "familiar spirit." John was allegedly the father of Katie.

On the evening of January 25, 1875, six people were present besides the Holmes couple. Three of the six were Olcott, Madame Blavatsky and a Dr. Fellger. On this occasion, Madame Blavatsky entered the cabinet with Colonel Olcott, watched him bag Mrs. Holmes in the prescribed manner, then used some hypnotic will power to throw the medium into a death-like trance. Yet as Henry and the Russian lady withdrew, they heard behind them the bolt inside the door slide into place as usual. Nelson Holmes, husband of the medium, was sitting out in front of the cabinet with the rest of the people.

Various phenomena occurred, and then came the climax. Writes Henry: "We heard the bolt drawn inside, and in breathless silence watched the cabinet door swing slowly open. I sat within a few feet of the entrance and plainly saw at the threshold a short, thin, girlish figure, clad in white from crown to sole. She stood there motionless for an instant, and then slowly stepped forward a pace or two." He goes on to say that the figure was shorter and more delicately built than the medium, and that whoever it might be, it certainly was not Mrs. Holmes—nor could it have been any confederate. In appearance the apparition was the Katie King described by Owen and General Lippitt, and shown by a photograph.

After a few moments, Madame Blavatsky, who was sitting next to Olcott, "uttered one word in a strange tongue and the specter withdrew as noiselessly as she had entered. When the meeting broke up, we found Mrs. Holmes in her bag, with its unbroken seals, and in so deep a catalepsy as to alarm Dr. Fellger at first. It was some minutes before she had either respiration or pulse . . ."

The Colonel felt that he had re-established the reality of something beyond any faking. Eliza White and the Holmes couple most probably *did* cheat at times when results were considered essential and psychic power was running low. But there *was* a genuine entity from the "other world," known as Katie King.

It is of interest that for two decades before, and for many decades after Eliza White played her infamous little role, John and Katie King were well-known characters in circles on both sides of the Atlantic. Katie's materializations were often observed by Sir William Crookes and other investigators. Sir Oliver Lodge, writing in 1928, said: "I have had many talks with John King; indeed my wife regards him as rather a friend." And the two "Kings" have persisted right up to recent times. Dr. Hans Gerloff, in a lecture in London in October 1963, stated that both John and Katie King had several times appeared at sittings with the Danish medium, Einer Nielsen, in the previous few years. They are usually, if not always, associated with powerful psychokinetic phenomena.

To the manuscript for his book, Henry Olcott added an account of his Holmes investigations, and some further research work he did on a remarkable transfiguration medium named Elizabeth Compton. Although the wave of interest in spiritualism had passed its crest, it was to some extent renewed, and the Colonel's book was accepted for publication. *People from the Other World,* as it was called, came off the press in March 1875, and is one of the most remarkable testimonials to the powerful "physical phenomena" of mediums of the last century.

The book went through seven editions, but what the Colonel appreciated most was the commendation he received from two great British scientists: Sir William Crookes and Sir Alfred Russell Wallace, both Fellows of the Royal Society.

Alfred Wallace said in a letter: "I only wish it [the book] could have as large a circulation in this country as it deserves. Its fair and impartial spirit, as well as its great literary merit, would greatly aid in that reaction of modern thought against modern materialism which is becoming every day more evident. . . . I think you underrate the value of your investigation at the Eddys' when you infer, almost to the last, that they *might* be imposters to some extent, and that anything is wanting to make the evidence conclusive."

But did spiritualistic phenomena, genuine though some of these appeared to be, and fantastic though they were, answer the million-dollar question haunting the mind of nineteenth-century man more than ever it had done before? Did they prove that man—even though he might be a son of the apes as Darwin maintained—had a nonphysical soul, or component, that survived death?

Some doubts remained in the minds of serious inquirers, including Henry Olcott. Such doubts are well expressed by

Sir William Crookes. A lady of St. Petersburg had written to him, asking if he really had proof of life after death. In his reply, dated August 1, 1874, he writes, *inter alia,* "During this whole time I have most earnestly desired to get the one proof you seek—the truth that the dead can return and communicate. I have never once had satisfactory proof that this is the case. I have had hundreds of communications *professing* to come from deceased friends, but whenever I try to get proof that they are really the individuals they profess to be, they break down. Not one has been able to answer the necessary questions to prove identity; and the great problem of the future is to me as impenetrable a mystery as ever it was. All I am satisfied of is that there exist invisible intelligent beings who *profess* to be spirits of deceased persons. . ."

This more or less expressed Henry Olcott's outlook and dilemma. Was, for instance, the black-bearded, handsome sprite, calling himself John King, really the spirit of Sir Henry Morgan, well-known buccaneer of Charles II's reign, as he claimed? Or something else? Was Katie his daughter, once known as Annie Owen Morgan, as both she and John said she was? Were the characters who glided onto the boards of the old Chittenden farmhouse actually the souls of humans dead and gone? Or were they pretenders, imposters from another realm of existence? Often he felt suspicious that they were the latter. At any rate they taught little, except that this physical existence is not the only form of intelligent life.

Madame Blavatsky, whom he now saw frequently, was sowing in his mind the seeds of an idea that spread beyond the horizons of the meager spiritualistic philosophy. Gradually she let him know that, scattered in different parts of the world, but united in aims and work, there was a secret Brotherhood of Adepts. These were advanced yogins with many supernormal powers. Even the *chelas* (pupils) of these Adepts had developed extrasensory powers. Adepts, and some of their *chelas,* could, for instance, travel astrally in full consciousness, and if necessary materialize their astral bodies. In other words they could, if they wished, appear as a phantom to anyone. So there were phantoms of the living as well as the dead.

Eventually she told him that this mysterious Brotherhood was, for its own high purposes, to some extent using this new upsurge of spiritism in the modern world. Some of the Brothers, she said, had been behind the Eddy phenomena. She was herself a lay *chela,* she claimed, and had called forth the phantoms from her past, just as she had ordered the appearance of Katie King at the Holmes test séance in Philadelphia.

Henry felt that much of this could be true, but one point he found hard to accept. If she had consciously called forth the spirits of people from her past at the Eddy farmhouse, why had she mistaken her uncle for her father, and found initial difficulty in recognizing the African juggler? Nevertheless, the notion of living Adepts pulling the strings at Chittenden was tenable. It tied up with what Frederick Evans had suggested—that the solidified spirits were controlled by highly intelligent agents *in the body,* as well as out of it.

Well, who could say what occult forces worked behind the scenes? If, as Madame said, a secret Brotherhood of White Magicians existed ("white" having nothing to do with color of skin) and was using its special powers, and spectacular phenomena, as shock tactics to lead to the spread of a non-materialistic philosophy of life, then that was just what the world of the 1870's needed.

Still, he could not go all the way with Madame Blavatsky's statements and explanations. Part of his mind clung to the belief that at least a proportion of the apparitions of the séance rooms were what they claimed to be—spirits of the dead. Yet the idea of the great unseen Brotherhood appealed to him. If it did in fact exist, might he, too, become one of its disciples or *chelas*? Might he be able to help in the great work of bringing some light into the dark woods in which mankind was lost? It was the only kind of work that was really worthwhile in the final analysis.

About the middle of May 1875, the Colonel received an envelope of glazed black paper addressed in gold ink and sent to him at his New York Office. It looked odd among his business mail. Inside the envelope was a sheet of thick green paper bearing a message in the same gold ink. It read:

> From the Brotherhood of Luxor, Section the Vth, to
> Henry S. Olcott.
>   Brother Neophyte, we greet thee.
>   He who seeks us finds us. TRY. Rest thy mind—
> banish all foul doubt. We keep watch over our faithful
> soldiers. Sister Helen is a valiant, trustworthy servant.
> Open thy Spirit to conviction, have faith and she will
> lead thee to the Golden Gate of truth. She neither fears
> sword nor fire but her soul is sensitive to dishonour
> and she hath reason to mistrust the future. . . . .

In short crisp sentences the letter went on to say that Dr.
Child must be given "an opprobrious punishment." This referred to Henry T. Child who as manager of the Holmes
mediums had taken public money for attendance at their
séances, and when they were exposed, joined loudly in the
hue and cry. Thus, by turning to hunt with the hounds, he
escaped being identified with the foxes. The letter also said
that Brother John (meaning, it seems, "John King" who
acted as a messenger of the Brotherhood) had brought three
of the Brothers to look at Olcott; these were Serapis Bey,
Polydorus Isurenus, and Robert More. Henry assumed that
this meant they had come in the astral form; he had been
completely unaware of any such scrutiny. The letter was
signed "Tuitit Bey, Observatory of Luxor."

"Brother Neophyte!" This must mean that he had been
accepted as a novice, a potential *chela* of the Brotherhood.
Henry felt very excited. But could it be a hoax by "Jack"
Blavatsky? Among that morning's letters was one from the
lady herself who was still in Philadelphia. In this she informed him that the message from the Brotherhood of Luxor
had come through her, and that she had read it with the
Brothers' permission. Then she gave him a warning:

> Beware, Henry, before you pitch headlong into it . . .
> you can decline the connection as yet. But if you keep
> the letter I send you and *agree* to the word *Neophyte,*
> you are cooked, my boy, and there is no return from it.
> Trials and temptations to your faith will shower on you
> first of all. (Remember *my* 7 years preliminary initia-
> tion, trials, dangers and fighting with all the Incarnated

> Evils and legions of Devils, and think before you accept).
> On the other hand if you are *decided*, remember my ad-
> vice . . . *patience, faith,* no *questioning,* thorough *obedi-
> ence* and *Silence.*

If the "Tuitit Bey" letter were a hoax, why did she paint
such a gloomy, unattractive picture? She knew that "no questioning," "obedience" and so on, would not appeal to an independent, outspoken Yankee such as he was. Still she knew
that his desire for occult knowledge and service was very
great, and that he did not lack courage. Well, he would put
his suspicions in his pocket for the time being, and accept
the offer.

A few days later he received another matey, colloquial letter from "Jack." Her style was quite different from the
somewhat archaic English of the Luxor letter. She was, she
said, ordered by the Brotherhood to begin giving esoteric instruction to Henry. The responsibility of this role seemed
to weigh heavily upon her. "I have been entrusted with an
arduous and dangerous task, Harry, to 'try' and teach you,
having to rely solely on my poor lame English. They *must*
have tremendous hopes in your intuitional gifts, 'pon my
word, I put very little hope myself in my powers of elocution,
and clear definite explanations. . . . I wish More would
undertake you; I wish he was appointed instead of me . . ."
This doubtless referred to Robert More, one of those who
had come to have a look at Olcott before he was offered the
chance of becoming a neophyte.

Everything his Russian friend wrote revealed that her
English was shaky. She was much more at home in French,
as was usual with members of the Russian aristocracy. He
had seen documentary proof of Helena Blavatsky's aristocratic
family background before writing about her in his book,
People from the Other World.

On her mother's side she belonged to a long line of Dolgorukov princes, one of whom had been a counselor to Peter
the Great. Her father, Colonel von Hahn, had descended
from a noble German family, the Counts von Hahn of Meck-
lenburg. Her mother having died when Helena was a child,
she had been brought up in the main by her maternal grand-
mother, Princess Helena Pavlovna Dolgorukov.

At the age of about 17 the tempestuous young Helena Petrovna von Hahn was married to a man for whom she had no love. This was Nikifor V. Blavatsky, twenty years older than herself, and acting Vice-Governor of the Province of Yerivan in the Caucasus. Within a few months she had left her husband and begun the world-wide wanderings which, through a quarter of a century, took her to many out-of-the-way parts of the globe. The main object of her tireless travels, it appeared, had been a search for the occult arts. She went in search of the miraculous, lured by reports of the esoteric, from voodooism to the high magic of Tibet. She claimed to have lived for a time in that forbidden country.

There had been many hair-raising adventures, some connected with her need to make money, others with her passion for freedom for all men. Once, for instance, in order to make a sum of money, she had ridden a wild "killer" horse in a Constantinople steeplechase, and had been almost crushed to death in a fall at the 18th fence. At another period she had joined Garibaldi's national liberation army, fought as a soldier at the battle of Mentana, been severely wounded with saber cuts and musket bullets, and left in a ditch for dead.

Until her arrival in New York from Paris in 1873, Madame Blavatsky had not been in an English-speaking country since she was about twenty. She was now forty-four. Still she was learning her English fast. Even before she began to give regular occult instruction to neophyte Henry, she had casually imparted a great deal of knowledge to him. He found her a great teacher—sympathetic, nondogmatic but with an air of true authority and power.

Even before he had received the letter from the Brotherhood, there had been strange signs of some invisible influence. Once, for instance, he wrote a circular which was to be printed in the journal, the *Spiritual Scientist*. When it was in proof form, he showed the circular to Madame Blavatsky for her approval or criticism. Reading through the printed matter, she laughed and pointed out something very strange. He had written six paragraphs and the first letter in each paragraph made up the name TUITIT. He had not been conscious of any telepathic direction while writing the circular, but this could have hardly been a coincidence. Shortly afterwards the letter arrived from Tuitit Bey.

Soon after he became a neophyte other letters began to arrive from a member of the Brotherhood, signing himself Serapis. These were largely concerned with the promotion of the *Spiritual Scientist* as an organ for the expression and promulgation of the esoteric philosophy—or at least some of it—which lay behind supernormal phenomena. The editor of this journal was a young man named E. Gerry Brown. For a time it began to look as though Brown, Madame Blavatsky and the Colonel had been selected as a triad for the attempted spread of this profound, perennial, but little-known spiritual philosophy.

During the next July when the Colonel was in Boston on business, he received several letters in the peculiar, highly characteristic handwriting of the Master Serapis. One of these set him thinking hard. It instructed him to find for H. P. Blavatsky a suitable apartment in New York City, install her there and "not let one day pass away without seeing her." It emphasized how important she was, not only to the work, but to Henry's own personal progress in occultism. It explained that at the present time she must be surrounded with the "best intellects of the country." Henry must bring these to her. She and he, together, were to become a channel for the work of the Brotherhood in the sharpening of the intuitions of a group of people, in the hope of bringing a new enlightenment to the world.

Madame herself was also in Boston at this time. She had gone there from Philadelphia on what she called urgent business. Exactly what that business was is not known, but part of it was, in her own words, "a mission to repair the damage done by that rascal Dr. Child in making poor old Owen mad." Robert Dale Owen had apparently gone out of his mind as a result of the worry over the exposure and bad publicity concerning Katie King and the Holmes mediums. At any rate it seems that she went to Boston on "orders" from her guru in the Brotherhood.

The Colonel and Madame Blavatsky spent some time in Boston investigating the remarkable phenomena of the medium Mrs. Thayer, whose specialty was the apport of flowers, plants, live birds, and sometimes fishes into a closed

Facsimile of letter (slightly reduced) received by H. S. Olcott
in New York in script of Master Serapis, June 11, 1875

séance room.

As far as the Colonel knew, his friend "Jack" intended to return from Boston to Philadelphia. There seemed good reason for this as she had recently been married again in that city, and her new husband, Michael C. Betanelly, was there awaiting her return.

It was an inexplicable marriage of which Olcott did not approve. He had first met Betanelly, a Georgian, in connection with the Eddy spooks. The man had come there to confirm the facts given out concerning the Georgian phantom, Michalko Guegidze. Betanelly said that he had known this man personally in Kutais, and that all the facts about the materialization were correct. He became very interested in spiritualism, but even more so in the Russian lady who was, incidentally, his senior by some years.

Betanelly begged Helena to marry him. She was not interested. He threatened to commit suicide if she did not accept him. Finally she consented on conditions that the marriage never be consummated, that she should retain the name "Blavatsky" and her present freedom of action, without interference or hindrance.

These were hard conditions for a passionate man in love, but Betanelly agreed. It was the only way. The wedding took place during one of Olcott's business trips to Philadelphia, but he did not attend. He considered that the Georgian was Madame Blavatsky's inferior in every important way, and that such a union was an act of madness on her part. Perhaps she thought that in this way she would attain economic independence, and be able to devote all her energies to the work of the Brotherhood. If so, she was holding to a feeble anchor, for Betanelly was struggling to establish an import-export business and his financial position was precarious. Besides, he was a crude fellow without education or any deep spiritual understanding.

As might have been expected, the husband soon forgot the terms of the marriage. He demanded his conjugal rights, and attempted to restrict Madame's freedom of action. This was an impossible situation for one of her nature, and especially for one who had special work to do under occult direction.

So the union—only three months old—had to be terminated.

The Master Serapis indicated this in his letters to the Colonel; he stated firmly that she must *not* return to the bad conditions and vibrations at Betanelly's house in Philadelphia. If necessary he must endeavor to prevent her return. "Tell her you are going to Phila., and instead of that take the tickets to New York City, NO FURTHER."

This was all very well, thought the Colonel; an apartment he could find, no doubt, but if he was to see her every day there, as directed, what were the gossips going to say? Of course, his feelings towards "Jack" were Platonic. The link between them had nothing to do with sex. But Mrs. Grundy would not understand that. And he had his sons to consider.

Reminiscing years later, after her death, and remarking that some people had, at various times, suggested a closer man-woman relationship between them, he states that any pure person, spending time with H. P. Blavatsky, would see "how her every look, word, and action proclaimed her sexlessness." Apparently, though, Betanelly did not find her so lacking in sex appeal.

The Master Serapis understood what the reaction of public opinion would be, and tried to steel Henry against it. He wrote: "Fear not, *immortal* man, scorn the evil whispers of the double-visaged Janus called public opinion."

Well, Henry was a neophyte of the Brotherhood. His was not to reason why, to ask questions, to hesitate. He was a "soldier" again and must carry out his superior's orders.

At the end of July he left Boston, taking Helena Petrovna Blavatsky with him to New York City.

Chapter 5

BIRTH OF THE THEOSOPHICAL MOVEMENT
1875

The Colonel found an apartment for his friend at 46 Irving Place, New York. His prescribed job of collecting good intellects around her did not require so much effort, for Madame herself was a magnet to such people. Her apartment soon became a kind of salon for gatherings of those interested in occultism, the old lore of the East and the new frontiers of thought.

Henry was very busy. Apart from his law practice and the center at Irving Place, he was still investigating any unusual events on the spiritualism front, and reporting them for the *New York Sun*. There seems to have been plenty of such events, and the Olcott articles helped to keep public interest in psychism simmering. Over their cups of coffee in the cafés, people discussed, constantly and controversially, the eternal questions of man's immortality, and the possibility of communication with those who had gone to that bourne from which no man is supposed to have returned.

Practically all the Colonel's leisure time was spent at No. 46, and this was much more than a duty. Apart from being his appointed teacher in occult philosophy, Madame was continually enthralling him with new evidence of magical powers. Back in Philadelphia, when he had stayed with her and her husband, he had seen many manifestations of these powers. One day for instance, seeing that the new bride was short of towels, he bought some toweling for her. Later he observed her hemming the towels, and decided that needlework could not have been part of the Russian noblewoman's education.

They were both sitting at a table, and presently Madame

gave an ejaculation as if someone under the table was annoying her.

"What's the matter?" asked Henry.

"Oh, it's only a little beast of an elemental that wants something to do."

"Capital!" he jested, "Make it hem those towels. It could scarcely be a worse hand with the needle than you."

She laughed, and abused him for his uncomplimentary remark, but at first she would not accede to the suggestion. Perhaps she could see that he did not really believe her about the presence of a "beastly little elemental," for, following his further pressing her to hand over the needlework chore, she agreed. She handed him the towels, needle and thread, telling him to lock them in a bookcase against the wall. The Colonel did so, and then returned to the table. The pair fell to talking on the inexhaustible theme of occult science. After about ten minutes she said:

"That nuisance has finished the towels. You can go and get them."

Henry, wondering what he would find, unlocked the bookcase and took out the dozen or so towels. He was startled, and thrilled, to find that they were actually hemmed—albeit the quality of workmanship was no better than "Jack's." Yet beyond doubt the sewing had been done by something in that locked, glass-fronted bookcase.

Writing of the incident, the Colonel says: "The time was about 4 p.m. and, of course, it was broad daylight. We were the only persons in the room, and no third person entered it until all was finished." He had proved himself as no mean sleuth during the Civil War, so one presumes that he made certain there was no access to the bookcase through the wall at its rear.

Henry had seen the so-called spirits of the dead do things equally amazing, but did these invisible elves, or elementals, really exist outside children's fairy tales? Andrew Jackson Davis, a great pioneer in spiritualism, believed that they did, calling such impish, "tricky little beings" *diakki*.

That they were impish, as well as sometimes helpful, was well known. In fact there is a tale that Madame Blavatsky herself had once been the victim of their impishness. Waking up one morning in New York, she had found herself sewn to the mattress—so securely that she could not come to breakfast until released by her hostess, a French widow named Mrs. Magnon. This incident took place before the fateful meeting at the Eddy farm in 1874, and comes to us through the writings of Miss Elizabeth Holt, a New York school teacher who lived with Helena Petrovna Blavatsky for a while during 1873.

Even the powerful "John King" who was frequently at hand to give timely help to Madame, was capable of mischievous tricks. She says of him in a letter to General Lippitt: "He plays me the most unexpected tricks—dangerous tricks sometimes; quarrels me with people, and then comes laughing and tells me all he has done . . ."

But she makes the point that, in spite of this, John was a "noble-hearted sprite"; that through the last 14 years: "Not a day but he is with me; he made acquaintance with all Petersburg and half of Russia under the name of *Janká,* or 'Johny,' he travelled with me all over the world. Saved my life *three* times, at Mentana, in a shipwreck, and last time near Spezia [Spetsai] when our steamer was blown in the air, to atoms and out of 400 passengers remained but 16 in 1871, 21 of June."

During her New York period John would rap messages on walls or furniture or, at night, materialize as a tall black-bearded figure, scaring the wits out of Madame's servant. On occasions he even conveyed money to people who required it for some worthy reason; such as Gerry Brown who was often in need of capital for the *Spiritual Scientist.* Once he brought to Mrs. Magnon a ruby ring she had lost months earlier; he put it under her bedclothes with a note from himself, saying that it was a reward for taking good care of his "lass Ellie" [Helena].

At her Philadelphia house, Madame kept a special writing desk for John King's exclusive use, and, she said, he would get mad if anyone interfered with the papers on it. He could sometimes write letters, himself, without the presence of a medium to give him "power." One of the people to whom he wrote was Colonel Olcott, whom he at times addressed as "My good friend Harry."

These written messages to Olcott were often produced in some curious way—to prove perhaps that they came from John and were not just tricks played by "Jack." Once, for instance, the Colonel walked into the house with a reporter's notebook that he had just bought on the way home. Finding Helena seated in the drawing room, he took the notebook from his pocket to show her. It was, he explained, specially for taking down the messages rapped out by John King when in the mood for rapping rather than writing. Without touching the notebook, Madame told him to put it back in his pocket. He did so. After a moment's pause, she bade him take it out again and look within. He turned the cover and on the first page he found written in pencil: *John King, Henry de Morgan, his book.* The handwriting was quaint, old-style, individualistic, as found in all John King's written messages to the Colonel.

Olcott states that no one else had touched this notebook from the time he bought it on the way home till the moment he found the written message, with, beneath it—produced at the same time—a complex, symbolic pencil sketch which would have taken a considerable time to draw by human hand.

A little later, while Henry was still staying at the Philadelphia house, John painted his own portrait on silk. It shows a black-bearded figure standing on a balcony with a suggestion of astral buildings and figures in the background. It is, the Colonel states, entirely the sprite's own work, apart from some floral decorations which John requested Madame Blavatsky to do. For the job a piece of silk was tacked on a drawing board and covered with a cloth, dry colors, water, and brushes being provided.

The painting, which shows considerable artistic talent, was presented to General Lippitt for whom it was executed. But eventually it found its way to The Theosophical Society's headquarters at Adyar, India, where today it hangs, the colors in the buoyant landscape and the handsome John as fresh and bright as if painted yesterday.

Puzzled by such incredible performances, Henry attempted to figure out just who and what this entity John King was. Finally he came to the conclusion that the name was used by three different other-world entities: one, an elemental in the employ of Madame Blavatsky; two, the earth-wandering astral body of the buccaneer, Sir Henry Morgan; and three, a messenger of the living Adept-Brothers whose pupils Olcott and Helena Blavatsky were.

The labyrinthine ways of the astral realm are hard to unravel, but there is little doubt that—as psychic research workers now say—the name John King was used, in the century between 1860 and 1960, by many different "spirits" or other types of entities, usually those with marked psychokinetic powers.

Among a number of bright young lawyers who frequented Madame's New York salon was William Quan Judge. He worked at the time for the firm of E. Delafield Smith, Attorney for the South District of New York. A short man, with a pointed beard and soft eyes, he had been a friend of Olcott for some time, but paid his first visit to Irving Place in August 1875. Though only twenty-four, Judge showed a keen interest in occult science. His notable talents in this direction were to give him a leading role in the future struggles and drama of the Theosophical Movement.

In addition to the young Irish-American lawyers like Judge, men of many professions and a variety of talents gathered around Madame Blavatsky at her Sunday evening receptions. There were writers and doctors and scholars, a Kabbalist, a few leading spiritualists, even one minister of the Church. Great talk was heard, strange, unheard-of theories were propounded in Irving Place, a quiet residential street that housed, in the seventies, some of New York's old, conservative families.

Word of her teachings, of her Oriental, "revolutionary" concepts soon spread beyond the quiet street. The mass of the spiritualists who had hailed her as a leader, could not accept the new ideas. She, and her star pupil Henry Olcott, were now suggesting that the sitters at the séances were being deceived; not so much by the mediums themselves—though this happened—but by the communicating entities; that these were not generally what they claimed to be, spirits of deceased relations and friends, but elementals, astral shells, and other classes of beings, impersonating and masquerading.

Relevant information they often seemed to have, but this was drawn from the minds of the sitters, for these psychic beings could read both the conscious and unconscious levels of mind. But, as Sir William Crookes had said, under stiff cross-questioning they mostly failed to establish their identities. They could fool the necromancers, the emotionally involved, who thought it sacrilege to question them too far, but not the scientific and detached investigators.

A few who had been ardent spiritualists found sense in this teaching and were prepared to go more deeply into the doctrines Madame Blavatsky was gradually disseminating. But the majority did not like it at all; it shocked and upset them to be told that the long-lost loved ones, found again at a séance, were, in fact imposters. This was especially so as the recent Civil War, like all wars, had created a widespread, emotionally-charged interest in death, survival, communication.

In a way it seems heartless to have shaken this new-found link between the quick and the dead. Why did the Russian woman attempt to do it, and why did she earlier identify herself with the spiritualists and help to fight their battles against materialistic opinion? She told Henry that she had been ordered to do both by the Brothers. Apparently the idea was first to establish the reality of psychic phenomena, and then, after breaking the tightening grip of scientific materialism, to try to spread the true explanation of the phenomena, and thus lead men to the esoteric philosophy that gave a deeper understanding of life, God and the universe.

Spiritism as practiced by ignorant mediums became, she said, "unconscious sorcery," and dangerous to all concerned. There was nothing spiritual about it; it tended to hold its adherents back rather than lead them forward to a wider, more evolved consciousness.

Noting in her scrapbook that she had been ordered to begin telling the public the truth about phenomena, she wrote: "And now my martyrdom will begin. I will have all the Spiritualists against me, in addition to the Christians & the Skeptics. Thy Will, Oh, M. [Master Morya] be done!"

The prophecy was correct. The battle of the press began. The spiritualists attacked through the *Banner of Light,* and other organs of their movement. The *Spiritual Scientist,* supported financially and in other ways by the hidden Brotherhood, carried the first trumpet calls of the new teachings. The controversy soon extended beyond the special journals and spilled over into the columns of the general press—the *Sun, Tribune, Graphic* and others. The Russian woman and Henry Olcott, lawyer and journalist in the outer world, neophytes of the Adept Brotherhood on the inner, became well-known public figures. But like all who dare to shatter complacency and cherished illusions, they were offered not a garland of flowers, but a cross.

In August 1875 Henry's training in the esoteric was coming to him in strange ways, and adepts in the occult arts crossed his path "by chance"—as it then seemed to him. One day he got into conversation with a stranger in New York and invited the man, who seemed of more than ordinary interest, to his rooms. There, after a while, the stranger, who looked like a fair-skinned Hindu, offered to show him something of great occult interest. The only preparation was that Henry should open the folding doors between the sitting room, where they were, and his small bedroom. This done, they both made themselves comfortable on chairs in the sitting room facing toward the wide doorway to the bedroom. The Colonel did not know what to expect, but it was only a few minutes before something happened. This is how he describes it in *Old Diary Leaves*:-

> I saw the bedroom converted, as it were, into a cube of empty space. The furniture had disappeared from my view, and there appeared alternately vivid scenes of water, cloudy atmosphere, subterranean caves, and an active volcano; each of the elements [water, air, earth and fire] teeming with beings and shapes and faces of which I caught more or less transient glimpses. Some of the forms were lovely, some malignant and fierce, some terrible. They would float into view as gently as bubbles on a smooth stream, or dart across the scene and disappear, or play and gambol together in flame or flood. Anon, a mis-shapen monster, as horrid to see as the pictures in Barrett's *Magus,* would glare at me and plunge forward, as though it wished to seize me as the

wounded tiger does its victim, yet faded out on reaching
the boundary of the cube of visualized *akash*, where the
two rooms joined. It was trying to one's nerves, but after
my experiences at Eddy's, I managed not to "weaken."

It was as though, by turning some switch in Henry's mind,
the stranger had enabled him to see a section of one of the
subplanes of the astral, apparently located within the physical
space of his small bedroom. Then suddenly the scene was
switched off, as a modern television show, and the stranger,
remarking that they might perchance meet again, took his
leave. Henry went to bed in his three-dimensional bedroom
where a window on another dimension had shown him much
to ponder upon.

A few days later the Colonel wrote what he called his first
extended journalistic contribution on esoteric philosophy.
This was a long letter, entitled "The Immortal Life" and
was published in the *New York Tribune* of August 30th.
The letter took the form of a commentary on a press review
of his book, *People from the Other World*. The reviewer
had queried the value of spiritualistic phenomena, saying
they often suggested to him a repugnant type of after-death
existence to which complete annihilation would be greatly
preferable.

Olcott states in reply that he had now discredited the assumed identification of the intelligences behind such phenomena with deceased human beings. Such intelligences
were, he states, really elemental spirits who had not yet lived
as humans, and in fact lived on a different plane from post-
mortem humanity. They (the elemental spirits) could be
controlled by an adept in occult science. In fact he had unexpectedly come into contact with living persons who performed "the very marvels that Paracelsus, Albertus and Apollonius are credited with." This letter from an old spiritualist is a milestone marking a definite stage in the transi-
tion of ideas that led toward the deep waters of occultism.

The months from this period onward were punctuated with
popping press guns in attack and counterattack. Madame
pasted her published articles, some of the Colonel's, and a
few of those of her antagonists, in voluminous scrapbooks,

of which there are now many volumes yellowing in the archives of The Theosophical Society at Adyar. How much
all this public controversy affected Olcott's personal and professional life is not recorded. Outwardly he retained the
calm of a seasoned veteran. "Colonel Olcott stands newspa-
perial fire nobly," wrote the Reverend Doctor Wiggin in
The Liberal Christian, the church journal he edited.

Wiggin, about the only church minister who dared associate with the group at Irving Place and write about the
meetings, gives us a picture of the personalities there. We
see a crowded room, people of all ages from the ancient
Kabbalist, Dr. Pancoast, to the youthful Mr. Judge. At the
center of the group is one who might be any age. Actually
she is forty-four and growing stout; her clothes are of startling
color and style, her jewels plentiful, from the many rings on
the delicate fingers to the Rosicrucian jewel about her neck.
She has the grand manner of her class—the Russian nobility.
When she speaks, the whole room is spellbound by the verve,
profundity, and wit of her words.

Yet Helena Blavatsky does not lecture; she does not mon-
opolize the talk. She is one of the great conversationalists of
the century, stimulating those around her to give of their
best. And so the talk ranges easily, brightly, excitingly over
many subjects: poetry, the soul of flowers, Crookes' new dis-
coveries about the force of light, the Carbonari (Italian Secret Society), the literature of magic, wonders of far-off
lands, such as the Siamese temple worship where the "dead"
are said to be brought to life, the phallic elements in religion,
recent mediumistic marvels on both sides of the Atlantic, and
what lies behind such marvels.

The Rev. Mr. Wiggin wrote: "If Madame Blavatsky can
bring order to modern spiritism, she will do the world a
service."

Colonel Olcott was growing more and more unhappy about
the spiritualistic movement with which he had been connected for over twenty years, writing, speaking and organizing. It was not only the empty, dead-end phenomenalism
that disgusted him, but such dangerous social drifts as "free
love" where so-called "soul mates" disregarded all moral re-
straints, and some mediumistic individuals of both sexes in-

dulged in intimate intercourse with beings of another world, such as the demon-lovers of old, the succubi and incubi of medieval witchcraft. It was a quagmire; surely the way out of it was not back into the desert of materialism, but rather onward and upward to the heights of the new—yet ancient—teachings of the Great Adept Brotherhood.

On the evening of the 7th of September, 17 people gathered in the apartment at Irving Place. Looking back on that evening years later, Henry noted the play of the sevens, a number he believed significant to his destiny and the special work he had to do. It was not the usual Sunday reception, but a Tuesday meeting to hear a lecture by George H. Felt, an engineer and architect who was considered a genius by many of his contemporaries. The subject of his lecture was, "The Lost Canon of Proportion of the Egyptians." Felt claimed to have discovered this "lost Canon" through his researches in Egyptology. It afforded, he said, not only the key to the marvels of the art and architecture of the ancient world, but also the formula for the evocation of the spirits of the elements (elementals).

The audience was the usual miscellany of journalists, editors, publishers, scholars, men of the law and others. W. Q. Judge was there, and a visitor was Mr. C. C. Massey, a Barrister-at-Law from England. Another present was Mrs. Emma Hardinge Britten, a well-known lecturer on spiritualism who was soon to write a book called *Nineteenth Century Miracles* in which she has left an account of that historic September evening at Irving Place.

Felt's lecture aroused a good deal of enthusiasm and animated discussion during which the Colonel had the idea that those present might launch a society for this kind of occult study. He wrote the idea on a slip of paper and handed it to Judge to pass to Madame Blavatsky. That lady who had, she states, recently received secret orders from the Brothers to "establish a philosophico-religious society and choose a name for it—also to choose Olcott," now nodded her head in agreement.

"Whereupon," wrote Mrs. Britten, "Colonel Olcott rose and after briefly sketching the present condition of the spiritualistic movement . . . and how the ancient theosophies could reconcile existing antagonisms, he proposed to form a nucleus around which might gather all the enlightened and brave souls who were willing to work together for the collection and diffusion of knowledge. . ." It was to be a society of occultists concerned with the study of "those secret laws of nature which were so familiar to the Chaldeans and the Egyptians, but are totally unknown to our modern world of science."

All present regarded this as an excellent suggestion. Several more meetings were held during September and October to discuss details. Various names were suggested for the new society, but not accepted. Finally someone came up with the word "theosophy." This, from its historical associations and general meaning, seemed to cover the aims and aspirations of the new body fairly well. It was adopted, and "The Theosophical Society" came into being.

The officers elected, initially, were: President, Colonel H. S. Olcott; Vice-Presidents, Dr. S. Pancoast and George Felt; Corresponding Secretary, Madame H. P. Blavatsky; Recording Secretary, John Storer Cobb (English barrister and Doctor of Laws); Treasurer, Henry J. Newton (manufacturer and inventor); Librarian, Charles Sotheran (author and bibliographer); Councilors, Rev. H. H. Wiggin, Judge R. B. Westbrook, L.L.D, Mrs. Emma Hardinge Britten, C. E. Simmons, M.D., Herbert D. Monachesi (journalist); Counsel to the Society, William Quan Judge.

In retrospect, this seemed to the Colonel a very casual, almost accidental, beginning of a movement that would eventually carry him off to the far corners of the earth, and set down roots in every continent. But actually it was neither casual nor accidental. Behind the scenes plans had been hatching for some time. This fact is revealed in letters written some time later to Mr. A. P. Sinnett* by members of the Brotherhood who were directly concerned in the founding of The Theosophical Society.

> One or two of us hoped that the world had so far
> advanced intellectually, if not intuitionally, that the
> Occult doctrines might gain an intellectual acceptance,

* See *The Mahatma Letters to A. P. Sinnett*, 3rd edition, p. 259, 24, and 267.

Henry S. Olcott in 1875

and the impulse given for a new cycle of occult research . . . So casting about we found in America the
man to stand as leader—a man of great moral courage,
unselfish, and having other good qualities [Olcott] . . .
With him we associated a woman of most exceptional
and wonderful endowments [H. P. Blavatsky] . . . We
sent her to America, brought them together—and the
trial began.

The *Chiefs* wanted a "Brotherhood of Humanity," a
real Universal Fraternity started; an institution which
would make itself known throughout the world and
arrest the attention of the highest minds.

Later the Master Morya made another interesting comment to Sinnett: "There is more of this movement than you
have yet had an inkling of, and the work of the T.S. is linked
in with similar work that is secretly going on in all parts of
the world." But the main spearhead of the movement in
the last quarter of the nineteenth century was the body known
as The Theosophical Society.

Although the egg had been incubating in great minds for
some time, and peckings at the shell began during September
and October 1875, it was on November 17th, at Mott Memorial Hall, New York, that the body emerged. On that date
the Society held its first regular meeting, and President-
Founder Olcott delivered the inaugural address.

If I understand the spirit of this Society, it consecrates
itself to the intrepid and conscientious study of truth,
and binds itself, individually as collectively, to suffer
nothing to stand in its way. . . . Come well, come ill,
my heart, my soul, my mind and my strength are pledged
to this cause, and I shall stand fast while I have a
breath of life in me, though all others shall retire and
leave me to stand alone. . .

In his address, which was a long one, the Colonel showed
that he had by then given some study to the ancient schools
of philosophy and mystery religions. Striving to find historical parallel for the new body, he reviewed the Neoplatonists,
the Stoics, the Hermetists and others. The new Society was

not like any of them. Nor could it be called a school of theurgy, for, unlike the members of such historic schools (the last one existed in old Alexandria) scarcely one of the members of the new Theosophical Society yet suspected that "the obtaining of occult knowledge requires any more sacrifice than any other branch of knowledge." Whereas, in fact, "a life of the strictest purity and self-abnegation . . . such as that of Jesus or Apollonius" is required.

"We are simply investigators, of earnest purpose and unbiased mind, who study all things, prove all things, and hold fast to that which is good." Emphasizing this point, he said: "We seek, enquire, reject nothing without cause, accept nothing without proof; we are students, not teachers." And again: "In some respects we resemble the Hermetists of the Middle Ages. But they had dogmas, and we, under our bylaws, have not. They believed in Theosophy—we are investigators."

One aim of the Society was to study religious questions from the standpoint of ancient beliefs, and discover all possible about the still-hidden laws of Nature. Other fields of study would be: "Mesmerism, Spiritualism, Od, the astral light of the ancients (now called universal ether)." Through such study and the spreading of the knowledge gained, the new Society would "aid in freeing the public mind of theological superstition and tame subservience to the arrogance of science."

Bold words, daring dreams, for a small band of people breasting the flood tide of materialism, drawn high by the bright moon of modern science! But their President, Henry Steel Olcott, had no doubts of their ultimate success: "Behind our little band," he said, "there gathers a mighty Power —the power of Truth."

Toward the end of November the Colonel took two suites of rooms at 433 West 34th Street, New York. Madame Blavatsky left Irving Place and moved into the ground floor suite. Henry occupied the suite above her. Let the gossips talk if they would! That was a small matter compared with the work the two had to do *together*—work vital to the future of humanity. They must live close to each other, for a busy lawyer had only his evenings free.

Perhaps his sons, whom he loved dearly, would turn against him. But it could not be helped; the work must be done, the ship of Theosophy must be got under way, whatever the cost. He had no idea, then, of the extent of the sacrifice he would be called upon to make for the cause he had embraced.

Chapter 6

THE VEIL OF ISIS
1876 - 1877

In the period following the formation of The Theosophical Society, Henry Olcott went through one of the most enthralling experiences of his eventful life. Writing of it some seventeen years later, he said: "The education of an ordinary lifetime of reading and thinking was, for me, crowded and compressed into this period of less than two years."

Madame Blavatsky was writing a book and he was helping with the English expression. English was a language with which she was far from familiar, while Henry was an experienced journalist and writer. After dinner each evening—when they were not "at home" to visitors—they would settle down on opposite sides of their big writing table and work at the book until sheer fatigue compelled them to stop—usually at about 2 a.m. It was what the Colonel witnessed across the table, as much as the material that came from Helena's pen, that comprised his concentrated course in occultism.

Madame admitted to him, and has left on record in her private letters, that she did not possess the archeological erudition and the deep knowledge of esoteric doctrines that were appearing on the pages of her manuscript. The book, which she tentatively called *The Veil of Isis,* was an attempt to break through the world of appearances to the eternal truths that lie beyond it. The physical universe around us is the temporary veil; beneath is the Divine Mother, the creative power of the Godhead, known to the ancient Egyptians as Isis. In her attempt to rend the veil, Madame dipped into remote ages and areas of ancient knowledge which she had never encountered in books.

How then did such knowledge come to her writing hand? Colonel Olcott was the nightly witness to what took place across the writing table. In *Old Diary Leaves,* written after many years of occult study, he gives as his firm conviction that most of the book was written *through* her by living Adepts—their guru, Master Morya, and others. For this she loaned her body "as one might one's typewriter." She was not a medium in the accepted spiritist sense of that term; there was no trance, no loss of consciousness. She, the normal occupier of the body, simply stepped aside, she said, and watched in full consciousness while her body was manipulated by whichever Adept had taken over.

The Colonel, observing closely, knew when there was a change of "tenancy." She would either walk out of the room, or go into an abstracted state. Following this there would be a distinct change of vocal expression, mannerisms, gait, and other idiosyncracies. But the most striking change was seen in the handwriting, and the style and subject matter of the manuscript.

Henry came to know some of the peculiarities of the personalities using "the old appearance," as they called the Blavatsky body. One of them, while thinking deeply, would twirl an imaginary moustache on Madame's lip; another, disliking English, would always converse across the table in French; a third would reel off, for the Colonel's entertainment, dozens of poetical stanzas of either sublime or humorous ideas. One personality was jovial and fond of good stories; another was reserved, dignified, with great erudition. "Oh, the evenings of high thinking . . . how shall I ever compare with them any other experiences of my life," writes Henry.

But sometimes, occupied in his own tasks, he did not notice the change of personality until too late. Once, for instance, when he thought that his chum "Jack" was still on the job, he remarked: "Well, old horse, let's get on with it!"

Silence greeted this. Looking up, he observed, from the transfiguration of the face, that a well-known staid and reserved philosopher was before him. The startled dignity on the features made Henry blush.

The Colonel came to know something of the personalities,

and—through Madame—the names, of all the *alter egos* who came and went. Only one, he says, was a spirit of the dead. The rest were living Adepts whose bodies were far away at the time. Extracorporeal travel at will is a well-known supernormal yogic power; another, more advanced perhaps, is the power of using the physical body of a suitable, specially-trained person. This practice is known in the East by the term *Avesa.*

The Adepts had other ways of helping the Russian occultist with the work assigned to her. When she was struggling along writing a few pages herself, perhaps under inspiration, and needed a quotation from some old rare book, it would appear before her in what she called the "astral light." Watching, Henry would see a far-away look come into the blue Blavatsky eyes. Then the gaze would shorten, as if looking at something a few inches from her nose, while her hand busily copied the quotation—as read in the astral light. This done, the expression in her eyes and face would return to normal.

Sometimes, instead of the required quotation being reflected for her, as in an astral mirror, the actual book containing it would be apported from some far-off library into the room where they worked. The Colonel describes such an event. On the occasion he was checking the printed proofs of her book, and came across a quotation that he felt, for some reason, could not be quite right. She must have made an error in copying it from the astral light. He told her so.

"Oh, don't bother; let it pass," she said.

But he refused. After some protests she said: "All right, keep still a minute and I'll try to get it."

A look of intense concentration and will power came into her face. Presently she pointed to a corner of the room and in a hollow voice said, "There!"

The Colonel went to the shelf in the corner, on which normally only a few curios and ornaments stood. There he found two volumes, bound in half calf, of a French work on physiology and psychology. He was sure that neither of the books had been in the house until that moment.

He was able to check Madame's quotation, and find that she had indeed been in error. Then he returned the books to the shelf in the corner. After a while he looked up from his proofreading to see if the volumes were still there. They had vanished. Madame Blavatsky had not moved from the table.

When *The Veil of Isis* was about ready for the publisher, Mr. Bouton, he informed her that the title had already been used for another book. He suggested she call hers, *Isis Unveiled*. This title perhaps had more sales appeal, but Madame felt it was rather presumptuous. She had not intended, nor had she succeeded, in lifting more than a little of the *mayavic* veil. But, unable to think of anything better, she reluctantly agreed.

* * *

While during 1876 the Colonel's nights had been so fascinatingly employed in occult education, his days had been occupied with a variety of activities—law practice, journalism and an event that created a great deal of public interest. This was the death, funeral service and cremation of Baron de Palm. The Colonel states in *Old Diary Leaves* that this was America's first cremation, and it stirred up a great deal of public hostility, being considered anti-Christian.

Few people had heard of Baron de Palm until his death, but then as soon as it became known that he was to be given a funeral service by The Theosophical Society—instead of the Church—and cremated, instead of being decently put under ground, articles began to appear in the leading newspapers, whipping public curiosity and animosity to a frenzy. This went on for about a week prior to the funeral service which took place in the hall of the Masonic Temple on Twenty-Third Street, New York.

The hall, which normally held about 2000, was overflowing, with people blocking every passage and lobby, and jamming the doorways. Actually, entrance was supposed to be for invitation holders only, but the public had rushed the doors as soon as they were opened and ticket holders had to fend for themselves.

The audience was in that uncertain, uneasy, semihostile mood when an unexpected sensational incident might transform it into something irrational and dangerous. The Colonel was standing on the platform delivering the funeral oration which some of the audience regarded as most un-Christian and revoltingly pagan. In the coffin beside him were the mortal remains of Joseph Henry Louis Charles, Baron de Palm, by now well publicized as the scion of an ancient baronial family of Bavaria, and a member of The Theosophical Society.

The Colonel had just pronounced the words: "There is but one First Cause, uncreated. . . ." when an excited individual jumped up and shouted: "That's a lie!"

Instantly the crowd was on its feet in an uproar. Some climbed on chairs ready to join in any fighting that might break out; others turned toward doorways and a stampede of escape was imminent. The Colonel writes that, fortunately, he had in the past studied the platform tactics of the great Abolitionist speaker, Wendell Philips. So now he quietly stepped forward a pace and, laying his hand dramatically on the coffin, stood motionless, waiting. . . . A dead silence of expectancy fell on the crowd. Slowly the Colonel raised his other hand and stated with great solemnity, "We are in the presence of the dead." Then he waited again in solemn silence.

The simple, sentimental phrase and symbolic gesture had the desired effect of quelling the excitement. The crowd settled down and the Colonel finished his interrupted sentence, ". . . eternal, infinite unknown."

By this time the police had arrived and were escorting away the man who had started the trouble. Tension was still high and more disturbances liable at this juncture, but Madame Blavatsky, who was in the audience, provided the necessary comic relief. She stood up and called out: "He's a bigot, that's what he is!" Everyone started laughing and she joined in heartily.

So the funeral service was concluded successfully, without benefit of clergy, as had been requested by the deceased. But the question remained; who was to cremate the body? Members of the recently-formed New York Cremation Society had, at the outset, been delighted with the prospect of their first corpse for burning, but they lost courage as outraged public sentiment began to show itself.

Such moral cowardice disgusted the Colonel. His friend the Baron had asked to be cremated, and cremated he would be! Olcott himself devised a scientific method of preserving the body for several months, and, while some means of cremation could be worked out, arranged for it to be kept in a vault at the Lutheran cemetery.

But the notorious "pagan service" at the Masonic Hall had, as Henry had feared, antagonized a bigoted Christian client, and cost him a professional connection worth, he estimated, about "£2000 a year". Quite a loss in those days! On the other hand there were hopes that The Theosophical Society would benefit from a substantial bequest in the Baron's will.

Interested in spiritualism, and apparently eager to learn about Theosophy, the old Bavarian nobleman had joined the T.S. early in 1876. He was living in a New York boarding house, and as he seemed lonely and miserable, Henry had offered him a room in his own apartment. The Baron had accepted eagerly.

Before his death the Baron had mentioned to Olcott that he planned to leave the major part of his fortune for the latter to use in the promotion of The Theosophical Society. Word of this promise had got around, and finally reached the columns of the daily press. Henry began receiving, as a result, congratulatory and begging letters.

An old will left with the Colonel showed Baron de Palm as owner of castles in Switzerland, gold and silver mines, as well as large tracts of land, in America. Hopes were high for the finances of the Society. But on investigation it was found that the land had been sold to pay taxes, the mining shares had less value than wallpaper, and the Swiss castles were "castles in the air."

Furthermore, there was no "cash in hand," no bank balance, no family jewels. When, with the T.S. Treasurer, Mr. Newton, the Colonel opened the dead man's trunk at the hospital where he had died, the most valuable items found were two of Henry's own shirts, from which the stitched name marks had been picked out.

So what kind of a man was the Baron? Official inquiries in various parts of Europe revealed him as one who had lived largely by swindling his fellow men. He had even served a jail sentence. He was indeed a Baron by birth, but a renegade.

Certain unprincipled enemies of Madame Blavatsky later spread the calumny that *Isis Unveiled* was "nothing but a compilation from the manuscripts of Baron de Palm, and without acknowledgement." But no manuscripts were found among his belongings, nor the slightest evidence, wrote the Colonel, "that he had either literary talent, erudition or scholastic tastes."

Henry, himself, far from gaining anything financially, was personally out of pocket through the old decadent nobleman who was, as one journalist put it, "principally famous as a corpse." Nevertheless, the Colonel was grimly determined to do as the dying man had requested, and at the same time pioneer in the West the Oriental method of corpse disposal, which for a number of reasons he considered infinitely superior to burial.

And so, on December 6, 1876, the cremation took place at the small town of Washington, Washington County, Pennsylvania. It was a public occasion although the body was burned in a private crematorium—that of a philanthropic physician who had recently constructed it for himself, and was considered an eccentric. Present at the ceremony were many scientists and members of boards of health and sanitation, also a swarm of reporters from all the leading American and some foreign journals.

Many of the editors had expected the event to provide the next day's main headlines, but that same evening about two hundred people were burned alive in the Brooklyn Theater fire. In the words of the Colonel: "The greater cremation weakened the public interest in the lesser one."

*   *   *

In the fall of 1876, between the Baron's funeral service and cremation, Henry and "Jack" moved to an apartment house on the corner of 47th Street and 8th Avenue. Here, above a shop that fronted onto 8th Avenue, they shared a large apartment, consisting of a writing and reception room, dining room, kitchen, bathroom, hallway, and three bedrooms. This was The Theosophical Society headquarters, and became known to the many visitors, and the public at large, as the "Lamasery."

Henry still regarded the Russian woman as sexless. She was his teacher in occultism, and at the same time his chum, engaged in the same work—a work which they, if few others, regarded as the most important thing in the world. In addition to the sobriquet "Jack," she answered to such nicknames as "Mulligan," "Latchkey" and "Old Horse." She obviously liked this chummy informality from Olcott, but the name she preferred her friends to use was "H.P.B." This, to her, seems to have signified the "co-operative society" that used the outer shell of Helena P. Blavatsky. Work accomplished, such as *Isis,* enlightening discourses delivered in her salon, "miracles" performed, were all done by H.P.B.., *not* Helena alone.

Sadly, the year 1876 saw the gradual dwindling away of the Society on which the Colonel and H.P.B. had pinned such high hopes. George Felt had extracted a hundred dollars from the Society's Treasurer Newton to defray, he said, the costs of the promised occult experiments for invoking elementals, and had delivered one or two lectures of an agreed program. But the Colonel writes: "He showed us nothing, not even the tip of a tail of the tiniest nature-spirit."

Olcott goes on to say that he believed Felt had previously done what he claimed, that is, actually brought forth the spirits of the elements; and H.P.B. backed up this belief. So in his inaugural address to The Theosophical Society Henry had spoken with confidence about Felt's ability to give such an epoch-making demonstration before the Fellows. Meetings were semipublic, in that Fellows of the Society did not feel bound to secrecy about what took place there. Consequently Felt's failure to do what he promised, and the mortifying disappointment of the little group, became publicly known. "He [Felt] left us to be mocked by the spiritualists and every other class of sceptic," wrote the Colonel much later.

Felt, however, in a letter to the *London Spiritualist,* maintained that he did begin to achieve success before The Theosophical Society. He claimed that some of the members saw lights and dark clouds moving across the drawings that formed part of his demonstration. "Certain members of lower degree were impressed with a feeling of dread, as though something awful were about to happen," he wrote, going on to say that some were rendered uncomfortable, others became hyper-critical and abusive, while others left the room: "Madame Blavatsky, who had seen unpleasant effects follow somewhat similar phenomena in the East, requested me to turn the drawings and change the subject." This showed, he maintained, the absolute necessity of forming the Society into degrees for such occult work.

If such events took place, Olcott seems to have forgotten all about them when he wrote of those earliest meetings years later. The fact is that Fellows who were in the Society primarily through their interest in phenomena, and their hope that such could be produced by Felt, drifted away. The Colonel writes that by the end of the year 1876 all that survived of the Society was "the form of a good organization, a clangorous notoriety, and a few more or less indolent members." He goes on to say that W. Q. Judge "was a loyal friend and willing helper, but he was so very much our junior that we could not regard him as an equal third party. He was more like the youngest son in a family. . . ."

Henry did not regard Judge as part of the vital focus that remained as the shell fell away. That focus was the American Colonel and the Russian noblewoman who never for a moment doubted the importance and excellence of the work delegated to them by their Masters. Nor did they doubt its ultimate success. There was just the pair, relying on each other and no one else. The only third party they could count on, they thought, was the big chandelier that hung over their writing table and gave them light into the small hours of the morning. They called themselves the Theosophical Twins.

The confidential talks that punctuated the writing chores beneath the chandelier turned gradually onto the possibility of taking the focus of the great movement-to-be to India. In that land, H.P.B. affirmed, the Society would take firm root, flourish and spread. Its branches would, like the Indian banyan tree, put down roots over a wide area—perhaps over many continents.

The Colonel listened and, deep down, longed to go to

India, longed to get away from the spiritual desert in which Western civilization was growing smug, proud and prosperous, while the empty dogma of the preachers drove more and more from the sinking raft of the traditional faith.

As Lord Lytton wrote of the contemporary scene: "Perhaps the saddest and dreariest thing in the ever-increasing materialism of the age is the ghostly squawking and gibbering of helpless lamentation made over it by the theologists, who croak about their old dry wells wherein no spiritual life is left."

Apart from the impossible struggle to get the Theosophical movement under way in this land of dry spiritual wells and croaking theologists, Henry had his own inner struggles. By now he had received all the proofs he needed, "alike of the existence of the Brothers, their Wisdom, their psychical powers, and their unselfish devotion to humanity." This made him want more and closer intercourse with them. But he had learned from his mentor, H.P.B., that the only road to that close intercourse was through self-conquest, self-denial and self-development; in short, through Raja Yoga.

That was easier said than done. Certainly the glittering colors were fading from the veil of Isis—the world of appearances. The old hungers for fame, wealth, and the pleasures of the flesh were almost dead. But not quite. He writes: "No one knows, until he really tries it, how awful a task it is to subdue *all* his evil passions and animal instincts, and develop his higher nature"*.

Although he had been taught by various Brothers, he says, there were periods when he relapsed into a lower state, with "an outbreak of my old earthly nature." This outbreak would keep away from him the very ones he longed for and needed. He knew that the intense battle for self-conquest, complete self-mastery, is one that a man must fight largely alone. But perhaps in India the interior struggle—as well as the exterior one—would be somewhat easier.

India had, for some hidden reason, always been the fountain of spiritual life. Were not many of the Brothers, the Masters—the modern *Rishis*—there, working behind the scenes for the good of mankind? One of them was their

* From a letter to A. O. Hume in *Hints on Esoteric Theosophy No. 1.*

own great Sadguru, the Master Morya. Yes, he longed to go and establish the headquarters of The Theosophical Society there, but how could he? What about his law practice, his sons, his need to make a living? He must provide for his boys, and even in India one had to eat!

In September 1877, *Isis Unveiled* was published in New York. Its reception from the critics was mixed: "a large dish of hash," "discarded rubbish" were the verdicts of two of them; others were more neutral, while several praised the book highly: "a valuable contribution to philosophic literature . . . with its striking peculiarities, its audacity, its versatility and the prodigious variety of subjects. . . ." wrote one critic. And another, "one of the most remarkable works for originality of thought, thoroughness of research, depth of philosophic exposition, and variety and extent of learning that has appeared for many years."

Henry felt that even the most favorable reviews fell short of the mark. It was pretty obvious that few, if any, of the critics had read the book thoroughly, and none, of course, knew who the real authors were. But he was pleasantly surprised at the reading public's reception of this two-volume, rambling, unusual work. The first edition of 1,000 copies was sold out in ten days. Within a year two reprints had been exhausted, and sales continued steadily. This was unprecedented for a work of such nature.

Later, looking back over two decades, the Colonel wrote of *Isis*: "If any book could ever have been said to make an epoch, this one could. Its effects have been as important in one way as those of Darwin's first great work have been in another: both were tidal waves in modern thought, and each tended to sweep away theological crudities. . . ."

*   *   *

One of H.P.B's favorite "miracles" at this period was the phenomenal production of portraits. No one knew *how* she did it; they simply watched the procedure and observed the effects. Sometimes she took a piece of white silk or paper, covered it with a sheet of clean blotting paper, and rested her elbows on it while she rolled a cigarette. Then she removed the blotter, and there on the upper side of the previously blank silk, or paper, would be a portrait. By this procedure she produced, for instance, an excellent head of their British friend, Professor, the Reverend Stainton Moses. He was in England at the time.

Once she asked Henry to give her a sheet of some crested note paper that he had just brought home from the Lotos Club. She then laid half of the sheet on a piece of blotting paper, scraped a grain of lead from a pencil onto it, and rubbed the surface with a circular motion of the palm of her hand. The Colonel, William Judge, and another visitor inspected the result of this rubbing of lead over a sheet of paper. What they saw was the head of an Indian yogi in *samadhi*. It looked like the work of a great artist—strong, sure, very individualistic. How did it come? They had watched her closely all the while, and the club crest was still on the paper.

But what Henry really desired was a portrait of Master Morya who had not yet shown himself physically or astrally to his devoted Yankee *chela*. H.P.B. promised to procure this, with the Master's permission, at a favorable time. But how long must he wait?

One evening when a French artist, Monsieur Harrisse, was present, Madame whispered to Henry that this was the right time to try. On instructions, Olcott went out to a shop nearby, bought some black and white crayons and a sheet of suitable paper, handed the shopkeeper a halfdollar coin—the price of the goods—and left the shop. "On reaching home," he said, "I unrolled my parcel, and as I finished doing it, two silver pieces of a quarter-dollar each dropped on the floor! The Master, it will be seen, meant to give me his portrait without cost to myself."

H.P.B. asked M. Harrisse to draw the head of a Hindu chieftain as he would conceive one *might* look. He protested that he had no clear idea of such a subject, and wanted to draw something else. But the Twins persuaded him and he finally went to work on an imaginary Hindu head. The Colonel describes the scene as follows:

"H.P.B. motioned me to remain quiet at the other side of the room, and herself went and sat down near the artist, and quietly smoked. From time to time she went softly behind him as if to watch the progress of the work, but did not speak until it was finished, say an hour later. I thankfully received it, had it framed, and hung it in my little bedroom. But a strange thing had happened. After we gave the picture a last glance as it lay before the artist, and while H.P.B. was taking it from him and handing it to me, the cryptograph signature of my Guru came upon the paper; thus affixing, as it were, his imprimatur upon, and largely enhancing the value of the gift. But at that time I did not know whether it resembled the Guru or not, as I had not yet seen him."

Madame declared it a fair likeness. If it were, thought Henry, then it represented a fine example of telepathic influence on the mind of the artist, perhaps from H.P.B., but more likely from the Master himself who may have been invisibly present. How soon, he wondered, could he check the likeness for himself? When the chance came, it proved to be the turning point of his life.

Late one night Henry was sitting in his small bedroom at the Lamasery, reading a book and smoking a pipe. To the left of the chair where he sat was a table, with a gas jet burning over it, and beyond the table another chair and the window that overlooked 8th Avenue. In front of him, on the other side of the room, was his camp cot. Immediately to his right was the door to the inner passage of the apartment. This was the only door of the room, and it was closed. Outside, at the far end of the passage was the exit door of the apartment leading onto the common stairway, and thence to the street. This outer apartment door was always kept locked.

H.P.B. was in her room, presumably asleep. There were no visitors staying in the Lamasery at the time, and all was silent.

Suddenly someone was standing near Henry. A flash of white came into the corner of his eye, and turning his head, he saw a man. But what a man! He writes: "I saw towering above me in his great stature an Oriental clad in white garments, and wearing a head-cloth, or turban, of amber-striped fabric. . . . Long raven hair hung from under his turban to his shoulders; his black beard, parted vertically on the chin

in the Rajput fashion, was twisted up at the ends and carried over the ears; his eyes were alive with soul-fire; eyes
which were at once benignant and piercing in glance; the
eyes of a mentor and a judge, but softened by the love of a
father who gazes on a son needing counsel and advice.

"He was so grand a man, so imbued with the majesty of
moral strength, so luminously spiritual, so evidently above
average humanity, that I felt abashed in his presence, and
bowed my head and bent my knee as one does before a god
or god-like personage. A hand was lightly laid on my head,
a sweet though strong voice bade me be seated, and when
I raised my eyes, the Presence was seated in the chair on the
other side of the table."

From Monsieur Harrisse's sketch, hanging on the bedroom
wall, Henry recognized his visitor. It was a fair likeness, as
H.P.B. had said, and undoubtedly here before him was his
own revered and beloved guru, Master Morya.

"He told me," the Colonel continues, "that he had come
at the crisis when I needed him; that my actions had brought
me to this point; that it lay with me alone whether he and
I should meet often in this life as co-workers for the good
of mankind; that a great work was to be done for humanity,
and I had the right to share in it if I wished; that a mysterious
tie, not now to be explained to me, had drawn my colleague
and myself together; a tie which could not be broken, however strained it might be at times. . .

"How long he was there I cannot tell: it might have been
a half-hour or an hour; it seemed but a minute, so little did
I take note of the flight of time."

When the Master rose to go, the Colonel wondered again
at his great height, estimating it to be about 6 feet, 7 inches,
and the splendor of his countenance. Then the thought
flashed across his mind—perhaps this is just an hallucination,
a *maya,* caused by H.P.B.'s occult hypnotic power. "If only I
had some tangible proof that the Master is really here as he
seems to be—something that I might handle after he has
gone, and show to others!" The Master smiled as he read his
chela's thought. Then he untwisted the *fehta* (turban) from
his head, placed it on the table, saluted benignantly, and was
gone. Olcott's description gives the impression that his guru

seemed to vanish into the air.

The turban remained on the table. It bore the same cryptograph as on Harrisse's crayon sketch. Olcott believed until the end of his life that this was an astral visit by his Master, who materialized his subtle body sufficiently for his pupil to see and feel him, and materialized his turban permanently.*

Afterwards when questioned by members of the Society for Psychical Research, London, Henry could not recall whether his bedroom door was bolted that night as usual, or not. But he was sure that the entrance door of the apartment was securely locked. If H.P.B. knew of the great Rajput's visit, she did not show any signs of it when Henry rushed to beat on her bedroom door and tell her of his wonderful experience. On later occasions when H.P.B. saw one of the visiting Masters before Olcott, she always told him so; this time the visit seemed to be news to her, and, Henry said, "she was as glad to hear my story as I was to tell her."

Returning to his room, he sat down and thought about the sweetness of his recent experience, about the shining Presence, before whom he, an independent Yankee, had spontaneously bent the knee. The grey dawn found him still there, still thinking about all the Master had said to him.

Before he turned out the gaslight, and went to the bathroom to freshen up for the office, he had made his great decision.

---

* Now, about a century later, the amber-striped turban with the cryptograph is still in one piece at the Headquarters of The Theosophical Society in India.

Chapter 7

LIFE AT THE LAMASERY
1878

Though Henry now had no doubts that he and H.P.B. must go to India and plant the theosophical sapling in the sacred soil, forces were still holding him in New York. For one thing he wanted to see his sons launched on careers before he left. He loved them and wanted them to think well of their father, even though, since they lived with their mother, he had not seen as much of them as he would have liked. He wrote in his diary for March 14th: "Dick Morgan at office, cordial and friendly as ever." It was an event to be noted with some satisfaction.

Dick had turned seventeen, and—according to a biographical sketch in the *National Cyclopedia of American Biography*—"had been given a good classical education abroad." This probably meant in Germany where Henry's brother Emmett Robinson (Bob) studied law at the University of Berlin, and stayed on into the '70's to cover the Franco-Prussian War for the *New York Tribune*. Now, however, presumably through the family link with the Pacific Coast, Richard Morgan had been found a post with a business house in San Francisco. Soon he would be going West to make his fame and fortune. Thus one of Henry's ties with New York was breaking.

The second son, William Topping, is not mentioned in any records, except in a letter written by W. Q. Judge who states briefly that William left college at the end of the year 1878. Judge claims that he helped obtain a position for the lad in a commercial firm, presumably in New York City. There seems to have been a close association between the

Henry Olcott's son, Richard Morgan Olcott

Olcott family and W. Q. Judge who later was a salaried employee in Emmett Olcott's law firm in New York.

So the promise of one of the Adepts in a letter to Henry—"Your boys will be provided for, fear naught for them"—was being fulfilled. There was no need to worry about them, but he would certainly miss them. Their mother was a greater problem. He was supplying her with money, and must organize his affairs in a way that would provide her with funds after he had gone to India. This, added to the difficulty of establishing some economic support for H.P.B. and himself after severing his professional ties with America, filled his days with pressing problems. It would be a great relief, of course, if Mary married again, as he hoped she might. But now, if she heard about his projected departure, she would doubtless do her utmost to obstruct it.

"Devote yourself to your main object," wrote the Master. This was difficult, but he knew that it was right, ethically and in every other way that mattered. The world would, of course, say that he was a fool to throw away the assets he had consolidated over so many years. But the world, as usual, was wrong. With his eyes toward the path he had chosen, he worked by a different law, a different measure, from what the world knew. Economic, social, family attachments must be broken if they stood in the way of the main object.

Not that it was duty alone that spurred him on. Before his mind rose a vision of the Sacred Land, and the yearning to learn its secrets, its hidden wisdom. A great new, wonderful adventure was awaiting him. But the question was: how to make the start? This would be the greatest of the many transitions of his life. In a material way, it would be a complete break from all his experience. All that he had learned of law, crime investigation, journalism and scientific agriculture would be of no use to him in British India. Although courageous, he had a cautious streak in him, too—especially now at the age of forty-six.

His father had been a business man; his two sons were going into business; perhaps commerce could provide the answer to his own immediate future problems. He decided to try to lay the foundations for an export-import business between India and America. He had many business contacts through his professional work; he would try to interest them and form a commercial syndicate, he, himself, taking care of the Indian end of the enterprise. But time was short, and time was needed for launching this new thing. Meantime there were his heavy professional duties, and he must play his part in keeping the theosophical fire burning at the Lamasery.

* * *

The bizarre Lamasery had become quite famous in 1878. Describing it, one journalist wrote: "Directly in the center [of the reception room] stood a stuffed ape, with a white 'dicky' and necktie around his throat, manuscript in paw, and spectacles on nose. . . . Over the door was the stuffed head of a lioness, with open jaws and threatening aspect. . . . A god in gold occupied the center of the mantlepiece; Chinese and Japanese cabinets, fans, pipes, implements and rugs, low divans and couches, a large desk, a mechanical bird which sang . . . albums, scrapbooks, and the inevitable cigarette holders, papers and ash-pots, made the loose, rich robe in which the Madame was apparelled seem in perfect harmony with her surroundings." The room had an oriental character, and held many of Madame Blavatsky's travel souvenirs.

From this center H.P.B. conducted her war with the materialists and spiritualists, writing, talking, clipping and pasting. . . . On most evenings the Colonel joined in the talking or wrote articles and lectures on theosophical subjects.

But work and serious discussion were sometimes relieved by the entertainment that both could provide for each other and visitors. Madame could tell strange, wonderful, sometimes terrible, tales of magic and mystery—often backed by personal experience. The Colonel was ready to enliven any party with one of his comic songs, of which he had a good repertoire. The most popular, especially to "Jack," was one that dealt with the Maloney family. It had in course of time, through Henry's inventions, "grown into a mock odyssey of the innumerable descents into matter, returns to the state of cosmic force, intermarriages, changes of creed, skin and capabilities" of the Irish family. The Colonel rendered it in the appropriate brogue, and Madame never seemed to tire

"The Lamasery," New York

of the crazy extravaganza. She nicknamed Henry, "Maloney," and he retaliated by calling her "Mulligan." Both names caught on among their close friends.

The menage in Eighth Avenue was, of course, an open invitation to the malicious tongues of the puritans. So to stem the flow of gossip about the lawyer and the Russian lady living in the same apartment, Henry's sister Belle made a helpful move. She persuaded her husband William Mitchell, a Presbyterian minister, to take the apartment on the floor above the Lamasery. Belle thus became a close friend of H.P.B.; she came to know the noble, self-sacrificing heart of the great Russian occultist, and experienced some of her incredible powers. Apart from lending respectability to the "irregular" arrangement, the wife of a minister of orthodox religion found herself defending the very unorthodox Helena against many slanderous attacks.

Helena rewarded her with undying affection and the privilege of witnessing some strange phenomena. Belle has left several of these experiences on record. Once H.P.B. pulled out a drawer and showed her a large collection of gold bracelets, lockets, rings and other jewelry, ablaze with precious stones. Belle was able to handle and examine them, and assure herself that they were "real." But when H.P.B. closed the drawer and told Belle to open it again, nothing was there. The treasure had all been illusory.

On another occasion Belle was examining a plain gold ring that H.P.B. had produced phenomenally. As it lay in her friend's palm, H.P.B., without touching it, closed Belle's fingers over it. Opening her hand when ordered a moment later, the parson's wife—and others around her—saw that the plain ring had somehow acquired three small diamonds imbedded in the gold in "Gipsy" fashion to form a triangle. This goldsmith work was no illusion, but very permanent. Eventually the ring came to the Colonel who wore it during the latter years of his life, and now it rests among the historic treasures at the international headquarters of The Theosophical Society.

A third phenomenal production for Mrs. Mitchell, in the early months of 1878, had a strange quality of semipermanency. Here is how Henry's sister herself describes it: "One day she [H.P.B.] showed me a string of perfumed beads made of brown clay that was stamped with figures." (Another witness called them "beautiful carved beads of some strange substance that looked like, but was not, hard wood.") Belle's description continues, "As I admired them very much, she asked: 'Dear, would you like to have some?' My reply brought them to me. . . . She charged me not to allow them to be fastened about any other neck than my own, assuring me that if I did they would melt. . ."

Mrs. Mitchell was delighted with the gift, and Henry wrote in his diary: "She is a gone coon and no mistakes—a spoilt Christian."

"Days and weeks passed," said Belle, "and the caution was forgotten, or unheeded. A child being sick, they were clasped around his neck to amuse him." That evening a noted medium was present, and a séance held to gratify Mrs. Mitchell. She was amazed, when the medium was in trance, to hear an Indian voice telling her to remove the beads from the child's neck before they vanished. She hastened to do so, but found that many had already melted away, and the rest were quite hot. Belle felt sure that the medium had known nothing about the beads, and that H.P.B. had not even been aware that the child was wearing them.

Phenomena were taking place every day, the most common one being the ringing of invisible bells—"astral bells," they were called. Henry writes: "In a pause in the conversation perhaps a guest would hold up a finger, say 'Hush!' and then, all listening in breathless silence, musical notes would be heard in the air . . . faintly far away in the distance . . . coming nearer and gaining volume until the elphin music would float around the room, near the ceiling, and finally die away again in a lost chord and be succeeded by silence. Or it might be that H.P.B. would fling out her hand with an imperious gesture and *ping! ping!* would come in the air, whither she pointed, the silvery tones of a bell."

H.P.B. usually gave credit to the unseen Masters for the production of her "miracles," but later in a letter to A. P. Sinnett one of them wrote that she, herself, was an adept in phenomena production, and much of what she attributed to the Masters was actually done by herself.

But, judging by his diary entries, Henry felt sure at the time that many of the "miracles" were the work of the Great Ones. And in addition that they graciously helped in many of the mundane domestic problems of the founders of the T.S.

As a housekeeper Madame was hopeless. Once she had placed an egg, not in a pan of water, but on live coals in order to boil it. A servant was a necessity, but a constant problem. One, named Lizzie, had to be sacked before all the house linen had vanished. Following this, come diary remarks such as: "Cooked my own breakfast," "Dad and I washed up the things. He made the bed, swept the floor, and generally covered himself with glory." The names "Dad" and "Daddy" several times appear in similar contexts. Who was he? Certainly not Henry's own father who had by this time passed away; a diary entry early in 1878 reads: "Burned the letters of my dead parents."

Henry looked upon his guru, the Master Morya, as his spiritual father, and frequently, in contexts that can leave no doubt, referred to him as "Father" or "Dad." It was an attitude that stunned the very respectful, worshipful Hindus, but Olcott meant only affection and love—never disrespect. One can only conclude that the "Dad" of the domestic chores was the benign and majestic Master Morya; that Olcott believed he was occupying "the old appearance" known as H.P.B. when that "appearance" was washing up, sweeping the floor, etc. The Colonel seems to have been quite serious in these diary comments.

But whatever his astral form may have been doing in New York, the guru's physical form was at this period far away in India. This is shown by an event that took place in April 1878. One day Helena suddenly fell unconscious. Nothing that the Colonel or Belle or any of their doctor friends could do would revive her. As the days passed and she remained unconscious, they became exceedingly alarmed. Then the Colonel received a cable from overseas. It read: "Fear nothing. She is neither dead nor ill, but has need of repose. She has overworked herself. . . . She will recover." It was signed by the usual cryptogram of the Master Morya, and had been sent from Bombay, India. After another five days, Madame returned to consciousness and continued her work.

Though The Theosophical Society as a body was now comparatively inactive, holding practically no meetings, a few influential people remained in the nucleus that held around the wonder-working magnet at the Lamasery. One of these was Dr. Alexander Wilder, a distinguished physician, author and Platonic scholar. Another was General Abner Doubleday who was also an author and is credited with being the inventor of the game of baseball. During April Henry was happy to receive as a Fellow of The Theosophical Society the great inventor Thomas Edison, who had just designed and built the first phonograph and made the first record. "Mary had a little lamb" came through the horn of his phonograph to startle his fellow scientists. Edison told Olcott that he was, himself, experimenting in occult fields with some success. Perhaps this was what drew him toward the work of the group at the Lamasery.

In May, 1878, William Quan Judge had returned to the fold after a long absence. The diary for the 12th of that month reads: "Judge's first visit since the grand row of a year ago. Called 'Daddy' the 'Great Unknown'—which rather pleased the old man."

Others, not much interested in either occult matters or altruism, buzzed around the Twins like bees around blooms that give the promise of life's hidden nectar. Nevertheless, some of these, such as Rosa Bates and an architect, Edward Wimbridge, became close friends of the Colonel and Madame Blavatsky. Rosa Bates was a schoolteacher, and Henry writes of her as, "the English lady with the long teeth."

In July New Yorkers were dying from a terrible heat wave. The Twins and the long-legged Wimbridge left the city and traveled by rail and stagecoach to East Hampton, Long Island. On the beach there H.P.B. paddled, "showing an infantile glee to be in such splendid magnetism," while the two men went swimming.

In the evenings the Colonel amused the company where they were lodging, at Captain Gardiner's hotel, by mesmerising his fellow boarders. H.P.B. entertained them on the piano, which she played superbly, and shocked them by her cigarette smoking and verbal attacks on the Christian church. Writes Henry: "Found Mrs. Gardiner, our hostess, in despair over the loss, and threatened loss, of boarders who have been shocked by H.P.B.'s rough-riding over Christianity." The short summer vacation ended after Henry's forty-sixth birthday on August second, and the party relieved the precarious situation at the hotel by returning to New York.

Soon afterward the Colonel received a letter from England to say that a British branch of The Theosophical Society had been formed in London. Six people had been present at its inaugural meeting in June. One of the six was the barrister-at-law, C. C. Massey who had been a visitor at the meeting in New York, in 1875, when the Society was founded. Massey was a serious student of psychic research and Theosophy.

The Colonel apparently knew the six British members individually, for he remarked that they were an "incongruous lot," and it would be a weighty problem to "steer them just right." Nevertheless he was delighted to hear that a branch had actually taken root abroad. When would he be able to transplant the shrunken stem of the main tree from the barren asphalt of New York to the fertile soil of India?

Chapter 8

DIFFICULT DEPARTURE
1878

In the first half of the nineteenth century the writings of the great Indian religious reformer of Bengal, Ramohan Roy, were being read and discussed in New England, which had close trading relations with Calcutta. A few years earlier Sir Charles Wilkins of the British East India Company had made the first translation of the *Bhagavad Gita* into English; Sir William Jones had founded the Royal Asiatic Society of Bengal, and rendered some of the Indian classics into English. Germans, like Schlegel, had initiated the historic dialogue between India and Germany which Max Müller carried on.

Hindu influence on America thus came not only directly from Ramohan Roy's works, but also indirectly through a few English and German writers impregnated with the Indian mystical thought that was slowly seeping into the West. Two fruits of the Eastern influences were: the transcendentalist school of American philosophy with its great literary figures, Emerson and Thoreau, and—on the religious side—the beginnings of a more liberal type of Christianity, usually called Unitarianism.

But though these leavening ingredients were there, working slowly on the old colonial Puritanism, they had not gone deeply enough to affect the mass of the people. The vast majority still followed the set dogmatism of their forefathers. Their angry God, breathing thunder and hell-fire on the wrongdoer, was still very much alive. It was a God-image that kept them trapped in a narrow sterile orthodoxy. The more liberal, open-minded concept had come to only a very few by the year 1878. Fewer still were ready for the profound penetration offered by the study and practice of Theosophy. The soil was too thin for the growth of this mystical tree.

India, itself, after centuries of domination by Western powers, was being steadily perverted with the purely materialistic outlook. But a strong substratum of the liberal, deep religio-philosophy of the sages was still there. It was the function of the new Theosophical movement, as Olcott saw it, to mine for that substratum, to unearth and develop its riches, and to spread them among the spiritually wilting peoples of India and the western world.

During this year a link was formed—in a strange way—between the Lamasery and the Indian people. On quite a different level from his channel with the Masters, another channel was opened which, Olcott thought, might facilitate their move and their work when they reached the great land.

One evening an old friend of Henry's spiritualist days, a Mr. Peebles, called to see him. Peebles had just returned from a trip to India, and had much to tell. As he talked, the Colonel's eyes strayed from his face to a photograph of two Hindus hanging on the wall. Walking across the room, Henry unhooked the photograph and handed it to his visitor.

"Did you happen to meet either of these in Bombay?" he asked, feeling rather foolish at such a question. They were just two of India's millions; Henry had met and become friends with them during his Atlantic crossing in 1870.

By one of the incredible "coincidences" that life sometimes provides, Peebles *had* indeed met one of them, named Moolji Thackersey. Furthermore, he had the Hindu's Bombay address in his pocket.

The Colonel immediately wrote to his old shipboard acquaintance, telling him about the Society, its great aims, and the two founders' plan to go to India. The result was that Moolji not only became a Fellow of The Theosophical Society, but told them of a strong movement in India for spiritual purification and the resuscitation of the Vedic teachings. The movement, called the Arya Samaj* was headed by a great Sanskrit pundit and reformer, named Swami Dayanand. At the same time Thackersey put the found-

* *Samaj* means "Society" and *Arya* may be translated as, "honorable, noble, faithful men."

ers in touch with the president of the Bombay branch of the
Arya Samaj, a man named Hurrychund Chintamon—later,
alas, to prove their first great Indian disillusionment.

As the weeks passed, there was an exchange of letters, books
and opinions between the Colonel and Hurrychund Chintamon. There was even some correspondence with the great
Swami Dayanand himself. Hurrychund, after a while, suggested that, as their aims and principles were the same, the
two groups—The Theosophical Society and the Arya Samaj—
should be amalgamated as one. This, he said, would increase
their power and usefulness. Suspecting nothing devious, the
Colonel found this an appealing idea. From all he had heard
and read of the Arya Samaj, it seemed to him to be almost
a "Hindu Theosophical Society."

So the union came about; the name of The Theosophical
Society was changed to "The Theosophical Society of the
Arya Samaj." Moreover, with misplaced trust, money sub-
scriptions received from members in America were sent to
Hurrychund for the funds of what was now considered the
main society—the Arya Samaj in India.

Before long, however, the Colonel received a document
which convinced him that, contrary to his original opinion,
the Samaj was not really identical in character with his beloved Theosophical Society, "but rather a new sect of Hinduism—a Vedic sect accepting Swami Dayanand's authority
as a supreme judge as to which portions of the Vedas and
Shastras were and were not fallible." This did not, of course,
suit The Theosophical Society. Its eclectic, open-minded
founders and fellows regarded themselves as students of ancient wisdom and modern learning; they were prepared to
consider all, but accept nothing as authoritative—be it from
the Vedas, the Bible, or Darwin. Everything was open to
question and consideration at the bar of one's own reason,
judgment and inner vision.

So the short-lived amalgamation was dissolved and the
name changed back to its original form. The founders took
the opportunity of issuing a circular defining The Theosophical Society's principles and aims. This is an interesting
document, showing that although the original objective,
studying occult science, was still uppermost, two other aims

were proclaimed. One was the formation of the nucleus of universal brotherhood, "wherein all good and pure men of every race shall recognize each other as the equal effects (upon this planet) of one Un-create, Universal, Infinite and Everlasting Cause." The other aim was the revival of Oriental literature and philosophy.

However, although The Theosophical Society felt that it could not run in double harness with the Arya Samaj, it was very sympathetic toward at least one object of the Indian organization: "to elevate mankind out of degenerate, idolatrous and impure forms of worship, wherever prevalent." So friendly association continued, as did the American subscription fees to the Samaj funds. There seemed no doubt that the Samaj, with its thousands of enthusiastic members, would provide a useful bridgehead for The Theosophical Society in India.

The Master Serapis told the founders that they must leave New York by the 17th of December. They set that as their target, but as the months passed, one obstacle after another blocked their path. One of the main causes of delay was Henry's battle to solve his many-sided economic problem; to put his affairs in order in New York, to make enough extra money for their journey, to lay the foundations of a business that would pay for their rent and rice in India. Of course, both he and H.P.B. could make a little money through free lance journalism, but that was a precarious business at best.

He tried desperately hard to form a syndicate of businessmen interested in the development of trade with India. He worked on the promotion of a company to develop a silver mine in Venezuela. If either of these projects succeeded it would give him financial independence. And a big insurance case in Albany held out promise of a large fee that should help tide the Twins over the lean early period in the new land. Henry's diary is a barometer showing the rise of his hopes with every sign of success, and his bitter disappointments with the failures, in the promotion of these enterprises.

One day he writes, "The Hartmann East India Scheme dissolves into thin air, and so one more staggering disappointment falls upon us. No matter. *Try.*" A little later—"Today, as on every preceding one, I was button-holing people to find someone to take Hartmann's capitalist place in the Indian speculation. Hard work and discouraging failures continually. But *Try."*

About a month later, early in October, he writes that business affairs are lively and promising with the Venezuela silver mine again looking up. A friend had "found parties to form a real working company."

One gathers from later entries that although most of the Colonel's big schemes failed to fructify in the short time left before December, he did, by dint of hard work and persistence, establish a few useful business links for future export-import trade with India. As departure day drew near, the silver mine scheme was still very much in the melting pot. If he stayed longer, he thought, he might succeed in getting the company on its feet. If he went—who could tell?

Though one part of his mind worried about economic matters, another part felt sure that the Masters whom they served would never let them suffer real privation. Henry had seen enough proofs that the Great Ones could produce money—from somewhere—when it was required for a good purpose.

On one occasion, while he was still a neophyte, Henry had gone on a special mission for the Brothers. This involved a long absence from his New York office, and a consequent loss of income of—he estimated—about a thousand dollars. When he returned from the mission, he found that this exact amount had been mysteriously credited to his bank account. It had been deposited, the bank officials said, by a very impressive-looking, not easily forgotten Hindu.

There had been several other instances of this sudden appearance of what he called "fairy gold." Where did it come from? he asked H.P.B. The Masters had renounced worldly activities; they were not engaged in any form of money making. How could they produce dollars or other forms of currency when required? All she would tell him was that there were hordes of hidden wealth, in one form or another, to which the Adepts had access. It belonged to no one. But it often had "bad karma" attached to it, and would thus bring harm and misfortune to any ordinary person who found and used it. But the Great Ones knew where it existed and could use it in their work for humanity. Even so, Henry felt it was wrong to expect such "manna from heaven"; it behooved an individual to make every effort for himself.

As December drew near, the Colonel's activities increased in volume and tempo. During the last weeks he did not even find time to write in his diary. Many of the entries for November and *all* for the first half of December were made by H.P.B. They carry a note of urgency, spiced by her characteristic robust humor.

On December 5 she writes that "Junior" [a nickname for Henry because he styled himself, "Morya Junior"] "has got hopes of making his *entree* into Bombay with the Govt. seal stamped upon his backside." Eight days later she writes that he has received "his regular nomination from the Govt. and appointed Commissioner with special passport."

He had received from the President of the United States a letter of recommendation to all American ambassadors and consuls, and the Secretary of State had provided him with a special diplomatic passport; his office (an honorary one) was to promote cultural and commercial relations between the United States of America and other countries of the world. This semiofficial appointment—the fruit of his faithful service in the past—though yielding none of the much-needed cash, gave him a certain status and respectability that was to prove valuable when he ran into political trouble in British India.

Four days before the sailing date set by the Master—December 17—they had still not bought their steamer tickets. But the Lamasery was getting empty of furniture and its miscellany of bric-a-brac. Most of it had gone under the auctioneer's hammer; even three of the landlord's window shades had been sold in error by one of their friends who, H.P.B. wrote, "surpassed himself in zeal" to raise money for them.

Henry had a farewell dinner with his brother Emmett Robinson (Bob), now practicing law in New York. He paid several visits to his dear Belle who had moved from the Lamasery to Orange. But he seems to have kept well away from his divorced wife. The diary shows that he occasionally got "moral essays" from her, indicating how much she disapproved of his "immoral" way of life. H.P.B. nicknamed her "Kali," after the Hindu goddess of destruction. Through newspaper hints of the proposed departure, Kali was probably on the alert. Presumably Henry was still providing her with money, for there were fears that she might take steps to prevent his departure. On December 13, H.P.B. wrote: "Kali suspects departure and thinks of arresting H.S.O." Probably some mutual acquaintance had warned H.P.B. of this.

Earlier in the month some of their trunks had been sent on ahead to Liverpool, England with Rosa Bates, who had decided to settle in India with the founders. Also to be of the India party was Edward Wimbridge. He, like Rosa, does not seem to have been particularly interested in the Theosophical movement as such, but he had strong personal reasons for wanting to get away from America and make a new start in life. Henry judged him to be "an honest, clever fellow." He was satisfied to have both him and Miss Bates as part of the group that would launch the T.S. in India. Being British, they might help the Society's image in official eyes.

Friends flowed in and out of the Lamasery until the very last—some helping, some hindering. Many brought parting gifts. Thomas Edison sent a phonograph, and though it weighed a hundred pounds, the Colonel was determined to take this wonderful new machine along. Some members of The Theosophical Society recorded gramophone greetings to fellow members in India.

At seven in the evening on the 17th Henry returned to the Lamasery with three tickets for voyages to England on the British steamship *Canada*. She was due to sail that very night. The end in New York was near—they hoped.

H.P.B. spent the last evening dining out with a friend. Henry stayed home and wrote letters. Toward midnight they were both ready to leave the apartment. Wimbridge was out carousing with friends and would join them aboard. Charles, their pet cat, had with feline foresight vanished earlier in the day. So they "took leave" of their old faithful friend, the chandelier, and drove off in a carriage to the *Canada*.

They were aboard before midnight, and H.P.B. notes with satisfaction in the diary: "Master S — — had the best of us and we *did* leave the American soil on the 17th." But although their feet were off the soil, they were still dangerously close to it when day broke on the 18th. The ship still lay at the wharf, and as the morning wore on, friends began coming aboard to see them. H.P.B. admits she feared that Kali might yet make some drastic move to prevent Henry from sailing.

At last, about three in the afternoon, the *Canada* loosed her moorings and swung slowly away from the dock. As the gap widened, H.P.B. began to breathe more freely, she said.

But after three or four miles the ship came to a stop off Coney Island, and dropped anchor. Waiting for the high tide, they were told. It would be the following day—the 19th—before they could cross the Sandy Hook bar. "Collapsed in fear again . . ." writes H.P.B. She adds, however, that it was not *real* fear, but a state of exhaustion through using a great deal of psychic power to ward off the danger. "The body is difficult to manage," she comments, "Spirit strong, but flesh very weak."

Evening and night passed, and then came the long morning of the 19th, while they still lay at anchor—vulnerable. Just after midday the pilot came aboard. The ship's engines sprang to life, and they moved toward the bar. H.P.B. held her breath in case they were stuck on the sand, though the Colonel assured her there was no danger of that.

They crossed, and a phase of their life faded away with the grey line of America's coast. The ship's bows cut the silken sea, under a cloudless sky, toward England, thence to India, and the new life.

Chapter 9

ON THE SACRED SOIL

It was sunrise. The Colonel on the deck of the *Speke Hall* gazed across the sparkling waters toward the coast of India, now emerging from the morning mist. Sixty days had elapsed since he sailed out of New York harbor. Fifteen of them had been spent in England; the rest aboard dirty ships, mostly in dirty weather.

England—now far behind—had been a pleasant interlude. He and H.P.B. had stayed at Norwood Park, London, with Dr. and Mrs. Billing—spiritualists-cum-theosophists. There had, of course, been meetings with members of the young British branch of the Society. Many visitors had called for discussions, and to enjoy the thrill of Madame conjuring objects from nowhere—a Japanese teapot for Mrs. Billing, an inlaid card case for Mr. C. C. Massey, and other items for other people. Also several spiritist séances with Mrs. Billing as medium had given evidence that her "guide" *Ski* was a messenger of the Indian Masters.

But the most striking incident happened one morning in a typical London fog. The Colonel and two friends were walking along Cannon Street in the City when one of the Masters passed close to them. They all noticed him, and Henry says: "I did not recognize him for an acquaintance, but I recognized the face as that of an Exalted One." The Master kept on his way and was immediately lost to sight in the fog. When sometime later the three friends returned to the Billings' house, they were told by both Mrs. Billing and H.P.B. that the Master had been there to talk to H.P.B. on occult business. He mentioned that he had seen the Colonel and his two companions on Cannon Street.

Henry had made a few purchases: a simple, light-weight

phonograph to replace the heavy American model which was giving trouble; a suit of clothes from a shop in Holborn Viaduct for £1-12-1—"very cheap." The most important purchase was tickets for the party aboard a ship leaving a week later for India. In Liverpool in the rain, on January 19th, 1879, they went aboard the unspeakable *Speke Hall*—"a narrow, dirty vessel with a cargo of coal."

The four of them (Rosa Bates had joined the party) brought the passenger list up to forty: "British army officers, civil service employees, Bombay brokers and merchants, and young women going out to fish for husbands." It was not a crowd calculated to take an interest in spiritual philosophy. In fact most were suspicious of it, and when one of their number—Ross Scott, a judge in the Indian Civil Service—joined The Theosophical Society, some threatened to report him to the British authorities for subversive activities. Ross Scott laughed with disdain.

Now, on February 16, Henry shaded his eyes to look across the Bombay harbor ablaze under the early Indian sun. He searched for the outline of Elephanta, "the type and visible representative of that Ancient India, that sacred Bharatavarsha, which our hearts had longed to see revived." But more obvious, on the promontory of Malabar Hill, was the symbol of the India they disliked—the sumptuous bungalows of the British, "the garish splendor of the new order of things . . . where the sincerest worship is paid to the Queen's idol on the current rupee."

The ship's anchor was hardly dropped before three Hindu gentlemen climbed aboard, and hurried toward the theosophical party on deck. They all seemed strangers to the Colonel, but he opened his arms and pressed them to his breast. Then he found that one of them was in fact his old friend Moolji Thackersey, unrecognizable in the clothes of his caste—"the dhoti and topcoat of white muslin and the red turban with its quaint helmet-like shape and horn pointing forward above the brow."

Another of the three was Pandit Shyamji Krishnavarma who was later to become famous as the coach of Professor Monier Williams, Orientalist of Oxford University. But where was the one who had been their chief correspondent in

India—Hurrychund Chintamon? The three, who had spent
the night on board a "bunder boat" waiting for the *Speke
Hall,* did not know.

The party went ashore on the bunder boat. "The first
thing I did on touching land," writes the Colonel, "was to
stoop down and kiss the granite step; my instinctive act of
pooja! For here we were at last on sacred soil . . . in a very
real sense to me they [the Indians] are my people, their
country my country; may the blessings of the Sages be and
abide with them and with it always!"

There were still no signs of Hurrychund among the color-
ful crowd. Before leaving New York, Olcott had written
asking him to find for them "a small, clean house in the
Hindu quarter, with only such servants as were indispensable. . ." So until he showed up, they did not know
where to go. They could only stand waiting in the gathering
heat.

At last he came and took them to the house. It was small
enough, situated in a forlorn compound, adjoining a glass-
roofed photographic studio. Both the studio and the house
proved to be Hurrychund's own property.

Visitors began pouring in soon after their arrival and on
the evening of the following day a reception was held in
the photographic studio at which 300 guests were present.
This was a deeply moving experience for the Theosophical
Twins. Addresses of welcome, accompanied by garlands,
limes, and rose-water, were given with that combination of
reverence and warmth which only the Indians know how to
achieve. The Colonel's diary says: "The occasion fairly
brought the water to my eyes. The long-expected moment
comes at last, and I am face to face with my spiritual kins-
men."

But soon came the rude awakening. They had been pressing the reluctant Hurrychund to tell them the rent of the
house. This was important, for their means were limited.
At last he presented an account that made the Colonel stare.
And this was immediately followed by another shocking
revelation. Here is Olcott's description of it.

"Our supposed hospitable entertainer [Hurrychund Chin-
tamon] put in an enormous bill for rent, food, attendance,

repairs to the house, even the hire of the three hundred chairs used at the reception, and the cost of a cablegram he had sent us, bidding us hasten our coming. . . . Protests came, one thing led to another and we finally discovered that the considerable sum of over six hundred rupees (not then a vanishing silver disk but a substantially valuable token) which we had sent through him to the Arya Samaj, had got no further than his hand, and a precious clamor arose among his Samajist colleagues. I shall never forget the scene when H.P.B., at a meeting of the Arya Samaj, let loose at him the bolts of her scorn, and forced him to promise restitution. The money was returned, but our dealings with the man came to a sudden stop. We set to work to find a house for ourselves, and got one for less than half the rent he was charging us for his own. . ."

Less than three weeks after their arrival in India they moved to the new house at 108 Girgaum Back Road. Moolji Thackersey found them a servant, a fifteen year old Gujerati boy named Babula. He spoke five languages, including English and French, and was to remain their faithful—and well-known—servant for many years.

In the palm-shaded Girgaum house almost every evening brought an impromptu durbar where people gathered to discuss philosophy, metaphysics, science, and The Theosophical Society. The Colonel was asked to give a public lecture to make known the purpose of this new, much-discussed—but somehow mysterious—society. The Hindus were thrilled to hear that its aim was to revive the ancient Eastern wisdom, and word had spread that behind the new movement was tremendous supernormal power. But centuries of foreign domination had created deep suspicion. Could people from the West come with a pure, disinterested purpose, or did some diabolical imperialistic intrigue lie hidden in the background?

At Framji Cowasji Hall, on the night of March 23rd, "the crowd was so dense as to pack the hall, balconies and stairways, until not one more man could have been crowded in." On the platform sat the new arrivals from the Western world, together with the leading figures of the different local communities of Bombay.

The Colonel, experienced in lecturing in America, was often inclined to speak "off the cuff," but for this occasion he had prepared his address carefully, writing it out in full. It was a long address, and when published some years later, it filled 25 printed pages. It must have taken nearly two hours to deliver.

Correspondents had previously sent him seventeen written questions, and Henry attempted to "cursorily glance at all" in the time at his disposal. Some of the questions concerned theosophical ideas about God, the immortality of the human soul, the next world, and the practical value of the study of occult sciences. Others asked what were the *concealed* aims of the Society.

The Colonel told his audience that there was room in the Society for members of all religions, that it did not offer any new creeds or dogmas, but was in fact for students who wished to search deeply into the latent nature of man, with the help of the occult sciences evolved by the rishis of old. He sketched the history of the Society and its conflict with established Christianity in the West. He pointed out how the young physical sciences, cocksure though they were, could not give the answers men sought to the profoundest question of existence. These answers could only come from within man himself through yogic self-mastery, guided by the ancient wisdom.

Frankly he attacked the degenerate state of Hinduism and the Indians of that day: their loss of faith in their ancient heritage of spiritual philosophy and culture, their toadying to the British and ruling classes, their impracticality and love of talk rather than action.

But at the end he struck a note of hope and confidence. Indians would awake to their responsibilities and another great leader would arise from among them. Then India would once more become the world fountain of true religion—and true science. He hoped he had made it clear that The Theosophical Society had no hidden aims beyond the altruistic ones stated openly. He emphasized the need for a reawakened India, and concluded with these words: "The youth of India will shake off their sloth, and be worthy of their sires. From every ruined temple, from every sculp-

tured corridor cut in the heart of the mountains, from every
secret vihara where the custodians of the Sacred Science keep
alive the torch of primitive wisdom, comes a whispering voice,
saying: 'Children, your Mother is not dead, but sleepeth.' "

Olcott notes in his diary that the lecture aroused "great
enthusiasm" and was a "grand success." Press comments were
on the whole good, the *Indian Spectator* declaring:

"A greater mission never was conceived. Let the Aryans
make common cause; let the Hindus, Parsis, Mohammedans,
Christians forget their differences, and the day of India's
regeneration is not far off." Even the Christian missionaries
who were present at the lecture were surprised and pleased
to find that the speech was, as one of their journals reported,
more an attack on Hinduism, as it had become, than on
Christianity.

On Good Friday, April 11, 1879, Olcott and H.P.B. set
off on their first long journey into the Indian interior. With
them went friend Moolji Thackersey and Babula. Their
main objects were twofold: to meet the famous Swami
Dayanand and to begin spreading the gospel of Theosophy.
At the same time they would be on the look-out for any interesting yogis, particularly wonder workers.

They traveled by train to the northern plains where the
heat made even Moolji catch his breath. At a station refresh-
ment room they met its manager, Babula's former master, a
lively Frenchman who had earlier been a steward of the
Byculla Club in Bombay. He had *not*—states the Colonel—
been a professional conjurer as later alleged by certain
Western cynics in an attempt to discredit H.P.B.'s powers.

In Rajputana: "We were on what to my 'chum' and myself
was classic ground, for it was associated with the history of
the splendid Solar Race of Rajputs, to which our own
Teacher [Master Morya] belongs and which enchains all our
sympathies."

The Colonel writes in his diary that on the train journey
to Jaipur they "passed the castle where my Father's [Master
M.'s] mother was born long ago."

After Jaipur they went to Saharanpore to meet Swami
Dayanand. The Arya Samaj gave them a formal reception
on the first evening when, in true Indian fashion, they ate

off leaf plates on the floor, using their right hands as the only cutlery.

Henry first met Swami Dayanand next morning as he completed his dawn bath at a well in a leafy grove. "His appearance, manners, harmonious voice, easy gestures and personal dignity" impressed the Colonel.

They sat together and exchanged a few compliments. Then later the Swami came to the dak bungalow where the party of Theosophists was staying, and made the acquaintance of H.P.B. Here there was a long conversation in which the leader of the Arya Samaj defined his views on nirvana, moksha and God in terms to which the founders of The Theosophical Society "could take no exception." Swami Dayanand accepted a place on the Council of The Theosophical Society, recommended the expulsion of Hurrychund Chintamon, and fully approved plans to have sections of the Society composed of sectarians—Buddhists, Parsis, Mohammedans, Hindus, and so on. He seemed to have been misrepresented to them earlier, for here was an eclecticism of which they happily approved.

Together the heads of the two organizations traveled to Meerut, where both the Swami and the Colonel lectured to a large gathering of Samajists. The leaders of the two societies agreed to work in close cooperation, and this seemed to give The Theosophical Society some ready-made audiences. Olcott was pleased, for the role of lecturer had fallen squarely on him. H.P.B. was a brilliant conversationalist, the mistress of the drawing room, but she never cared to address a large public audience. Both the founders felt that the courageous, if pugnacious, Swami, fervently intent on purging and purifying Hindu religious practices, was a worthwhile ally to have in the great work that lay ahead of them.

The cementing of this alliance seemed to them at the time the greatest achievement of their first Indian safari. They had been feted by some wealthy Indians and princes, but insulted by others who had scented the bad official odor about the couple. There was small wonder for this as rumors had gone around, and, anyway, a British government sleuth had been clumsily dogging their footsteps for the whole 3000 miles of their northern journey. With one thing and another, the trip had been tiresome, unbearably hot, and most uncomfortable—especially for H.P.B.

They were glad to see the Bombay railway station again. But before attending to her bags, H.P.B. marched up to the adhesive detective, who had just alighted on the platform, and gave him a piece of her mind. With biting irony she complimented him on the results he must have achieved from his long expensive journeys in first class carriages, bearing his large wardrobe and fine selection of false beards and moustaches. She sent her compliments to his superiors, adding that she would be glad to give a recommendation for his promotion.

The man blushed and stammered, at which she felt sorry, for his only fault was the foolish inefficiency with which he had carried out his assignment. His government was to blame for sending him on such a senseless mission. Consequently, before going home the Twins drove to the United States Consulate and "demanded that the Consul should send a vigorous protest to the Chief of Police for his insulting treatment of inoffensive American citizens." H.P.B. had taken out papers as an American citizen before leaving New York.

Notwithstanding her official American citizenship, however, Helena Petrovna Blavatsky was considered a Russian by the British Intelligence people—a Russian of the ruling class, and therefore suspect. The old fears of Russian designs on India were as strong as ever. Stronger perhaps, with the recent troubles in Afghanistan, where the lion and the bear maneuvered as always for positions of strategic power. Many in India preferred to try the devil they did *not* know rather than suffer any more from the one they did; so the British disarmed the people and gagged the press.

To the official mind neither the Russian lady nor the Yankee Colonel could be fitted into any known category that was respectable. They did not mix with the Western sahibs and memsahibs. They did not observe the color line, "drawn across the gateway of almost every Anglo-Indian [British] bungalow." Their publicly-stated purposes in India were not very credible. Their so-called Theosophy was most likely a cover for something else—perhaps spying for Russia. After all, the Colonel could not be expected to have any love for a Britain whose official sympathies had been with his recent enemies—the slave states of the South. To say the least, the Yankee and the Russian were an odd pair, and their activities must be closely watched.

Documents in the National Archives of America show that the Colonel was, in the spare time available, carrying out some official jobs requested by his own government. He sent back reams of information about tents and equipment used by the British East India Army. This information was obtained officially and openly from the right quarters. He furnished long reports to the Secretary of State on his efforts to promote better trade relations between India and America— a very difficult task at the time.

There were no personal gains from this hard work. If the Colonel hoped that some financial rewards would come, he was bitterly disappointed. His principals in Washington, though they had given him commissions, would not even let him use the title "United States Commissioner"—which would have, at least, been a help in his work, and increased his prestige with both British and Indians.

Money was their big problem in their first year in India, as Henry had feared. For their long journey north the Masters had provided the funds (some 2000 rupees), but they had to earn their own bread in Bombay—somehow. Using the business contacts he had established in New York, Olcott managed to earn some money through exports and imports. His diary shows that he exported tiger skins and curios, and imported clocks. And there may have been other items of merchandise. Both founders were able to make a little with their pens, H.P.B. writing for the Russian papers, and Henry doing an occasional article for a New York daily . . ."$15 per column from *N.Y. World,* measured after publication, and *Graphic,* $10 per week." Indian news was not of much interest to America at that time.

Thus, exuding pints of perspiration in the Bombay summer heat, Henry battled to earn what they needed. So tight things were that he even "regretted the money" spent on buying himself a bed. To add to the gloom of his financial horizon, he received word that his hopes of the silver mine had come to nought, and that he had been cheated out of his $10,000 fee in the Albany insurance case.

Sometimes he called himself a fool for coming to India before making adequate material preparations; at times he felt sorry for himself; at others he felt confident that the Masters would never see them in real want. But his guru pointed out that he was wrong in all these reactions and attitudes. In a stern letter he reminded Henry that it had been his "own fervent desire to go to India," and said: "do not hope that at the last moment you will be helped. If you are unfit to pass your first probation and assert your rights of a future Adept by forcing circumstances to bow before you—you are totally unfit for further trials." In other words, give up vain regrets and self-pity, put your shoulder to the wheel and count on no one but yourself.

Nevertheless, beneath the surface, the Masters were incubating economic assistance. Soon after the receipt of his guru's chastening letter, the Colonel was inspired with an idea that might eventually solve their financial and also other problems.

The volume of written inquiries about Theosophy and The Theosophical Society had been growing to such an extent that by the middle of the year 1879 both Olcott and H.P.B. often found themselves working until two or three o'clock in the morning in order to cope with the necessary replies. It would be impossible to bear the strain much longer. Furthermore, the same questions were repeated by many of the correspondents, and the founders were constantly repeating the same written answers.

Then came the idea of publishing their own magazine, through the columns of which they could answer the many queries, and generally spread the theosophical teachings. But there were risks involved. Some capital, as well as much work, would be needed to launch the magazine, and it might not sell.

On July 4, 1879, they made their great decision to go ahead with preparations. Henry wrote the prospectus; some active Indian members worked to get subscribers; H.P.B. wrote articles and obtained others; Wimbridge designed the cover; Master Morya came in his physical body on July 15, to talk to the leaders; other members of the great Brotherhood took an active interest in the project—Master Narayan ("the revered Old Gentleman") even ordering certain changes four days prior to publication date.

On October 1 the first issue of *The Theosophist* appeared. It was unique and vital. Behind the magazine in the early days was the enthusiasm of the founders and the inspiration of several Masters, some of whom, using pseudonyms, contributed articles from time to time. In fact—like the Society itself—the monthly journal was in reality the child of those who worked behind the facade.

With its fourth issue—January 1880—*The Theosophist* began to show a profit, and went on from strength to strength. It was not long before the Colonel was able to forget his pressing financial worries, forget his distasteful export-import business, and concentrate on the work for which he had come to India. The work itself, through the medium of the new magazine, provided him and H.P.B. with a modest but adequate and steady income.

*   *   *

The first twelve months of The Theosophical Society in India saw the arrival of some of its important future workers. One of these was Damodar K. Mavalankar, a young man who soon became a frequent visitor. The Colonel describes his arrival in the evenings, out of the Bombay rains, "clad in a white rubber waterproof and leggings, a cap with flaps to match, a lantern in his hand, and the water streaming from the end of his long nose." When all the waterproofs were peeled off, one saw a thin frame, lantern jaws, and legs "like two lead pencils."

Damodar was a serious-minded, intense young Brahmin, interested in nothing but the search for occult knowledge and spiritual development. He was one of the few who, through dogged determination, found the gateway to his highest aspirations.

The year also struck the keynote and set the pattern for the Colonel's constant traveling. From the time he came to India until his death he seems to have been, like Ulysses, "forever wandering with a hungry heart." But it was not so much hunger for something elusive as the urge to get on with his inspired mission—the spread of Theosophy.

On December 2, 1879, Olcott and Madame Blavatsky, accompanied by Damodar and the servant Babula, left for the north again. This time the prime object of the journey was to visit Mr. and Mrs. Sinnett at Allahabad—two more of the vital future workers in Theosophy.

As Editor of the *Pioneer,* the most influential newspaper in India, Alfred Percy Sinnett held a key position in British-Indian society at this time. As well as being a first class journalist, he was keenly interested in the occult questions of the day. In fact the Colonel had only been nine days in India when he received his first letter from Sinnett. It asked for information about The Theosophical Society and promised to publish any interesting facts in the *Pioneer.* He would, Sinnett said, be happy to make the personal acquaintance of the two founders. Correspondence eventually led to an invitation from the Sinnetts to come and spend a time at their residence at Allahabad.

Early on the morning of December 4 the travelers reached Allahabad railway station, and found Mr. Sinnett there, "with his barouche and pair, coachman and two footmen in handsome liveries." At the house Mrs. Sinnett received the visitors charmingly, and "before she had spoken a dozen sentences," wrote Henry, "we knew that we had won a friend beyond price."

Patience Sinnett noted in her diary for the day that Madame Blavatsky was: "a most original old lady who promises great amusement." Mr. Sinnett's impressions were also good, but after a time this rather conservative Britisher began to be disturbed by the Russian lady's behavior which, he said, "offended against good taste in many ways, especially in her treatment of Colonel Olcott, to whom she dealt out very rough language from time to time and tyrannized over to an exasperating degree."

Why, wondered Sinnett, did this veteran of the Civil War, this ex-lawyer put up with such vile treatment. The Colonel, he says, once gave him an answer to this: "Do you think I would stand going about with that mad Frenchwoman if I did not know what lies behind her!"* He would be re-

---

* See *The Early Days of Theosophy in Europe,* by A. P. Sinnett.

Alfred P. Sinnett (1840-1921)

ferring, of course, to the Masters behind her, but would he make a mistake about her nationality? This casts some doubt on the authenticity of the remark.

Many important people came to the Sinnett's to meet the Theosophists. And despite her unorthodox manners, H.P.B. so intrigued the company that she and the Colonel were invited out to a number of houses; they began to make the acquaintance of the British rulers of India. Such social gatherings were not, however, to the taste of either of the founders, though two of the people they met were destined to play a part in their Society, and their lives.

One of these was Mr. A. O. Hume who had been Secretary to the Government, and now held an important position in the Indian Civil Service. Later he was to become known as the "Father of the Indian Congress." The second person was Mrs. Gordon, the wife of Major-General W. Gordon. She was at this time, the Colonel says, "in the prime of her beauty and sparkling with intelligence." He goes on to say that it was worth the whole voyage to India just to get to know Mrs. Gordon and the Sinnetts.

The founders spent eleven days at Allahabad, talking Theosophy and producing miraculous phenomena for people, most of whom, no doubt, thought it merely some kind of clever conjuring trick. Then accompanied by the Sinnetts and Mrs. Gordon, the Twins took train for Benares. At the station to meet them were Damodar and Babula—who had gone on ahead—and an agent of the Maharaja of Vizianagram, whose guests they were to be.

At Benares they met "Majji,"* a famous yogini who lived in a cave on the banks of the Ganges. She was well versed in Vedanta, and "appeared to be about forty years of age, fair-skinned, with a calm dignity and grace of gesture that commanded respect. . . . She refused to show us phenomena (always, it will be recollected, our first request on such occasions)," wrote Henry.

During another visit to Majji by the Colonel, Mrs. Gordon, and Damodar, she said that H.P.B.'s body was occupied by a yogi who was working, so far as he could, for the spread of Eastern philosophy. The Colonel writes that, "What is cer-

---

* Sometimes also spelled "Maji."

tain is that the occupant of her [H.P.B.'s] body had a most recalcitrant one to manage." He spoke from hard experience. But he suffered the tempers and tantrums of the Russian temperament not only because of "what was behind her," but because he observed that she dealt out the rough treatment only to those who were close to her, to those whose faith in the cause would stand up to any test. Others she treated with gloved hands. In a way, then, her abuse was a compliment; she drew the sword of her tongue only on those she deemed worthy.

The Colonel lectured a number of times in the holy city, once to a meeting of the Literary Society of the Benares pandits, convened in his honor. In this he pleaded for the revival of Sanskrit learning, and for the invention of Sanskrit equivalents for the many words derived from Latin and Greek employed in modern scientific writing. The need of the hour, he said, was to show every student "how much the Aryan thought was in harmony with modern scientific discovery, how his ancestors had traversed the whole field of knowledge, and how proud and glad he ought to be that he was . . . the heir of their wisdom." Olcott was elected as an honorary member of the Literary Society.

That evening some of the pandits came to the palace where the theosophical party was staying. One of the visitors was the principal of Benares College, Professor G. Thibaut, a German and an old pupil of Max Müller. Swami Dayanand, Damodar, and Mrs. Gordon were also present. Professor Thibaut sat on Madame Blavatsky's right on a sofa, frock coat buttoned to his chin, his intellectual face looking very solemn, his cropped hair standing up like spikes on his head. Toward the close of the evening, devoted to the discussion of Indian themes, Thibaut remarked to H.P.B.: "These pandits tell me that in ancient times there were yogis who had actually developed the *siddhis* described in the *Shastras*, that they could do wonderful things, such as making a shower of roses fall in a room like this; but that nobody can do such things now."

Perhaps he had heard of H.P.B.'s powers, and was making a subtle challenge. If so, his challenge was accepted. H.P.B. gave him a scornful look, and replied:

"Oh, they say no one can do it now? Well, I'll show them. If the modern Hindus were less sycophantic to their Western masters, less in love with their vices, and more like their ancestors, they would not have to get an old Western hippopotamus of a woman to prove the truth of their *Shastras*."

Setting her lips, and muttering something, she swept her right hand through the air with an imperious gesture. Onto the heads of the startled pandits fell about a dozen roses.

The professor was so dumbfounded that, in the scramble for the *apported* blooms, he failed to get one.

A discussion on the Sankhya philosophy followed this phenomenon, Dr. Thibaut putting many searching questions to H.P.B. At the end of it he declared that neither Max Müller, nor any other Orientalist, had made the *real* meaning of the philosophy as clear to him as she had. He thanked her with a little Teutonic bow, and fixing his eyes on the floor, as was his habit, he said:

"I unfortunately did not obtain one of those unexpected roses, so would you kindly produce another for me as a souvenir of this delightful evening?" Perhaps he suspected that the first fall was a trick, and that she would not be prepared for a second production.

But Madame replied promptly: "Yes, certainly—as many as you like."

She made another sweeping gesture and down came another shower of roses, one of them hitting the professor on the top of his spikey head and bouncing onto his lap. The effect was so comical to the Colonel that he collapsed in laughter.

But there was yet another surprise in store for the solemn Sanskrit scholar who seemed so anxious to prove to himself that the ancient *Shastras* spoke the truth about the potential powers in man. As the Colonel and Madame Blavatsky bade goodnight to him on a veranda outside the doorway, where Damodar was standing with an oil lamp to light the way, H.P.B. took the lamp, held it up in her left hand, pointed her right forefinger at the flame, and commanded imperiously: "Go up!"

The flame rose and rose until it came to the top of the chimney. Then, "Go down!" She ordered, and it slowly descended until it burned bluish at the wick. A second time, at her command, it rose to the top, and sank again almost to the point of extinction. Then she handed the lamp back to Damodar, nodded farewell to the stunned Professor Thibaut, and walked inside.

The next day the party returned to Allahabad. On December 26 the Colonel, as President, received Mr. and Mrs. Sinnett into The Theosophical Society. One of the questions in the initiation ceremony at that time was directed to the unseen Masters, and asked if they approved of the candidate's admission. On this occasion, says Henry, there was an audible reply—"Yes, we do." Time would show that the Masters had planned a key role in the Theosophical movement for the Sinnetts.

Four days later the theosophical party left for Bombay, reaching there on New Years Day, 1880. Their first year on the "sacred soil" was over. What had it brought? Friends gained, some enemies baffled, money problems solved, the foundations for the Society in India laid, and "621 subscribers to *The Theosophist*" after only four months. In a country where leading dailies had only between one and two thousand names on their mailing registers, this was a good circulation for a young magazine devoted to occult subjects.

Chapter 10

SIMLA AND THE SAHIBS
1880

The first few months of 1880 were occupied with the routine work of getting out *The Theosophist,* lecturing, admitting new members, and general administration. Punctuating this was the excitement of more unexpected contacts with the hidden Brotherhood. A diary entry for March 24 reads:

"Evening. H.P.B. took Damodar and myself to Worlee Bridge. A superb and striking electric storm raged. As we sat in the carriage enjoying the scene and the sea-breeze, Hamlet, one of our Brothers and a pupil of T. (Tuitit) Bey's, showed himself, came to the carriage, touched H.P.B.'s hand, and saluted us. He moved in silence and with such dignity as to deeply impress me. Then he walked off fifty yards and disappeared." Henry explains that there were no bushes, buildings or other objects behind which the Brother could have walked. He excitedly jumped out of the carriage and ran ahead to the spot where the Great One had vanished, hoping to catch a glimpse of him somewhere. But there was no one to be seen.

H.P.B. later wore a large gold locket in which was a portrait of this Master seen at the Worlee Bridge.

It was three days after this event that Mr. and Mrs. Coulomb, who were to be antagonists in the theosophical drama, stepped onto the stage, appearing unexpectedly at the doorway of the founders' Bombay residence. One who knew them described Mrs. Coulomb as a "wrinkled and witch-like" creature, and her husband as a "ghostly-looking Frenchman with the complexion of an ash-barrel to which is attached a black beard and with a glass eye that transfixed you while its mate wandered about uncertainly."

Alexis Coulomb was of a French family that had settled in Egypt, while his wife—formerly Emma Cutting—was British by birth. They had just arrived in Bombay by ship from Ceylon. Their fares had been paid by the French Consul in Ceylon. They were penniless.

Some years earlier—H.P.B. told the Colonel—this couple had given her some timely help when she had landed in Egypt after suffering shipwreck and the loss of her worldly possessions. They had certainly been friends in need, and now she must do her best to return the good service. The Colonel agreed heartily. Poor though they were, they invited the destitute couple to stay with them, and Henry dashed off to the bazaar to hire furniture for their use.

Soon afterwards he found Alexis a job as a machinist in a cotton mill. But this did not last long; Coulomb was "very quick-tempered and hard to please in the matter of employers." So in the end it was decided that the couple could stay on indefinitely at the headquarters of the Society at Girgaum Back Road, Alexis as handy man, doing repairs, alterations and so on, Emma as assistant housekeeper to Rosa Bates. Neither of the founders suspected at this time that "Coulomb" spelled "Calamity."

It was during this year that the founders made their historic first journey to Ceylon, and the Colonel began his epic battle for the revival of Buddhism. But that theme belongs to another chapter.

Before setting off, the Colonel, with an unusual lack of diplomacy for him, put Emma Coulomb in charge of household affairs during their absence. In other words, he promoted her over the spinster schoolteacher, Rosa Bates, who had been of the original party. Doubtless Emma was more experienced in housekeeping matters, but the situation was hardly likely to foster harmony and happy relations.

The founders returned from Ceylon to find a domestic cyclone brewing. The two women were at daggers drawn, with Rosa Bates even accusing the Coulomb woman of attempting to poison her. The Colonel thought this accusation quite absurd, and said so. Then the storm burst. "Hell of an explosion between Rosa and us. . . . This settles her hash;

she must go." Wimbridge sided with Rosa, his compatriot, and went too.

She was offered a return ticket to New York, but she rejected it and moved off somewhere—out of the records. Olcott helped Wimbridge to start an art-furniture business in Bombay. Apparently he at last met with success here and, it is said, made his fortune.

August brought the Colonel's 48th birthday and a present of a pair of gold-framed spectacles from "Latchkey," as he usually called H.P.B. at this period. Toward the end of the month he and H.P.B. and Babula left Bombay on another trip to the north. They planned to join the Sinnetts at Simla.

En route to the Himalayas, at Meerut, Olcott had a long discussion with Swami Dayanand on various aspects of yoga, including the *siddhis*. At the end of it Henry asked the Swami what he would call phenomena such as the ringing of invisible bells, the shower of roses from the ceiling, and the rise and fall of the lamp flames on command, as he had witnessed from H.P.B. at Benares.

"They are genuine phenomena of yoga," Dayanand replied.

Simla in the summer season was the headquarters of the Viceroy's government, and here the British sahibs who ruled India, along with their loud-speaking memsahibs, were seen at their snobbish worst. "It was a hierarchical society, some civilians and their wives ranking first, then the army officers, and finally the businessmen. The Simla Government issued an elaborate warrant of precedence with 63 ranks—the Viceroy at the top and a superintendent of a telegraph workshop at the bottom. It included military as well as civil ranks, the Archdeacon of Calcutta ranking immediately below a brigadier and immediately above the Tea Controller of India."*

Mr. Sinnett was very much afraid that the eccentric, tempestuous Russian occultist would upset the strict code of good taste and decorum in this imperial snobocracy. He pleaded with her to say nothing about Theosophy—or the "spy business" which unfortunately still tormented the founders—for the first few days. She must keep a calm, reserved unexcitable mien if she would impress the sahibs and memsahibs.

---

* *The Fall of The British Empire"*, by Colin Cross.

Olcott backed Sinnett up in this advice; he felt it important to make this "heart of Anglo-India . . . send life-blood
into our Society." Also this was perhaps their golden opportunity to get clear of the spy suspicion once and for all.

So the social round began. To "Brightlands"—the Sinnett's house—came important civil servants, including Mr.
Hogg, the Director General of the Postal Department; Mr.
Kipling, Director of the Lahore School of Arts and father
of Rudyard Kipling; and Mr. A. C. Lyall, Government Secretary in the Foreign Department. Among the army officers
who came was a Major P. C. Henderson, "our old foe of the
Secret Service who sent the detective after us."

Of course H.P.B. soon forgot her promises to behave in
a seemly and circumspect manner. At the dinner parties held
at "Brightlands," "Rothney Castle" (Mr. Hume's house on
Jakko Hill), Mr. Hogg's mansion, and other places, she began
to display her magical powers again. She rang her fairy bells,
caused raps to be heard on ceilings, furniture, and other
places, including the Government Secretary's head. At first
no harm to public opinion seemed to arise from these "magical phenomena." On the contrary, the Anglo-Indian memsahibs began to expect them as the main feature of their
social gatherings. For a time Madame Blavatsky was the
"lion" of Simla, and Henry had great hopes for the formation
of a branch of The Theosophical Society in the heart of imperial India with a good proportion of the "important people" as members.

Moreover, conversations with people such as Major Henderson and Mr. Lyall, written statements to the Foreign Department, and the display of the Colonel's credentials from
the United States President and Secretary of State, led at last
to an official countermanding of orders to have the couple
watched as possible spies. No longer would they have the embarrassment of a clumsy detective tailing them around India.
On the surface all suspicion about their purpose in the country seemed to be dropped. But most likely, under the surface, the counterespionage people were still keeping tabs on
them in case they were not quite so crazy and harmless as
they seemed to be.

Social entertainment apart, H.P.B. performed, in these

Himalayan heights, a series of remarkable yogic phenomena that have since found their way into many reports and books. The incident sometimes called the "magical picnic" is a fair sample of their dramatic nature and of the double-edged reactions they caused. From eye-witness reports by Olcott and Sinnett, the following seem to be the salient points. Mrs. Sinnett possessed, among her household crockery, a set of attractive cups and saucers purchased in London. Of the original dozen in the set only nine were left, three having been broken. They were unmatchable from the shops in Simla.

On the evening of October 2, it was decided to go out in the hills next morning for a picnic breakfast. Six people were to be in the picnic party—the Colonel, H.P.B., the two Sinnetts, Major Henderson, and Mrs. Reed, who turned out to be, as Olcott puts it, "Major H.'s sweetheart and an intriguante."

Just as they were about to leave in the morning, another acquaintance rode up—Mr. Syed Mahmood, a District Judge. He was invited to join the party, which consequently numbered seven people, plus the necessary servants.

They set off. Sinnett says that neither H.P.B. nor Olcott had any share in the selection of the path taken. But, once they were on the path, according to the Colonel, H.P.B. and Major Henderson led the way, although, he says, H.P.B. had never been in that direction before during their stay at Simla. After walking four or five miles through the forest they came to a waterfall, and decided to have their picnic there on the edge of a grassy slope under some trees. This spot was chosen, Sinnett states, not by H.P.B., but by himself and Major Henderson.

It was now about ten o'clock in the morning, and the servants, who had carried the hampers, began to spread out the food and crockery. Then the Sinnetts' butler came up to his mistress in some consternation. They were one cup and saucer short, he said; none had been put in for the District Judge who had joined the party at the last moment.

Patience Sinnett reprimanded him for his neglect. She noticed that he had brought six cups from the nine left of the London set. Well, what can be done? she asked.

One of the party said to H.P.B. jestingly: "This is your chance, Madame, to do some useful magic: produce another cup and saucer."

All laughed. But the laugh died away as they saw H.P.B.'s face grow intense and serious. Would she really do it? They watched as she stood up and walked about the ground within a radius of about a dozen yards from the picnic center, pointing the big seal ring on her finger toward one spot after another. One or two people stood up and followed her, among them Major Henderson who was suspicious of tricks.

Presently, she touched a spot and said: "Dig there!"

The Major snatched up a tableknife and began to dig. Beneath the thick mat of grass was a network of fine roots from the trees. He cut through these and dug deeper. About six inches down his blade struck something hard. Scooping the earth from around it, he found a cup. The watchers caught their breath in awe as he brought it into the sunlight, and they beheld a cup matching precisely the distinctive green and gold set.

"Keep digging!" H.P.B. ordered him. He did so, cut through a root as thick as his little finger, went deeper, and finally brought out a matching saucer.

A silence fell on the party. Then everyone began talking excitedly. Among the most enthusiastic in his praise was the doubting Major of the "cloak-and-dagger" department. He declared that he would even join The Theosophical Society if she would perform another miracle on the spot, specified by himself.

As H.P.B. seemed willing to try, he said that she must produce phenomenally his completed Theosophical diploma of membership.

H.P.B. sat on the edge of the slope and seemed to go into communion with herself—or with some invisible helper. After a time she said: "All right. I'll do it, but you must hunt for the diploma yourself. The Brother helping me says that it's rolled up, tied with blue twine, and hidden under some creepers."

Henderson started his hunt among the vines, and soon came out with a roll tied with blue twine. Opening it, he found his diploma of membership, the name Major Phillip

Henderson already filled in. Moreover, there was a letter to him, written in Colonel Olcott's handwriting on The Theosophical Society letterhead. It was signed in Tibetan characters, "for H. S. Olcott, President." The Colonel stated emphatically that he, himself, did not write that letter.

The picnic proceeded happily. It seemed to be a great achievement to win the greatest skeptic as a member of The Theosophical Society in this way. But during the walk home the Major seemed deep in thought. At a halt where they all rested, he excused himself and invited Syed Mahmood to go with him back to the scene of the picnic: there was something he wanted to check, he said.

When the two men joined the party again, Henderson informed H.P.B. that he suspected someone might have put the cup and saucer where he had found them by means of a tunnel from the edge of the bank. He and Mahmood had searched for such a tunnel, and though they could not find one, he felt that it could have been obliterated by his own digging and people trampling about on the spot. To convince him that the two miracles she had performed were genuine, she must do yet another one under conditions dictated by himself and the District Judge.

This sounded very much like an ultimatum, and the imperious Russian lady reacted as might have been expected. She "poured out upon the two unfortunate skeptics the thunder of her wrath," writes Henry, "And so our pleasant party ended in an angry tempest."

This did no good, of course. The skeptics were offended and left the party. A few days later the Major resigned from The Theosophical Society and, as reports of the "magical picnic" had reached the press, he wrote a letter to the *Times of India* in which he stated:

> I declared the saucer to be an incomplete and unsatisfactory manifestation, as not fulfilling proper test conditions. My reasonable doubt was construed as a personal insult . . . I am not a Theosophist, not a believer in phenomena, which I entirely discredit, nor have I any intention of furthering the objects of the Society in any way.

H.P.B. had thrown her psychic seeds on very stony soil.

Henry had seen enough of his friend's phenomena to know that her powers were genuine, but he always liked to check the facts in each case, for the benefit of those who had not enjoyed his advantage of close association, over a long period, with the worker of wonders. Concerning their return home to the Sinnett house after the picnic he writes: "Mrs. Sinnett and I, reaching the house first, on the return of our party, went straight to the butler's pantry, and found the three other cups, of the nine which she had left of the original dozen, put away on an upper shelf." So the one excavated was obviously not from the set, nor could it have come from any shop in Simla.

In *The Occult World* Sinnett discusses objectively the hypothesis of fraud in this case, and rules it out as against all common sense. H.P.B. would need to have seen in advance that an extra cup would be required, because an unexpected visitor would join them; that the butler would forget to obtain an extra cup for him. She would have to arrange somehow that the butler would bring the green and gold set, manufacture a cup and saucer to match, have a confederate tunnel into the spot, and bury the extra crockery there. She would have to influence the party to go in the right direction and stop just at the right spot, without making it obvious. Finally, she would need to efface all signs of such a tunnel so that a suspicious major, trained in security work, could find no traces of it.

Even imagining that all this was possible, who could have done the tunneling and burying? He was sure that his visitors staying at "Brightlands"—H.P.B., the Colonel, and Babula —had not left the house from the time the picnic was first suggested in the evening until the party left the next morning. And H.P.B. knew no one else in the area likely to act as a confederate in trickery. Come to think of it, he did not consider the Old Lady herself (as he called her) morally capable of carrying out such an imposture.

The press publicity and much talk about the picnic set all Simla discussing Madame's "miracles." Half called them fakes; the other half said they were the work of the devil. The British sahibs and memsahibs found it very difficult to square such things with their religion and philosophy of life. If they believed in Christ's miracles, it was because they believed that he was God. How could a mere mortal—and a Russian at that—do such things? A mortal was full of sin; Madame Blavatsky was no exception; how could she have a Godlike command over nature? If she was *really* interfering with God's laws, it must be the devil.

The Hindus, on the other hand, had no difficulty in believing in the possibility of such powers in a human being. It was part of their ancient religio-philosophy that through yogic training man could develop the *siddhis*—powers that are supernormal, but not supernatural. They are part of the broader concept of nature. All men in the course of spiritual evolution will develop such powers. Some individuals through yogic disciplines, either during their present lives or in former ones, have already acquired them.

It was part of the philosophy of the perfectibility of man that the Mahatmas, or Great Souls, existed. It thrilled the Hindus that Madame Blavatsky and Colonel Olcott had come to tell them that the Great Ones were still among them. Most were prepared to accept H.P.B. as an agent of the Mahatmas, and therefore one capable of performing so-called miracles. Some of the Hindus, however, aping the British overlords, scoffed at such old "superstitions" and were ready to proclaim the Russian woman a fraud.

The founders' stay of six weeks in the "heart of Anglo-India" was perhaps not an entire waste of time. Enough of the Britishers showed sufficient interest in the esoteric philosophy for a branch of the Society to be formed there—The Simla Eclectic Theosophical Society—with Mr. Hume as its first President. And, more important, during this visit the famous correspondence between Sinnett and the Mahatmas began*.

Thirsting for the deep knowledge which he felt must lie behind such great psychic powers as he had witnessed from H.P.B., Sinnett told her that he wished he could get into direct communication with one of the Adepts.

Somewhat to his surprise, she replied that, though it might be difficult, she would try for him. So he wrote a letter ad-

---

* See *The Mahatma Letters to A. P. Sinnett,* The Theosophical Publishing House, Adyar, Madras, India.

dressed "To the Unknown Brother" and handed it to her. It was some days before he received a reply, and when it came it was not from H.P.B.'s guru, as he had half expected. It was from a Master known as Koot Hoomi Lal Singh— usually called Master K.H.

The correspondence continued, Sinnett writing questions, mostly on esoteric philosophy, and receiving written answers from Master K.H.—with a few from Master Morya also. The letters often came in odd ways. "Koot Hoomi letter put inside a sealed letter of Sinnett's—to his entire satisfaction," writes the Colonel on December 2, 1880.

"The answers would often be found in locked drawers, sometimes inside his own letter, the seal of which had not been broken. On occasion the Mahatma's reply dropped from the open air upon his desk while he was watching."*

A. P. Sinnett put the substance of the Mahatma teachings thus received into his book, *Esoteric Buddhism*. This, published in London in 1883, caused something of a stir in the West, where Darwinism and other iconoclastic theories of advancing science were lowering man's traditional image of himself. The book tended to reverse the process, offering a deeper, more acceptable concept of the old idea that man was made in the image of God.

After leaving the Sinnetts, the founders toured several centers in the north of India, Olcott lecturing to the Arya Samaj and other groups. At Benares he lectured to a meeting of leading pandits, where a resolution was passed for a cordial entente between The Theosophical Society and the Sanskrit Samaja. Also, while guests at the palace of the Maharaja of Benares, they decided that his family motto—"There is no religion higher than truth"—would be a very suitable one for The Theosophical Society. The Maharaja readily consented to their adopting it, and it has remained the Society's motto ever since.

At the close of the year 1880—December 30—the travel-weary couple finally reached Bombay railway station, and drove by carriage to the new house that had been found for them in their absence. It stood in a lovely position on the

---

* *Theosophy,* by Alvin Boyd Kuhn, Henry Holt and Company, New York, 1930.

Beyond asking you to tell Mr Sinnett that I have received all his letters (that of Feb. 15ª included) but have had not even a moment's time to give him, I have nothing of the nature of a "commission" for you to execute at London (That, of course, is ill.) I province; and he has, under the orders of the Maha Chohan, left you the widest discretion in the full knowledge that you will vindicate the policy of the Society.

If you will recall our conversation of the _second_ night at Lahore you will

Facsimile of letter (slightly reduced) received by H. S. Olcott in script of Mahatma K.H., 1884

Facsimile of letter (slightly reduced) received by H. S. Olcott hill overlooking the sea at Breach Candy, and was known as "Crow's Nest." For such a palatial, well-situated bungalow the rent was conveniently low. This was because the house was reputedly haunted. But even if it were, what did that matter? To students of the occult, ghosts were no disadvantage; in fact they were more grist to the mill.

Chapter 11

THE STRUGGLE FOR BUDDHISM

"Buddhism, stripped of its superstitions, is eternal truth,
and he who strives for the latter is striving for Theos-
Sophia, Divine Wisdom, which is a synonym of Truth."

(From the Maha Chohan's letter: *Letters
from the Masters of the Wisdom,* First Series.)

The Colonel's interest in Buddhism seems to have begun
at about the same time as his interest in Eastern occultism.
Dr. J. M. Peebles, whose meeting with Moolji Thackersey in
Bombay led to the link with the Arya Samaj, brought back
significant news from Ceylon. This was a printed report of
a three-day public debate, between the Christian missionaries
on the one hand, and a Buddhist orator on the other. The
subject of the debate was the relative merits of the two religions, and the monk—Meggittuwatte—had soundly thrashed
the missionaries.

The Colonel, being very much against the role the Christian church was playing in colonialism, and always on the
side of the underdog anyway, was delighted about this event
and its result. He opened a correspondence with Meggittuwatte and also with the High Priest of Adam's Peak, Sumangala, who was known as the representative and embodiment
of Pali scholarship in Ceylon.

From this correspondence Henry learned of the unhappy
situation of the Ceylonese Buddhists. The British, in more
subtle ways than the Dutch before them, were suppressing
the Buddhist religion and using the Christian religion as a
political tool to bring the Sinhalese completely under their
domination.

This was effected by devious measures. For instance, mar-
riages had to be performed in a Christian church in order to
be easily proved legal (essential for obtaining many kinds of

official positions and advantages). Christian baptism was a necessary precedent to the marriage ceremony in a Christian church. Child education was, however, the chief means of proselytizing Christianity, and eliminating the Buddhist culture of the island.

Unlike the earlier Dutch colonists of Ceylon, the British made a show of tolerance. Theoretically, the Buddhists were permitted to open their own schools, but in practice this was well-nigh impossible. Schools could not be opened without a license from the British Governor of the island, and—more important as a restricting factor —no school was eligible for grants of aid from the government unless it devoted the first hour of the day to the teaching of the Authorized Version of the Bible. The result was that in 1880, the year Olcott first came to the island, there were only four Buddhist schools as against 805 Christian schools.

Earlier, the Christian missionaries had begun employing another weapon in order to break the hold of Buddhism on the islanders. A few of the missionaries studied translations of the Buddha's teachings and began public controversies with the Buddhist priests in order—they hoped—to ridicule Buddhism and prove it a false religion. This open war between the creeds raged hottest during the years from 1860 to 1880. The most notable and famous of the many verbal battles was the Panadura debate in which the brilliant orator Meggittuwatte figured. There was no doubt to which side the laurels went on this and other occasions, and the missionaries began to see, and to admit, that it had been a mistake to challenge the Buddhists in rational arguments. In fact, the challenge had the reverse of the desired effect; it reawakened interest and zest among the Sinhalese for their own ancient religion.

It was at this juncture that Colonel Olcott arrived on the scene to throw the force of his enthusiasm, his great energy, and marked organizing ability into a nascent Buddhist revival.

When Henry sailed from Bombay to Ceylon on the 7th of May, 1880, he was in appearance much as his statue, now standing in a main street of Colombo, shows him: strong and sturdy of build, with hair thinning above the broad, no-

Unveiling of Olcott statue in Colombo, February 17, 1967, by His Excellency William Gopallawa, Governor General of Ceylon. On the right at the back is His Excellency Cecil B. Lyon, Ambassador of the United States to Ceylon. Others in the group include: Senator Y. R. Piyasena (far left), Mr. R. Premadasa, Hon. Minister for Local Government (second from left), Dr. Saddhamangala Karunaratne, Assistant Archaeological Commissioner (third from left), Ven. Hottimulle Vajirabuddhi Thero (fifth from left), Mr. D. L. F. Pedris, President of The Theosophical Society in Ceylon (sixth from left).

ble brow, but luxurious on the chin, and forming a wedge-shaped beard well down his chest.

With him to Ceylon went H.P.B., Damodar, Wimbridge, the servant Babula, and several Indian delegates from the Bombay branch of The Theosophical Society. Galle, then the main center of the island, was the ship's destination, and it was the 17th of May when it dropped anchor in the harbor there. Henry noted with pleasure the play of what he considered his fateful number—seven—at his departure and arrival.

The theosophical party had a right royal welcome, passing on the way to the shore by small boat through a laneway of brightly-decked fishing boats, their prows all pointing inward toward the laneway. On the jetty a huge crowd waited. A white cloth, spread for their feet, ran from jetty to waiting carriages. Then a thousand flags waved welcome along the roads as their carriages moved slowly through the great multitude to the house appointed as their place of residence in Galle.

Chief priests of the Buddhist faith received and blessed the party at the threshold. At last they were able to enter the house, but this did not mean they were allowed a much-needed rest. For the whole of the day the house was crowded with welcoming visitors—yellow-robed monks and gaily-dressed laity.

One of the first things the founders did in the island was to become Buddhists officially. This was not just to please the Sinhalese people; even before they had left the shores of America they had declared their preference for this religion. Now at a temple in Galle, before a Buddhist priest, they publicly "took pansil." Kneeling in front of a great statue of Lord Buddha, they repeated the Pali words of the Panchala Sila after the priest. A great crowd was present and, writes Olcott, "When we had finished the last of the Silas, and offered flowers in the customary way, there came a mighty shout to make one's nerves tingle." He also states plainly their attitude to the faith: "Our Buddhism was that of the Master-Adept Gautama Buddha, which was identically the Wisdom Religion of the Aryan Upanishads, and the soul of all the ancient world-faiths. Our Buddhism was, in a

Colonel Olcott in Ceylon with Buddhist priests, 1880

word, a philosophy, not a creed."

As the theosophical party moved slowly through village after village toward Colombo, and later visited other centers, including Kandy, the crowds snowballed in numbers and enthusiasm. The Colonel lectured to many thousands in temples, halls, and in the open air. He attempted to fire them with the zeal and self-respect that would encourage them to fight for the rights of Buddhists against the injustices and oppression of their "Christian" overlords. His lecturing tour was a huge success in spite of—or perhaps helped by—the obstructive tactics of missionaries and some government agents.

Apart from the lectures, there were long discussions with priests on Buddhist metaphysics, in some of which H.P.B. was allowed to play a part, despite the handicap of being a woman. She often illustrated her points, and enlivened the proceedings, with flashes of her psychic powers. Interest and enthusiasm among the Sinhalese reached a very high pitch. Seven new branches of The Theosophical Society were formed during this first two-months tour, and the Colonel regretted afterward that he had not, then and there, begun collecting money for a Buddhist education fund.

He had soon discerned that the real solution to the problems of the Sinhalese lay in education, and that there had to be a fund to establish Buddhist schools. But he unfortunately failed to discern that the time to strike was during this first tour, when enthusiasm was at its zenith. By losing that opportunity he brought himself a tough struggle for the future.

At Kandy the founders were shown a great relic kept in the temple there—the supposed tooth of the Buddha. This was an honor indeed, for the last person allowed to see it had been the Prince of Wales. Olcott writes in *Old Diary Leaves* that the tooth was about the size of an alligator's, and was "supported by a gold wire stem rising from a lotus flower of the same metal. . ." He gives an interesting dissertation on the beliefs and legends surrounding this famous relic.

After viewing the tooth, the founders returned to their lodgings, and there a group of educated Sinhalese asked H.P.B. her opinion as to the genuineness or otherwise of the relic. Was it really a tooth of Lord Buddha? This was rather a delicate question, but H.P.B. was equal to the occasion.

"Of course it's his tooth," she replied, jovially; "One he had when he was born as a tiger." This gave something for both the credulous and the skeptics to chew over.

In April of the next year—1881—the Colonel went again to Ceylon—this time without H.P.B. who remained behind to take care of *The Theosophist.* Henry's main object was "the raising of an Education Fund and the rousing of popular interest in the subject of education generally." For this purpose he spent nearly eight strenuous months in the island, traveling through the jungle from village to village, mainly in a two-wheeled bullock cart which he had fitted out to his own design, with dining room, writing room and bedroom.

On one part of the journey he had to travel 57 miles by paddy boat—a mere platform across two canoes—shooting rapids, and sleeping under the stars on the rough bamboo deck amid the jungle noises.

The "white Buddhist," as he was often called, met with continual difficulties. The high public emotions of the previous year had waned. Moreover, the vast majority of the Sinhalese were poor people, and those who did have money vacillated, promising subscriptions to the fund readily, but usually not fulfilling their promises.

Yet there were individuals of open, generous heart—sometimes in excess of their means. One memorable example was a poor, miserably-clad village woman who offered a single rupee for the fund. This, she apologized, was all she had and it represented six-months savings from her labors. She had intended to buy herself a decent cloth to wear. But now she wanted instead to help the noble work being done for the Sublime One. She would save for another six months for the new garment, she said cheerfully.

The Colonel could see that the woman was a pauper and the offer brought tears to his eyes. To the assembled people he said: "This woman has earned good karma by her pious deed. Now let us earn the same by relieving her distress." Taking a rupee from his pocket, he threw it on the floor. Other coins began to spin through the air and soon thirty rupees were collected for the self-sacrificing woman.

Later enquiries showed Henry that she was a very poorly-paid cleaner, and that her story of poverty was quite genuine. He felt that her action should be an inspiration to others, so a few days later, at one of his lectures, he asked her to sit close to the stage on which sat, besides himself, several Buddhist monks and high dignitaries. Then addressing the large audience, he mentioned some goodly sums that had been given by various people—naming them—and added: "But I will show you one who has given more than all of these combined." Then he told the story of the Buddhist "widow's mite" and called the woman concerned onto the platform. The applause was thunderous, and a large subscription was collected for the Education Fund that day.

It was during this second visit to Ceylon that the Colonel wrote his famous *Buddhist Catechism*. Experience had shown him the shocking ignorance of the Sinhalese about the fundamentals of their own religion—not only among children and the laity, but among many monks as well. Failing to get some well-informed priests to do the job, he took it on himself, writing at odd times during his travels, lectures, and labors.

His object was to produce an elementary handbook on lines similar to those used so effectively by Christian sects. To fit himself for the task, this indefatigable American read 10,000 pages of Buddhist books (in English and French translations). After the manuscript of the Catechism was completed, Olcott had to go over it word by word with High Priest Sumangala, because the latter's certificate of approval was essential to acceptance of the book by the Buddhists. This was a difficult and touchy business, taking many long days of conference, with many metaphysical snags to be negotiated. Olcott had, for instance, touched lightly on a difference of opinion between the Northern and Southern Buddhist schools with regard to Nirvana, but the High Priest denied that there was *any* difference at all. Finally, the Colonel had to give way, as he writes, "to force *majeure*" and change his wording in order to get on with his vital project.

The book appeared, in both English and Sinhalese versions on July 24, 1881, the money for the original printing being supplied by a "saintly woman and sweet friend, Mrs. Ilangakoon of Matara, Ceylon."

The *Catechism* became a best-seller, the money for its sales going to Buddhist educational and other work. In Ceylon it found its way into practically every home and became a text-book in the Buddhist schools. But its influence spread far beyond Ceylon; it went through more than forty printings,* and was finally translated into over twenty different languages. It earned praise from some leading Orientalists of the West.

Apart from the raising of an Education Fund, political action was necessary if the wrongs of the Buddhists were to be righted. So Olcott became a lobbyist for the Sinhalese people—something they could not have done for themselves. He interviewed the Governor of Ceylon, Sir Arthur Gordon, who, fortunately, was interested in occultism and comparative religion. Henry was impressed, for instance, to find that he knew all about H.P.B.'s Simla miracles. Sir Arthur was quite sympathetic to the Buddhist cause, but it was necessary, even so, for someone to go to England and put the whole question before the Secretary of State for the Colonies. This the Colonel did later in 1884.

As a result of Henry's tireless work on their behalf, the Sinhalese were eventually given back their religious freedoms and rights. It was no longer necessary, for example, that couples should borrow tail coats, top hats, corsets, and crinolines and go to a Christian church in order to be legally wed. Wesak, the birthday of Lord Buddha, was declared a public holiday. Educationists from the West, sympathetic with the work Olcott was doing, came out to help in establishing Buddhist schools and colleges. Where but two schools had existed in 1880, by the turn of the century there were over two hundred.**

---

* See Quest Book Miniature edition, The Theosophical Publishing House, 1970.
** Ceylon honors the memory of Colonel Olcott in many ways. In 1967, for instance, its government issued a special postage stamp to commemorate the sixtieth anniversary of his death, stating in an official bulletin, "Ceylon remembers with gratitude and veneration Col. Olcott, a great American who has been a source of inspiration and guidance to the Buddhists of Ceylon." (See photo opposite page.) Also in that same year a statue was unveiled in Colombo by His Excellency the Governor General of Ceylon. (See photo opposite page 135.)

Issued to Commemorate 60th Death Anniversary
of
COLONEL HENRY STEEL OLCOTT

DATE OF ISSUE: DECEMBER 8th 1967
Denomination: 15c
PRINTERS: BRUDER. ROSENBAUM, AUSTRIA

DESIGN: PORTRAIT OF COLONEL H. S. OLCOTT, AND BUDDHIST FLAG
COLOURS: Blue, Yellow, Red, White, Reddish Orange, and   Shades of Blue

Format: HORIZONTAL
SIZE: 25x36 mm
PRINTING PROCESS: Photogravure

Facsimile of Olcott Stamp affixed to first day cover
issued in Ceylon December 8, 1967,
and announcement of stamp issue (slightly reduced)

With the advice and help of the Colonel, an international Buddhist flag was designed. It was meant to be a symbol of unity; it became also an emblem of Buddhist renascence in Ceylon and elsewhere. Hearing of the "white Buddhist" and the miracles he had worked in religious revival, it was not long before other countries were asking for him to come and help them, too.

In 1884 the Colonel had an invitation from King Theebaw III of Burma to go there for conversations on the Buddhist movement. In 1885 he went, and seems to have enjoyed Burma with its wonderful temples and pagodas, friendly people, and admirable priests. Of the Burmese he writes that they were a "lovable people, and a manly, self-respecting, albeit awfully lazy, people." With regard to the monks, he agreed wholeheartedly with a travel writer of his time who said: "The tone of the monks is undoubtedly good. Any infractions of the law . . . are severely punished. . . . In return for their self-denial, the monks are highly honored by the people. . . . Religion pervades Burma in a way that is seen in hardly any other country."

Yet the personality who impressed Henry most in Burma was a Christian. Accustomed to the Protestant missionaries who made scurrilous attacks on him, and the native "Christian" rowdies who tried to break up his meetings, Olcott was happy to meet a venerable Roman Catholic Bishop—Father Bigandet—who had spent years in Burma, studied Buddhism and written a fine book on the Buddha's life—the *Legend of Gaudama.*

Remarking that this book was the earliest Western introduction to the life of Lord Buddha, the Colonel praised it as being "learned, exhaustive and impartial." He was pleased, in turn, to hear the old prelate and scholar, who had read Olcott's *Buddhist Catechism,* comment that "there was no more useful book on the religion of Sakhya Muni."

Discussing with respectable elders at Rangoon Theebaw's invitation to Mandalay for conversations at the Court, the Colonel learned that that monarch was "a monster of vice and cruelty, and his motive was not to satisfy his thirst for religious knowledge, but only to gratify an idle curiosity to see the white Buddhist." So Olcott decided not to visit the

Court, although urgently pressed again to do so by the King. With blunt American frankness, he made no secret in Burma of his reasons for not accepting the invitation of a "debauched tyrant."

Olcott lectured and formed a number of branches of The Theosophical Society in Burma, but with such a religious-minded people and high standard of priesthood, there was little need for a zealous Buddhist revivalist of his stamp. Yet something important did come out of his Burmese adventure. Some six years after his first two visits to the country —that is, early in 1891—the Colonel heard that a Burmese Buddhist League had raised a large sum of money and was anxious to send a preaching mission for Buddhism to Europe. Delegates were on their way to India in order to get The Theosophical Society President's concurrence and blessing for the mission.

Though this was the kind of zeal that Henry admired, he felt that it would be a wrong action—at that particular time. Before Buddhism was proselyted abroad, there should be unity in its ranks and a common platform from which it could speak. The creation of such a platform was a dream that had been occupying his mind for some time.

Now he would take some action in the matter. He had visited Japan in the interests of Buddhism during the intervening years, so he asked delegates from there, and from Ceylon, to come to The Theosophical Society's headquarters at Adyar to meet the Burmese delegates. As a result a committee was formed representing the two great Schools of Buddhism—Northern and Southern, Mahayana and Theravada. The Committee met on January 8, 1891, at Adyar. This in itself was a historic event.

Henry put before the committee his views concerning the vital need of a common platform on which the mighty spiritual forces from the Enlightened One could converge, focus, and then spread their message of light across the world. He invited full discussion on the matter. The idea in general was agreed upon quickly and enthusiastically, but a fortnight was then spent in comparing all the points of belief in the *Mahayana* School, represented by Japanese delegates, and the *Theravada* School, represented by the monks from Ceylon and

Burma. After this discussion the Colonel drafted a document, "embracing fourteen clauses, upon which all Buddhist sects could agree if disposed to promote brotherly feeling and a mutual sympathy between themselves. A fair copy of this document was signed by the delegates and myself."

This agreement could be only tentative, for the delegates had no real authority to speak for the great and powerful Buddhist priesthoods of their countries. It therefore behooved the father of the idea—Henry Olcott—to visit the countries concerned and gain concurrence of the highest priestly authorities.

The platform, if finally adopted, would be a historic achievement, for never before, in the many centuries since Buddhism had spread throughout Asia, had a mutual ground of compromise and cooperation been found. The Colonel had become a popular and respected figure in Buddhist countries and his chances of building the bridge of unity seemed fairly bright.

It was for this purpose that he made his third visit to Burma in January 1891 and spent time discussing the subtleties of Buddhist metaphysics with monks and laymen there. "They are a clever people the Burmans. . . ." he writes, "every man of them has passed his time in *kyoung* (monastery) according to the inflexible national custom. . . ."

The Colonel set himself to win the approval of the leading priests for his compromise platform. There was much heated discussion and debate at Rangoon, but the upshot was that the white Buddhist's several propositions "were found orthodox and according to the Tripitakas."

The real test, however, would come in Mandalay itself where he must meet, in council, the greatest of the Burmese monks, together with their acknowledged leader, the Royal High Priest. This was no other than the brother of King Thebaw III whose invitation Olcott had spurned six years earlier.

But the priest was the antithesis of his debauched brother. He was learned, high-minded, and very humble, wearing a plain cotton robe "like that of the poorest monk in the Council." In striking contrast to the plain robes of the monks was the great Council Hall at Mandalay where the meeting took place. It was a place of splendor and beauty, with a lofty ceiling supported by straight shafts of teak, painted or lacquered in venetian red and embellished with gold leaf.

The meeting lasted for four hours, the Colonel and the priests kneeling—as was customary—the whole of this time. With aching knees and leg muscles, Henry made his impassioned appeal for unity. He described the work done in Ceylon—the schools and colleges opened, the new Buddhist journals, pamphlets and tracts in circulation there. He talked of his visit to Japan and dwelt on the noble qualities of that nation of brother Buddhists. Then to the venerable elders kneeling around him he broached the main object of his mission to Burma—the platform of unity with all brother Buddhists.

The wrinkled old monks and the high-minded Royal Priest seemed deeply impressed by this sincere, straight-talking American who had come to them with nothing but love in his heart and the selfless desire to help the great cause of Buddhism. They agreed unanimously and wholeheartedly with all the points of his platform, and the Royal Priest signed the document as "Accepted on behalf of the Buddhists of Burma."

There was no difficulty about obtaining the agreement of the Buddhists in Ceylon where the Colonel was already something of a national religious hero. In fact, seven leading Buddhist priests of the island had given him a Letter of Authorization to admit people into the Buddhist faith—an honor never before conferred upon a Westerner.

The tough problem, however, would be to get the fourteen point platform accepted by the Northern School, as represented by Japan.

Henry's first visit to the land of the Rising Sun had taken place two years earlier, that is, in 1889. The reason for his going had been a pressing invitation from a national committee of younger Buddhist priests of Japan. This had been brought to Adyar by a delegate—Mr. Noguchi—who planned to escort the Colonel back to Japan.

Noguchi had arrived in time for the annual convention of The Theosophical Society in December 1888, and had made a memorable speech to that assembly. In the address he spoke

of the deplorable condition of Buddhism in his own country, where it had for centuries been the national religion. For
the demoralized state of the priesthood, and the religious
apathy of the people, he put the blame on Western civilization which was spreading its blight over Japan.

The only one who could save the situation, he said, was
Colonel Olcott who had worked such wonders in Ceylon. He
begged the theosophical assembly for a "loan" of their President—"this worker of social miracles, this defender of religion, this teacher of tolerance. . . . We are" he said, "praying Colonel Olcott to come and help us; to come and revive
the hope of our old men, to put courage in the hearts of
our young men, to prove to the graduates of our colleges and
universities, and to those who have been sent to America
and Europe for education, that Western science is not in-
fallible, and not a substitute, but the natural sister of religion. . . ."

When Olcott and Noguchi and Dharmapala (a young
monk from Ceylon) reached Kobe in Japan, the Buddhist
priests of all sects (there were nine main ones) were lined
up on the pier to welcome the white Buddhist visitor, "with
that exquisite politeness for which the nation is celebrated."

At first the Shin Shu sect, the most powerful, wanted to
finance the Colonel's lecture tour. But Olcott saw that this
would give an entirely wrong impression. He had come not
to promote further enmity between the sects, but tolerance,
brotherhood and unity. So he called the heads of all the
sects to a meeting at the Choo-in Temple in Kyoto.

He gave them a stirring speech on the theme of Buddhist
unity and the need of concerted action for spreading the
teachings abroad. Good beginnings had already been made
in the West, he told them. Several great authors had written
of Lord Buddha in sympathetic terms. One book in particular had done more for Buddhism, Henry thought, than any
other agency. This was *The Light of Asia,** by Sir Edwin
Arnold. Olcott's own *Buddhist Catechism* was already in
fifteen languages and was being used as a textbook in the
Sorbonne, Paris. He had heard that in France there were
some 12,000 professed Buddhists, and he felt sure that there

_____
* See Quest Book edition, The Theosophical Publishing House, 1969.

were at least 50,000 in America. These were all signs of the really tremendous potential for the spread of Lord Buddha's sublime message.

So now was the time to be up and doing. But the first thing—the very first—was to put their own house in order. He suggested the formation of a General Committee, representative of all sects, to act for the overall interests of Buddhism.

"I added," he says, "that I positively refused to make the tour of Japan unless I could do it under their conjoint auspices. . . Finally I gave notice that unless they did form such a Joint Committee, I would take the next steamer back to my place of departure. . . . I am not sure that those venerable pontiffs, spiritual teachers of 39,000,000 Japanese, and incumbents of about 70,000 temples, must have thought me as dictatorial a fellow as my countryman Commodore Perry. It doesn't matter now, since my terms were accepted; the Joint Committee was formed . . . and thenceforth my program was laid out by the Committee so as to take me to every important Buddhist center throughout the empire, and to have me become the guest of each of the sects, and give my lectures at selected temples of each."

The Colonel's four-months' tour through the length and breadth of Japan stimulated public interest until it took on the aspect of a national event. Every paper and magazine in the country gave accounts of his mission and the physical appearance of the "American Buddhist."

"Since Colonel Olcott's arrival in Japan," ran one typical press report, "Buddhism has wonderfully revived. . . . He has been everywhere received with remarkable enthusiasm. . . . He has taught our people to appreciate Buddhism, and to see our duty to impart it to all nations. Since his discourse in Tokyo, the young men of the Imperial University and High Schools have organized a young men's Buddhist Association, after the model of the Young Men's Christian Association, to propagate our religion."

In Tokyo the Governor entertained him at dinner at the Nobles' Club, where he met the Prime Minister and members of the cabinet and gave an after-dinner speech on the subject of education.

Colonel Olcott in Japan with Buddhist priests, 1891

As he traveled about the country, he was delighted with the courtesy and friendliness of the people and their ingenuity in finding novel and spectacular ways of expressing their welcome. At one place, for instance, a kite bomb was exploded and sent out a streamer declaring in giant letters that "Olcott San is come." This, as well as being a form of welcome and celebration, had a practical value, he was informed. It notified people in surrounding districts that the great white Buddhist had arrived, so that they might come to town to see him and hear his inspiring words.

During the 107 days of this first Japanese tour the Colonel gave 75 lectures. Some of his audiences were small select groups, but most of them numbered from two to five thousand people. He calculated later that he had given his spoken message to some 187,500 people all told.

Early in the tour, he was requested to recite, before the high altar and the statue of Buddha, the service of the Pancha Sila in Pali, as it is done in Ceylon. Not a sound was heard from the hundreds of priests and thousands of laymen present as the "white Buddhist" intoned the simple sentences. The uniqueness of the occasion appealed to Henry's fancy. He writes: "I could not help smiling to myself when thinking of the horror that would have been felt by any of my Puritan ancestors of the seventeenth century, could they have looked forward to this calamitous day! I am sure that if I had been born among them at Boston or Hartford, I should have been hanged for heresy on the tallest tree. . . ."

Near the end of this tour he tried to form a Theosophical branch in which the various Buddhist sects might be led to work in brotherly union. But he was told by some of the most sagacious leaders that the spirit of sectarianism was far too strong. Only a foreigner, outside all their sects and social groups, could carry on such work successfully. And the foreigner would have to be a sincere Buddhist.

"You are the only man we know who possesses these requirements," they told him. "If you will come and settle in Japan, we will give you as many branches and as many thousand members as you wish."

The Colonel was sorely tempted. He now knew the Buddhist countries intimately and if he could be spared from the

Theosophical movement proper, he would "very soon build up an International Buddhist League that might send the Dharma like a tidal wave around the world."

So to put the matter to the test, he offered his resignation of the Presidency of The Theosophical Society, passing it over to H.P.B. But she resisted the suggestion vigorously, cabling that if he resigned, she would at once quit the Society. No doubt she hoped thus to frighten him into remaining. "Still," he writes, "this would not have stopped me if a far higher personage than she had not come and told me that the Buddhist scheme must be postponed, and that I must not leave the post confided to me." The high personage was presumably one of the Masters of the Great Brotherhood.

"The Buddhist League is, therefore," the Colonel goes on, "a great and splendid work that lies in the closed hand of the future . . ."

So leaving his dream in that "closed hand," Henry returned to India and his Theosophical headquarters. But until the end of his life he strove for the welfare of the Buddhist religion, regarding it as an important part of his theosophical work.

Two and a half years after leaving Japan—that is at the end of October 1891—Henry was a second time approaching its shores. In his pocket was an important document—the Buddhist Fourteen Point Platform—signed earlier that year by the Buddhists of Burma and Ceylon. He was hoping to get the signatures of the nine main sects of Japan.

But quite apart from differences between the sects in Japan, a much wider gap divided them from the Southern School of Burma, Ceylon, and Siam, which the Northerners called the Hinayana, meaning the "Smaller Vehicle." The Japanese, themselves, belonged to the Mahayana (Large Vehicle). The Southern Buddhists, however, honored their school with the name Thera Vada (Way of the Elders).

Writing about the two great schools half a century after Olcott's time, Christmas Humphreys, President of The Buddhist Society, London, says "As compared with the Mahayana the Hinayana is more practical, rationalistic, ethical and 'Protestant' in feeling. The Northern School of Tibet, Mongolia, and millions of Chinese, Koreans and Japanese, is more mystical, metaphysical, and devotional, including schools of esoteric ritual, schools of pure faith, and the school of Zen Buddhism. . . ."*

This describes briefly the nature of the differences that have always stood between the two schools. But Colonel Olcott had studied deeply the history and basic principles of Buddhism, and he felt that the fundamentals of both are the same, and the two schools are complementary parts of one whole. They should, therefore, he felt, emphasize their common base, be tolerant toward each other, and work in unison. In his fourteen point platform he had of necessity laid stress on the practical, ethical, rationalistic aspects as embraced by the Southern School. How then, he wondered, would the Japanese High Priests react to the document.

Arriving at Yokohama on October 28, 1891, he learned—and was inexpressibly shocked to learn—"that on the morning of that very day one of the most disastrous earthquakes in the history of Japan had spread devastation over a wide area: thousands of buildings, including some of the strongest temples, had been destroyed. . . . It was not a promising time for me to get the High Priests together to consider my fourteen propositions. . . ." In fact many of the priests were away, busy at the devastated areas. They would hardly be in the mood for discussion on basic Buddhist principles.

In Kyoto he talked with the highly-influential priest, Shaku Genyu San of the Shin-gon sect, who was also a leading member of the General Committee of all the sects, formed during Olcott's earlier visit.

When this priest read the fourteen propositions, he said that there was infinitely more in Mahayana Buddhism than in these condensed bits of doctrine. What then was the point in signing them, he asked. To this the Colonel replied: "If I should bring you a basketful of earth dug from Fuji San, would that be a part of your sacred mountain?"

"Of course it would!"

"Well, then, all I ask is that you will accept these propositions as included within the body of Northern Buddhism—as a basketful of its mountain so to speak."

---

* *Thus Have I Heard,* by Christmas Humphreys. The Buddhist Society, London, 1948.

This analogy seemed to appeal to the priest and when the Colonel argued further about the necessity of a united Buddhist front, he agreed to do his best to promote the acceptance of the platform.

Finally, during a nine day stay in Kyoto, the determined Colonel obtained signatures from eight of the leading sects. Shaku Genyu San also had the authority to sign "on behalf of the General Committee," representing the nine sects. This he did.

So the Colonel felt that he virtually had the agreement of the whole body of the Japanese Buddhists. It was a great achievement, bringing to a close the eventful year of 1891. It had also been a tragic year seeing the passing of his dear friend and fellow worker, H. P. Blavatsky. But many battles were fought on other fronts before the coming of that sad day.

Chapter 12

MAGNETIC HEALING

Commenting on Henry Olcott's horoscope, an American astrologer wrote: "The joint influence of the moon in Scorpio and the sun in Leo would indicate much ability as a magnetic healer."

All his life Henry was deeply interested in the subject of mesmerism. He read all he could about its progress, met its practitioners, and investigated both mesmeric and hypnotic phenomena. When his travels took him to Europe he would visit the great French pioneers of medical and psychological research into hypnotism—Liebault and Bernheim at Nancy, and Charcot in Paris.

Although some of the leading hypnotists discounted the theory of a vital fluid or energy flowing between the operator and the patient, the Colonel held to it—more especially as the theory agreed with the teachings of the early occult science. Trained clairvoyants today confirm that there is such an etheric energy, and practitioners claim that it can be directed by the human mind and will to flow to any part of the body—either the patient's or their own.

This energy is part of every person's etheric mechanism. As well as supplying the vitality necessary for life, health and strength, it forms a bridge between mind and body. Having this double purpose the mechanism is used for both mesmeric (magnetic) and hypnotic (suggestive) healing, but in a different way for each.

In the "Transactions of the Medical Research Group of the Theosophical Research Centre," we read: "The magnetic healer deliberately avoids throwing the patient into a trance. He directs vital energy through his hands to the patient's body . . . the patient meanwhile remaining fully conscious of what is going on. . . . While the magnetic healer thus pours vitality into the patient, he is careful not to drive out the patient's own vital energy: on the contrary his aim is to feed the sick person with healthy magnetism and ultimately so to restore the normal flow of vitality in the diseased body that health may re-assert itself.''

On the other hand the hypnotist replaces some of the patient's vital energy by his own with the intention of breaking the etheric bridge between body and mind. He thus puts the patient into a degree of hypnotic trance. In this state the patient accepts from the operator positive suggestions calculated to overcome the disease and create conditions conducive to health.

The Colonel's life-long hobby of mesmerism was to bear valuable fruit for the great cause which he now served. During his third visit to Ceylon—in August 1882—he began, without planning or intending it, a phase of extraordinary mesmeric healing.

It came about in this way. He was informed by the Buddhist High Priest that the Roman Catholic missionaries had converted a house well near Kelanie into a healing shrine, after the fashion of Lourdes. The Colonel felt that if healing actually got under way—through either suggestion or coincidence—there might be a rush of Buddhists into Roman Catholicism. He did not want good Buddhists thus lured by superstition. "It's a serious matter. You must do something about it," he said to the High Priest.

"But, what can I do?"

"You, or some other monk, must cure people in the name of Lord Buddha, of course." Henry told him.

"But—but, we know nothing about such things!"

"Nevertheless, something must be done."

Soon after this conversation the Colonel was sitting at a table in China Garden in Galle receiving subscriptions to the Buddhist Education Fund. A cripple named Cornelius Appu was brought forward and introduced. Cornelius offered a rupee. His subscription was so small, he apologized, because he had not been able to work at his trade for the last eight years owing to the fact that he had one arm paralyzed and one leg partially so.

The Colonel felt a strong sympathy for this good-hearted cripple, and a Voice within him said, "Here's your chance for the holy well!" Impulsively he made a few mesmeric passes over the man's arm without speaking; then the latter hobbled away.

But that same evening Cornelius appeared at the Colonel's quarters by the seashore. He came, he explained, to give thanks to the great white Buddhist for making his arm feel much better. He could now move it a little. Thus encouraged, Henry gave some more healing to the arm, and told the patient to return in the morning for further treatment. This went on for eight days, by which time the arm and leg were both completely cured.

Cornelius was able to "jump with both feet, hop on the paralyzed one, kick equally high against the wall with both, and run freely. With the hand that had been useless for eight years he was able to hold a pen easily and sign a statement about his cure for publication in a Buddhist journal.

A few days later Olcott gave a lecture at a place twelve miles outside Galle, where there were rumors that the missionaries planned to attack him. Among the enthusiastic Buddhists who walked the dozen miles to protect their beloved Colonel, was the ex-cripple Cornelius Appu.

As a match to dry jungle, the news of the healing spread; other patients came, "by twos and threes first," writes Olcott, "then by dozens, and within a week or so my house was besieged by sick persons from dawn until late at night, all clamoring for the laying on of my hands." Many were crippled with paralysis, rheumatism or lumbago, some were blind, some deaf or dumb, and there were cases of epilepsy and other diseases.

From then on the Colonel worked at his healing for many hours each day, until he felt that his vitality was exhausted. Not all cases were susceptible to his healing powers, but many were. There were dozens of cures that appeared to the islanders nothing short of miraculous.

The word that their great, white Buddhist benefactor had become a miracle-healer traveled ahead from village to village as Olcott moved through the countryside. Reaching a stopping place for the night, he would find patients waiting for him on verandahs and lawns or sitting in carts, wagons, palanquins and other conveyances. Later when his fame had spread throughout all Ceylon and India, he was to find them waiting for him even on railway platforms where his train was due to halt for ten minutes or so.

He observed after a time that, though he was able to cure hundreds, his long labors had no visible effect on hundreds more. So he must find a way to prevent waste of time and conserve his vital energy. It was necessary to have a test by which he could select those applicants whose auric vibrations were in harmony with his own, those for whom there was thus good hope for a cure. Such a test should produce visible phenomena in order to indicate to all concerned, as well as to himself, which ones were potentially curable by his methods. In this way the inevitable audience would know why he worked on some people and sent others away without attempting to heal them.

The test he devised was based on those he had seen used by other practitioners. It was this: he would ask the candidate to stand upright and firm facing a wall. Then Henry, standing directly behind, would raise his hand and point it at the back of the candidate's head. Holding it there, he would will with great concentration that his hand become a powerful magnet to draw the person's head backwards. Without speaking, he would keep up this concentrated effort of will for several minutes, observing closely for any physical effects of the magnetic experiment on the candidate.

Some people proved completely impervious to the "magnet"; some began to sway slightly after a period of exposure to the concentrated will power, increasing the oscillation, perhaps, after a time; others responded almost immediately; falling backwards into the Colonel's arms.

The first class he sent home as unsuitable for his treatment. The third he started work on immediately; they were very readily curable—sometimes instantaneously. Then if time was available, he would attempt to heal those who had shown most sensitivity in the second class of candidates. The test had the desired effect; it separated the sheep from the goats as far as Olcott's mesmeric healing was concerned, and it saved the healer from wasting precious time and vitality.

As the months of 1882 rolled on, Olcott continued with this arduous healing work—in both Ceylon and India. The unexpected appearance of such a *siddhi* in the Colonel— added to H.P.B.'s phenomenal powers—brought many more people to The Theosophical Society. The President was glad of this, but he did not regard his cures as miraculous. They were scientific, he maintained, following laws well known to occult science. And, though his original motive had been to promote the interests of Buddhism, he soon found that what drove him on and kept him going, more than anything else, was compassion for the sufferers.

This compassion, this heartfelt sympathy in the healer, is, he stated, an absolute essential for successful healing work. In *Old Diary Leaves* he cites a strange case which, he considers, proves this point. In Ceylon a man with one side of his body paralyzed was brought for cure. The Colonel began on the cripple's arm, making his usual passes along the nerves and muscles, occasionally breathing upon them, the while sending by thought and will power currents of his own vital energy into the paralyzed limb. In less than half an hour the cripple was able to "whirl his arm around his head, open and close his fingers at will, grasp and hold a pen or even a pin, and, in fact, do anything he liked with the limb."

Then he was sent aside while the Colonel had a break, smoking his pipe and chatting with members of his committee. During the chat he learned that the cripple was wealthy and had spent 1,500 rupees on doctors without getting any relief. He was, however, well known for his avarice and meanness.

Olcott's feeling toward the man underwent an immediate change; one thing that disgusted him was money greed. He told someone to ask the wealthy cripple how much he had decided to give the Buddhist National Fund for schools. At this, the man whined that he was poor and had spent much on doctors; he could not afford more than a rupee, he said. That capped Olcott's disgust.

"Take the creature out of my sight!" he told the committee.

But finally, realizing what his enemies would make of such an action, his discretion prevailed. He went to work on the miser's crippled leg. Within half an hour he had removed the paralysis and sent the fellow away, walking as well as anybody.

About a fortnight later Henry was, after a short tour, back at the same center. He inquired after certain patients, among them the miser. Was the fellow still in good health? The reply surprised him. Though the arm was quite normal, he was told, the leg had relapsed to its previous paralytic state.

Why had this happened? It could not be a result of suggestion because the man had not been near enough to hear Henry's harsh words; he could not understand a word of English anyway. After much reflection Henry decided that the key to the mystery was "sympathy." While treating the arm he had been inspired by great sympathy, lively interest and benevolent intent toward the sick man. By the time he came to the leg, these feelings had changed. He could feel no sympathy with the miserly creature, and did the healing job for reasons of policy only.

Probably the most interesting cure of paralysis was that of a young Brahmin whose face had been paralyzed for two years; so much so that he was unable to close his eyelids or use tongue and lips. His speech was just an incomprehensible noise in his throat.

The cure took place in Calcutta in the house of Sir Jotendra Tagore (father of the famous Indian poet) where so many sick people had gathered for the Colonel's ministrations that "the place looked like a hospital." Henry was standing at one end of a long room when the young Brahmin was brought in at the other. The patient stood with an eager expression, indicating in dumb show the nature of his affliction.

That morning the Colonel was feeling full of power—sufficient to "mesmerize an elephant," he said. Raising his right arm above his head, he looked piercingly at the patient in the doorway. Then sweeping his arm down to the horizontal, and pointing his fingers at the Brahmin, he pronounced in Bengali (the man's own language) the command: "Be healed!"

A tremor went through the patient, his eyelids closed and

opened, his tongue was thrust out and withdrawn. He realized that he was healed, and with a wild cry of joy, rushed forward and flung himself at the Colonel's feet. He placed his savior's foot on his head, embraced his knees and poured forth his gratitude in fluent speech.

Olcott writes: "Every person in the room partook of the young Brahmin's emotion, and there was not an eye unmoistened with tears. Not even mine, and that is saying a good deal."

Epilepsy was a disease which, Olcott found, succumbed speedily to his mesmeric passes. One of his first cases of this came to him at Tagore's house. The patient was a twelve-year-old boy who had been suffering from epilepsy for six or seven years. Good physicians had treated him, with no effect. The disease had become so violent that in one day and night he had had no less than sixty fits, and was unable to get up and walk. In this state he was brought to the Colonel.

After seven days of the latter's mesmeric treatment, a relative of the patient wrote to the *Indian Mirror,* "The boy has so much improved that he can run and walk without difficulty . . . and appears perfectly healthy; besides which he has had no fits during this period [of treatment]. His appetite has returned, costiveness is gone, and he gets sound sleep, and is enjoying life like other boys for the first time in seven years. I consider from his general appearance that the disease has gone, and it is now only a question of his more or less rapid convalescence."

Many blind people came to Olcott and some he was able to cure. One of the most dramatic cases was that of a pleader of the District Court in Bhagalpore, Bengal. The man's name was Babu Badrinath Banerji. He was completely blind, and had to be led by a boy. The Colonel found that he was suffering from glaucoma, with atrophy of the optic disc. The cleverest eye surgeons of Calcutta had discharged him from the hospital as incurable.

Henry put the blind man through his mesmeric test and found him a sensitive patient. So he decided to try the formidable task of bringing atrophied optic nerves back to life. He describes something of his method: "I held the thumb of my clenched right hand before one of his eyes, and that of the left over his neck, and willed a vital current to run from the one to the other, completing with my body a magnetic circuit, of which one glaucomic eye and the optic tract, to its seat of development in the brain, formed parts. This process was continued for about half an hour. . . At the end of the experiment he could see a reddish glimmer of light in that eye. The other was then operated on similarly with the same result. He returned the next day for further treatment, and this time the light lost its reddish color and became white. Persevering for ten days, I was finally rewarded by seeing him with restored sight, able to read with one eye the smallest type in a newspaper or book, to dispense with his leader, and go about like anybody else."

This case created much talk as the man was well known to the whole community of Bhagalpore. Two medical men, graduates of the Calcutta Medical College, studied the eyes through an ophthalmoscope during treatment, and wrote a report of their observations, which appeared in the *Indian Mirror.*

The report states that Babu Badrinath Banerji's case had been pronounced incurable by two of the best oculists in India, and that the patient possessed certificates to this effect. It then described what the ophthalmoscope revealed after several treatments from the Colonel: "We found that the atrophied discs were becoming healthy, the shrivelled blood-vessels admitting blood to circulate in and nourish the discs. . . He can easily walk about without anybody's help, and the glaucomic tension of the eye-ball is gone. . . Every ophthalmic surgeon among your readers will admit this cure to be unprecedented." The doctor goes on to challenge the medical world "to produce the record of a duplicate to this case."

Another physician, Dr. Ladli Mohun Ghose reports on ten remarkable cases which the Colonel had cured, among them his own, which was blindness in the left eye. Leading eye specialists of Calcutta had pronounced Ghose's case incurable, and probably congenital. "But today," he writes, "after a few minutes of simple mesmeric treatment, by breathing through a small silver tube [one method of treatment], Col.

Olcott has restored my sight. He has˙ made me close the right eye, and with my hitherto useless left one read ordinary print. My feelings may be better imagined than described."

Writing his *Old Diary Leaves* a decade after these healings, Olcott states that Badrinath Banerji's sight "faded out twice and was twice restored by me; the first time after it had lasted six months, the second time after a whole twelve months. In each case I found him totally blind and restored his sight with half an hour's treatment. To cure him permanently I should need to have had him by me, where I could have given him daily treatments until the glaucomic tendency had been completely extirpated."

Both deafness and dumbness succumbed readily to the mesmeric treatment, and many people regained their hearing and speech through the power of the Colonel's hands. One of these, a man of about twenty-five or thirty, had been completely dumb for three years. He was among the sick brought to Olcott at Tinnevelly in South India. Writing of this cure, Mr. S. Ramaswamier, who acted for a time as the Colonel's secretary and was an eyewitness, says:

"Amidst a great crowd, right in front of the Nelliappa temple the Colonel laid his hands on the unfortunate dumb man. Seven circular passes on the head and seven long passes, all occupying less than five minutes, and speech was restored... The Colonel, amidst deafening shouts of applause and thunderous clapping of hands, made him pronounce the names of Siva, Gopala, Rama, Ramachandra and other deities as glibly as any bystander could. The news . . . spread at once through the town and created a great sensation." Olcott adds that people rushed from their houses, waving their arms in excitement and shouting: *"Wah! Wah! Wah!"*

Casting out demons was also not beyond the healing power that flowed through Henry Olcott in the year 1882. He describes the case of the "Demon Lover." A young Buddhist monk had for some two or three years been obsessed by a female demon who was playing the part of a spirit lover of the nymphomaniac type. The monk was "thus obsessed seven or eight times a day and had become reduced to almost a skeleton." The Chief Priest of the monastery asked the Colonel to cure the monk.

Water, which he had magnetized, was often used by Olcott in his cures. In this case he decided to put the obsessed monk on a course of magnetized water, making him come every morning for a fresh supply. After a month of this treatment, the man was completely free of his demon lover. Nevertheless, to prevent future obsession, the Colonel advised that he return to the world and marry. This the young monk did.

As could be expected, the attitude of many of the British medical men in authority was most hostile toward all this spectacular, "unscientific" healing. One example typifies their reaction. A young civil surgeon came one day to observe the Colonel treating twenty odd patients and making some wonderful cures. The surgeon became enthusiastic and assisted Olcott as a diagnostician. He offered to return on the morrow to help the healing in whatever way he could.

Then going home he reported to the Chief Medical Officer. His chief listened coldly to the enthusiastic report; then pronounced sentence of excommunication on Colonel Olcott as a charlatan and swindler. The young surgeon was forbidden, on pain of losing his job, to have anything more to do with Olcott and his "money tricks." The young man lost courage and did not return.

The fact was that the Colonel never took a fee for healing though he was frequently offered money by the wealthy. A Muslim in Bengal, for instance, promised him 10,000 rupees if he would but turn aside from his route, come to the man's house, and cure his wife of paralysis. The Colonel refused to go. "I might have done," he said: "if he had been a pauper, and no friend of his had pronounced the word 'money' to me."

Olcott felt that, though it was in order for doctors and certain other professional healers to charge reasonable fees for their time and skills, he himself must never exploit this wonderful *siddhi* of compassion with which he had been suddenly endowed (by the Masters, he believed). It must be used solely for the benefit of his fellow men, never for personal gain.

Looking back on his healing period some ten years afterwards, he felt glad, indeed, that he had never accepted any of the sums of money offered him. "If we [he and H.P.B.] had ever taken a present for ourselves," he writes, "the whole Indian public would have abandoned us in the Coulomb crisis." This foundation-shaking affair was almost upon them at the time of his healing mission.

It seems to have been a superhuman power that Henry wielded for a little over a year, during which he treated some 8,000 patients. In one 2,000-mile circuit in India—traveling by rail, canal boat, horse gharry, horseback, palanquin, and elephant—he treated 2,812 sick persons in fifty-seven days. This was in addition to giving many lectures on Theosophy and organizing twelve new Theosophical Society branches. He was told that professional mesmeric healers of the time would not have attempted half that number—except, perhaps, prodigies such as Schlatter, Newton, the Cure d'Ars, and Zouave Jacob. But these professed to be working under an overshadowing spiritual control.

"So far as that is concerned," writes Olcott, "I frankly confess my belief that I could not have gone through such a great and sustained outpouring of my vitality, unless I had been helped by our Teachers, although I was never so told by them."

There were signs, however, that the Masters were giving their help, and were actually present on occasions. For instance, the blind patient Badrinath Banerji seemed to develop a degree of clairvoyant power under treatment. On several occasions he saw, through closed eyelids, "a shining man with blue eyes, light flowing hair, light beard, European features and complexion." The man looked at Badrinath with a kindly, benevolent expression.

The Colonel recognized the astral visitor from his patient's description as "one of the most revered of our Masters . . . a *Paramaguru*. . ." Noting the recurrent vision in his diary for April 21, 1883, he says: "Badrinath saw S . . . again," by which, one presumes, he meant Master Serapis who was, as the reader will remember, one of Henry's earliest Teachers in America. Others who knew this great Adept have described him as, "a fair Greek by birth, blue-eyed, with sunny red-gold hair"—which fits Badrinath's vision quite well.

During the latter half of 1883 the Colonel's remarkable healing powers began to wane. In a healing tour from Madras to Bombay during October it took a great deal of time and energy to effect any cures, and there was a much larger percentage of failures.

In Bombay he made the following entry in his diary for October 19, 1883: "Returned to quarters in a torrent of rain. Through D.K.M. (Damodar) got an order from the Chohans not to heal any more until further notice."

Later he writes that the prohibition had come none too soon as, if he had kept up the strain, he might easily have become paralyzed himself. Just before starting on the journey to Bombay, he had had a warning sign: his left forefinger had become temporarily devoid of sensation. Also there was a loss of tone in his spine. It felt, he said, "like an uncoiled spring, without elasticity."

Swimming in the sea, which he had done as often as possible as a restorer of his vitality during the heaviest periods of his healing work, no longer had the desired effect. He was still in a condition of depleted vitality early next year when he sailed for Europe with Madame Blavatsky. But one bright day in Bavaria, on the shores of a lovely lake, he recalled a thing taught him long before by his guru— nervous power may be regained by lying flat on one's back on the ground beneath a healthy fir, pine, cedar or spruce tree, putting the soles of one's feet against the trunk, and making oneself absorptive to the magnetism of the earth and the tree's aura.

There were plenty of suitable trees around, so Henry put the strange therapy to the test. It worked wonders, bringing him back to normal health and vigor.

During the months when the healing force flowing through him seemed to work miracles, the Colonel realized that the world would simply not believe what was happening—except those people who either benefited or personally witnessed the cures. So to help his cause in spreading Theosophy, he obtained testimonials of the most striking cases. These, handwritten long ago in Ceylon or India, signed by the healed patient and one or two eyewitnesses, may still be seen in The Theosophical Society archives at Adyar, India.

A truly kind-hearted man, the Colonel felt deep sympathy for all suffering. Yet he was wise enough to know that all he could do was as nothing against the tremendous mass of disease and affliction in the world. It behooved him to do all he could, of course, for the immediate cause of compassion, and the long-term cause of enlightenment. But fundamentally there was only one cure for suffering humanity; that was to change the nature and understanding, and thereby the karma of man. Only thus could the disharmony and disease of the generations ahead eventually be eradicated.

Chapter 13

AN ADEPT COMES TO THE COLONEL'S TENT
1883

During Henry's mesmeric healing crusade described in
the last chapter, the founders had moved their headquarters
from Bombay to Madras. It came about in this way. In
May 1882, before the healing started, Olcott and H.P.B.
had made their first visit to Madras, drawn there by that
city's evident interest in matters theosophical. They received
a tumultuous welcome, made many friends and formed a
promising branch of the Society.

Among the new friends was a brilliant young lawyer
named T. Subba Row. A Pleader in the High Court of
Madras, he had, for some time before the Madras visit, been
in correspondence with H.P.B. and Damodar at Bombay,
evincing great interest in esoteric philosophy.

Afterwards he confessed, in private conversations and
writings, that when he met H.P.B. an inner door opened to
a storehouse of forgotten occult knowledge. He remembered
his last life on earth, and recognized his Sadguru—the Master
Morya. Both the founders felt a great love for this exceptional young man—as they did for Damodar.

The Colonel writes: "I cannot recall one equal to T.
Subba Row of Madras in bright genius for grasping the
spirit of the Ancient Wisdom. And his being at Madras
was one of the causes of our fixing upon that Presidency
town for our official residence."

Their first view of their home-to-be, on the outskirts of
Madras at Adyar, was on May 31 when, according to the
diary, Olcott and H.P.B. "went to see a splendid bungalow
by the river bank." The bungalow, and surrounding estate
of about 25 acres called Huddlestone's Gardens, was up for
sale at what was considered a ridiculously cheap price—9,000
rupees, or about 600 pounds sterling.

The Twins did not have even that amount of money, but the new-found friends were anxious to have them residing at Madras. So, one of them—Mr. P. Iyaloo Naidu—advanced the 3,500 rupees needed for a deposit, and another—Judge Muttuswamy Chetty—secured a loan for the rest of the money required, on easy terms.

The Adyar estate was theirs by the time the Colonel returned in November 1882 from his first healing safari in Ceylon. Early the next month "Monsieur Coulomb began boxing H.P.B.'s furniture for shipment to Madras." A week before Christmas the founders left Bombay by train, taking the Coulombs, Damodar, Babula, and their two dogs Djin and Pudhi with them. Arriving in Madras in the early morning, they were met by some fifty Theosophical Fellows who escorted them the seven or eight miles to Adyar—across the river by the quaint, pink bridge, and along the private drive through mango trees to the pallatial, pillared house. The quiet Adyar river flowed a few feet behind the house, and not far away was a long yellow beach on the Bay of Bengal. "Happy days are in store for us here," wrote the Colonel.

January 1883 brought them the delightful sunny weather of perhaps the best winter climate in the world. It also brought busy days: desk work in connection with *The Theosophist* and the swiftly-expanding Society, discussions with many visitors, settling the staff into new quarters, buying furniture for H.P.B.'s room on the terraced roof of the bungalow.

In the early days at Adyar the diary reports that Master Morya paid visits to H.P.B. every day. These were evidently astral visits, and—perhaps as a result of them—Madame announced that there must be a special room prepared—a secret or shrine room.

"Helping get Morya's room ready," writes Olcott in the diary on February 11. Then three days later: "Finished the hangings on the wall of the secret room. Day before yesterday there dropped in that room, in Madame Coulomb's presence, a note from K.H. and Rs.150, with the plan of a sanctuary for Buddha, and orders to have it constructed." This seems to have been the first phenomenon in the famous

An early picture of The Theosophical Society headquarters building at Adyar, 1887

shrine room. Aware that no one at headquarters had this amount of money (150 rupees) to spare for such a project, the Colonel never for a moment doubted the genuineness of the phenomenal letter which was addressed to him.

Upstairs, at the beginning, there was a large room used by H.P.B. as a bed-sitting room, and a small one over the stairs given to Damodar. The shrine room was a new construction, adjoining H.P.B.'s room, with a door connecting the two. A specially-made cabinet was hung in the shrine room against the wall dividing it from H.P.B.'s room.

This cabinet was used as a kind of astral post office, psychic power being concentrated within it. Written messages to the Mahatmas—instead of being given to H.P.B., as had been the usual practice—were now placed inside the cabinet. And into the same place came written replies. Sometimes such replies appeared in a few seconds; sometimes after many days. On occasions messages from the Mahatmas were received in the astral post office without any previous queries or requests having been placed there. This was so, for instance, in the case of the initial message to Henry with its 150 rupees.

At about the middle of February 1883, Henry left by ship for Calcutta and places north, where he healed, lectured, and organized new branches of the Society. Among old friends met at Calcutta were Major-General and the beautiful Mrs. Gordon, and the Sinnetts. Alfred P. Sinnett had by then lost his job as Editor of the *Pioneer*. His dismissal was to a large extent, it seems, a result of his theosophical activities, the proprietors of the paper being antipathetic toward things occult and other worldly.

Sinnett, however, did not seem unduly worried about the situation. He returned soon afterward to England, full of bright hopes for a distinguished future in journalism, creative writing, and the promotion of Theosophy in the "right circles" there. After all, was he not the man to whom the Mahatmas had written scores of letters revealing much of the Ancient Wisdom!* His correspondence with the Masters, which had begun toward the end of 1880, continued for

* Over 120 letters were published in *The Mahatma Letters to A. P. Sinnett*, the originals of which may be seen at the British Museum.

a time sporadically after he went to England, then dwindled and came to an end in 1885.

The Colonel's sandals and wide Indian cotton trousers collected much traveler's dust during the whole of the year 1883. Though May found him back from Calcutta, he was off again in June for a tour of Ceylon and Southern India. Toward the end of August he went to Ootacamund, a fashionable holiday resort in the Nilgiri Mountains. There he joined his chum who was staying at the home of Major General and Mrs. Morgan. This couple were duly initiated into The Theosophical Society, and proved themselves to be among its staunchest friends when the big troubles came.

Late in September Henry was on his way to Bombay; after there was to be a tour of northwest India. With him went Damodar who had been working strenuously as the Society's Recording Secretary. Coming from a wealthy Brahmin family, Damodar had received a good education in English and a strict training in the orthodox religious practices of his high caste. Also, following tradition, he had been married by his parents in childhood to a girl of their choice.

But after finding his guru—the Master Koot Hoomi—through the help of H.P.B. and The Theosophical Society, he abandoned his caste and left home. His young wife, Lakshmibai, agreed that he should part from her to live the life of an ascetic. Damodar gave up his worldly wealth (worth some 50,000 rupees), assigning it to his father on condition that Lakshmibai should be taken care of in the family home.

Through his devotional work at The Theosophical Society and ascetic practices, Damodar was beginning to develop some yogic *siddhis,* and was able to travel consciously outside his body. Sometimes he acted as an astral courier for messages to and from the Masters. It was, for instance, on this tour with Olcott that the Mahatmic messages came, through Damodar, ordering the Colonel to suspend healing—as related in the last chapter.

Another young man who joined Henry Olcott on this never-to-be-forgotten journey to the northwest was William T. Brown, a law graduate of Glasgow University. Brown had met Alfred Sinnett in London and had come out to

Damodar K. Mavalankar

India, determined to work with the founders, and if possible make contact with the Himalayan teachers themselves. At the outset Olcott warned him of the sharp thorns in the petal path of occultism, and the terrible rigors and trials of discipleship to the Masters. But Brown seemed undaunted by this.

During the journey to the northwest, Damodar made three out-of-the-body journeys to Adyar which convinced the Colonel that these experiences were no mere dreams or hallucinations. In the first journey he found himself, in his astral body, at Headquarters conversing with H.P.B. in her room there. One of the Masters was present and gave a message for the Colonel. Before leaving to take the message, Damodar asked H.P.B. to telegraph the substance of it. Perhaps he lacked faith in his own astral memory, or Olcott's belief in his powers of astral travel.

On returning to his body where he had left it at Moradabad, he gave the Master's message to the Colonel. The latter wrote it down on the spot and had it signed by several witnesses who were present. Next day the telegram arrived from H.P.B. at Adyar, corroborating Damodar's words.

The second astral trip involved a more difficult feature. Damodar, wanting to take a letter to his guru, went to sleep holding it in his hand. But instead of going to the Master's ashrama as he had expected, he found himself at Adyar, drawn there by the fact that Master K.H. was himself there astrally. Having read the apported letter from the hand of Damodar, the Master left it at Adyar. H.P.B.—perhaps to furnish more evidence of Damodar's developing occult powers—enclosed the letter in an envelope with one of her own, and posted it back to Olcott. The date and place name stamped by the post-office on the envelope proved that it had been sent from Adyar on November 5, which was the day following Damodar's nocturnal journey, carrying the letter across the length of India. In those days before airmail, such a quick delivery could have been made only by some supernormal, occult method. The letter's return journey by train from Adyar to the far north took the usual time for mail at that period—five days.

Damodar's third extracorporeal experience took place

while he was dozing in a train traveling from Delhi to Lahore. When he awoke from his sleep, it was six o'clock in the evening; he immediately informed the Colonel, and an Indian member of the Society who was in the carriage, that he had just returned from an astral trip to Adyar where he had seen H.P.B. have an accident. She had fallen and, he thought, hurt her right knee.

As soon as possible Henry wired H.P.B. the query: "What accident happened at headquarters at about six o'clock?" Her reply, telegraphed from Adyar, is preserved in The Theosophical Society archives. It reads: "Nearly broke my right leg. Tumbled from Bishop's chair, dragging Coulomb, and frightening Morgans. Damodar startled us."

On the open ground to the north of Lahore a camp of canvas tents and pavilions had been erected for the theosophical party to live and hold their meetings. The sleeping tents were divided into two compartments. Henry shared one of these with William T. Brown. During his second night in the tent—November 19—the Colonel had a happy, unforgettable experience: "I was sleeping in my tent," he said, "when I rushed back toward external consciousness on feeling a hand laid upon me. The camp being on the open plain, and beyond the protection of the Lahore police, my first animal instinct was to protect myself from a possible religious fanatical assassin, so I clutched the stranger by the upper arms and asked him in Hindustani who he was and what he wanted. . . I held the man tight as would one who might be attacked the next moment and have to defend his life. But the next instant a kind, sweet voice said:

"Do you not know me? Do you not remember me?" It was the voice of the Master K.H.

"I relaxed my hold on his arms, joined my palms in reverential salutation, and wanted to jump out of bed to show him respect. But his hand and voice stayed me, and after a few sentences had been exchanged, he took my left hand in his, gathered the fingers of his right into the palm, and stood quiet beside my cot, from which I could see his divinely benignant face by the light of the lamp that burned on a packing-case at his back. Presently I felt some soft substance forming in my hand, and the next minute the Master laid his kind hand on my forehead, uttered a blessing, and left my half of the large tent to visit Mr. W. T. Brown who slept in the other half. . ."*

The object formed in Henry's hand was a paper wrapped in silk. Going over to the lamp, he found it was a message in the Master K.H.'s handwriting. While studying it, he heard an exclamation from Brown's side of the canvas screen, and went in. The young man held another silk-wrapped message, received, he said, in the same manner as Olcott's.

In a pamphlet, *My Life,* W. T. Brown states that the letter and silk wrapper appeared to "grow out of nothing. I feel a stream of magnetism and lo! it is materialized." The silk was a fine handkerchief with the initials "K.H." marked in blue.

Returning to the reading of his own message, the Colonel found that it was mainly one of private counsel, but Master K.H. also prophesied the early death of two active enemies of The Theosophical Society. Finally he elated Henry with these words: "Tomorrow night, when the camp is quiet and the worst of the emanations from your audience have passed away, I shall visit you again for a longer conversation, as you must be forewarned against certain things in the future."

Next evening after Olcott's lecture, he sat with Damodar and Brown expectantly awaiting the arrival of the Great One. The crowd had dispersed, and the rest of the Colonel's party had gone off to Lahore. It was ten o'clock and all was quiet. From the tent they presently saw a tall, white-clad figure approaching. He came within a few yards of where the three sat in the doorway of Olcott's tent. They saw that it was not the Master K.H. after all. Henry recognized the visitor as Djwal Khul, who was then an advanced *chela* of the Great Brotherhood of Adepts. Olcott had seen him physically in Darjeeling only a few months earlier.

The *chela* beckoned to Damodar who went forward. Then the Master himself appeared before the tent and took the young man off a little distance. Olcott and Brown quietly kept their places. After a few minutes Damodar returned to his friends, and the king-like figure of K.H. walked away. Djwal Khul had already disappeared.

* *Old Diary Leaves Vol. 3.*

Now Henry began to fear that he would not have the supreme joy of a talk with the Master that night after all. But later, while he sat alone in his tent writing in his diary, Djwal Khul returned, lifted the *portiere,* beckoned, and pointed to a stately figure waiting in the starlight. Henry dropped his pen and hurried out to the Master K.H.

The Benign One took him away for some distance to a place where interruptions were unlikely, and for about half an hour Henry had the joy of hearing the Master's sweet, gentle voice. Among many things—some personal—he told Olcott of troubles that were brewing in England at the London Lodge, warning him of what might happen to the Theosophical movement there. Grave difficulties lay ahead, but whatever happened, he (the President) must never lose faith and confidence.

Henry's heart leapt and tears of happiness sprang to his eyes when he heard the Master say, finally, that One higher than himself, namely the Maha Chohan, had sent him to have this talk and instructed him to say that he was well satisfied with Henry Olcott's fidelity to the great cause.

Next day the theosophical party moved from Lahore to Jammu, where they occupied bungalows as guests of the Maharaja of Kashmir. Rising early on the morning of November 25, the Colonel went into the adjoining room to speak to Damodar who was sleeping there. But Damodar was absent. Henry went to look for him, asking the servants if they had seen anything of him. Finally one servant said he had seen Damodar leave the bungalow at daybreak—alone.

But surely, thought Henry, he cannot have gone far; his belongings are still in the room, and he has not left any message. He returned to Damodar's room to have another look. There, lying conspicuously on the table, was a note from the Master K.H. It could hardly have been there when he entered the room before, or he would surely have seen it. He felt that it had appeared phenomenally on the table while he was outside searching for the missing youth.

The note simply told Olcott not to worry, as Damodar was under the Master's protection. The Colonel felt rather excited about the new development, and sent a telegram to H.P.B., telling her what had happened. Her reply came the same day. Apparently—through her "psychic radio" with the Masters—she was aware of the situation and knew that Damodar would soon return.

Two days passed with no further word. Then, on the evening of the third day after his disappearance, Damodar walked in, "looking haggard yet more wiry and tough than before. He is now a new man indeed. Brought me a message from Hilarion. His complexion seems two or three shades darker." So wrote Henry in his diary.

Damodar whispered a message from Master Morya in the Colonel's ear. It was accompanied by a password by which Henry knew that the message was a genuine one—from his own guru.

During his three-day absence, Damodar had, it seemed, been with the Master K.H., and some other members of the Brotherhood at a retreat not far away. He had been given some special training and health treatment there which had quite obviously made a new man of him. No longer frail and timid, he was now, on the contrary, "robust, bold and energetic in manner." On most of what had taken place his lips were sealed, but he told a little, and later on wrote something of the experience in *The Theosophist*: "There I met not only my beloved Gurudeva [K.H.] and Col. Olcott's Master, but several others of the Fraternity, including One of the Highest. . . . Thus I saw my beloved Guru not only as a *living* man, but actually as a young one in comparison with some other Sadhus of the blessed company. . ."*

The Colonel arrived back in Madras on December 15, 1883, in time to prepare for the annual convention of The Theosophical Society. "Home never seemed so delightful, nor my old chum so dear," he told his diary.

But frightful headaches were bothering him again as they had, on and off, over a long period. About ten days after his return he received an occult message that, if he slept in the shrine room, his Master would remove the headaches once and for all. In complete faith he carried out the instruction immediately. "Slept in the Occult Room," says the diary for December 27, "and my Guru cured my agonizing headaches 'forever.'"

---

* See *The Theosophist* Vol. V, Nos. 3-4, Dec.-Jan. 1883-4. pp. 61-62.

Strange things were happening daily in the shrine room. Christmas Day, 1883, was special—"six or seven notes to different persons simultaneously appear in the silver bowl [in the shrine room cabinet]—one in Marathi to Tookaram, in which his secret name was given."

But three days later something more dramatic occurred. The Colonel and H.P.B. were standing together on the lawn. He said to her: "I'm sorry other members have not helped Judge Sreenevas Row on the matter of Convention expenses. He has given 500 rupees out of his own pocket. I feel sure he can't afford that much." H.P.B., after reflecting a while on this, called Damodar who was standing talking to a nearby group. She said to him:

"Go to the shrine and bring me a packet you'll find there."

In less than five minutes Damodar was back with a sealed envelope. It was addressed to "P. Sreenevas Row" who opened it and found inside Government Promissory Notes to the value of 500 rupees. On the back of each note was written the initials "K.H." in the Master's customary blue pencil. Together with the money was a kind letter of thanks from the Master to the Judge.

On the last day of the year, 1883, Henry wrote that it had been "the most active and fortunate of all for our Society," and that he had covered 16,500 miles touring India and Ceylon. He was well satisfied with the way things were going. The next year—1884—he thought should be devoted mainly to theosophical work in Europe. He felt that he must go there personally. Such a trip would cost a lot, but Judge Sreenevas Row had told him that he could raise the necessary funds at a month's notice.

From what the Master K.H. had told him, the money would not be wasted on such a journey. His presence was necessary to deal with the situation at the London Lodge. Dark clouds banking on the horizon there could bring serious damage to the Society if not dispelled before the storm burst.

Chapter 14

THE DANGEROUS BOOM IN THEOSOPHY
1884

The Colonel began the year 1884 with a quick trip to Ceylon. There he persuaded the persecuted Buddhists to form a Buddhist Defence Committee, and agreed to act as the committee's special envoy to the appropriate governmental authorities in England.

On February 20 he and H.P.B. boarded in Bombay a French ship bound for Marseilles. With the founders went 26-year-old Mohini M. Chatterjee, an attorney-at-law from Calcutta who could lecture brilliantly in English on Theosophic and Vedic themes. Another in the party was Mr. B. J. Padshah, whom the Colonel described as "one of the cleverest Parsi graduates of Bombay University." A third was the Moslem servant Babula.

Behind them the Twins were leaving a highly combustible mixture of elements in the Adyar test tube. President Olcott had put the administration of the Society's affairs in the hands of a council, the most active and effective members of which were two new arrivals. One was a wealthy British electrical engineer named Mr. St. George Lane-Fox, and the other a Bavarian doctor of medicine and great traveler— Dr. Franz Hartmann. The latter had arrived during the preceding December as the delegate from America for the convention. He had, however, been in correspondence with the founders for some time before that on the subject of his deepest interest—occultism.

Oddly, the Colonel had also put on the Adyar Council the semiliterate, quick-tempered Alexis Coulomb. Later he wrote that he did so because the wife, Emma Coulomb, had begged him to, saying that her husband "was a proud man" and that his feelings would be hurt if he were left out.

The dour and dutiful Damodar remained behind as Recording Secretary of the Society. Now the oldest pillar of that body left at headquarters, Damodar was not of the temperament to make for mutual understanding and tolerance between himself and the two new European "managers"—Lane-Fox and Hartmann, who were also residing at the Society headquarters.

But the real Iago of the coming drama was Emma Coulomb. She was by now completely fed up with working for something she neither understood nor believed in. The Theosophical Society, in her eyes, was anti-Christian and anti-British. (She was officially both by birth.) The paranormal phenomena were, she considered, either the work of the devil or faked. The faking would be all right if there were money in it. But the only money she ever got her hands on was what she could manage to pilfer from the housekeeping funds. That was something, but not enough to fulfill her dream—a new start in the hotel business.

There had been some good opportunities, but these had slipped through her fingers—thanks to Madame Blavatsky. For instance, Prince Hurisinghji, a wealthy member of The Theosophical Society, had been all set to give her the 2,000-rupee "loan" she had asked for when he was at Adyar. She had gone to see H.P.B. off in Bombay in February expressly because the journey through India would include a visit to the Prince. At his house she had reminded him of the promise, and the money was almost in her hands, when Madame Blavatsky found out and put a brusque end to the deal.

Aboard the ship Madame Coulomb bade a fond and tearful *bon voyage* to her employer, but a moment later expressed her real feelings to Babula. Perhaps she thought that he, too, shared her hatred of a mistress he was often threatening to leave because of "unjust demands." Now Emma muttered to him:

"I'll never forgive your mistress for that last interference. She will certainly pay for it—dearly."

Madame Blavatsky had given Emma charge of the keys to

the upstairs rooms at Adyar; so now she and her husband had a free hand and plenty of time to plan a revenge that would wreck the imperious Russian woman and her Society—and at the same time put the funds they needed in their own pockets. It would be done!

At Marseilles the theosophical party was met by Baron J. Spedalieri, a Kabbalist and pupil of the late Eliphas Levi. From there, while Mohini and Padshah went on ahead to Paris, the founders proceeded to Nice as guests of Lady Caithness, Duchess de Pomar and Fellow of The Theosophical Society.

There H.P.B. was delighted to meet again some of her compatriots—members of the Russian nobility who were still on the Riviera at the tail end of the season. The Colonel, too, enjoyed a taste of Continental high life. Not that empty talk or visits to the Monte Carlo casino interested him, but he was ever a student of human nature and, moreover, some members of the international set were beginning to show an interest in Theosophy. Besides, their hostess, Lady Caithness —a Cuban-born beauty and heiress, surviving her titled husband—was a fascinating character, even if a bit eccentric, believing firmly that she was a reincarnation of Mary, Queen of Scots.

After about twelve days in Nice they took train to Paris where Lady Caithness had hired an apartment for them at 46 Rue Notre Dame des Champs. Awaiting them there was William Q. Judge who was passing through the French capital en route to India.

The Colonel found a good deal to interest him in the city. He visited and studied the methods of the famous hypnotic healer Zouave Jacob, and met other healers—mediumistic and clairvoyant—who were becoming celebrated. It was a very pleasant week that he spent in Paris on this occasion, but urgent problems were awaiting solution across the Channel. So on April 5 he left by train for Calais and the ferryboat to England. With him went Mohini Chatterjee, while H.P.B. and Padshah remained in Paris.

In order to get full information on the London situation, the Colonel had sent a circular letter to members of the London Lodge, asking each to send his or her views to him in confidence. Many replies had come while he was still in Paris, and now as the train rumbled through the flat French farmlands, he began to study the various viewpoints expressed.

In a letter from an active member of the lodge, Mr. Bertram Keightley, he had just come to a passage where the writer affirmed his confidence that the Masters would order all things well, when he happened to glance up. He saw a piece of paper fluttering down as if from the roof of the carriage. It fell on the floor between him and Mohini, who was the only other person in the carriage. Picking it up, he found to his joy that it was an envelope addressed to him in the handwriting of the Master K.H.

He eagerly tore open the envelope and read the letter inside.* Referring to the London problem, it expressed confidence that Henry would "vindicate the policy of the Society." It pointed out that everything had happened as foretold by the Master five months earlier at Lahore, and stated that the best interests of the movement would be served by bringing all latent potentialities (for destruction as well as construction) to the surface. Let all the cards be put on the table—"As your charming new friends at Nice who frequent Monte Carlo and the gambling *cercles,* would say, the players have now—*cartes sur table.*"

The letter then sounded a note of warning about affairs back at Adyar. "You have harbored a traitor and an enemy under your roof for years, and the missionary party are more than ready to avail of any help she may be induced to give. A regular conspiracy is on foot. She is maddened by the appearance of Mr. Lane-Fox and the powers you have given to the Board of Control. . ."

Already letters from Damodar and others at headquarters had complained that Emma Coulomb was being more than troublesome. She was apparently spreading stories around that H.P.B.'s phenomena were fakes, and hinting broadly at trap doors and sliding panels in the shrine room. She was now openly expressing to all and sundry her hostility toward the Society.

---

* *Letters from the Masters of the Wisdom, First Series,* Letter 18. The Theosophical Publishing House, Adyar, Madras, India.

The Colonel was very perturbed by all this. Of course Emma had said these things to him personally several times in the past; she was undoubtedly a foolish, ignorant, and prejudiced woman; but prattling to outsiders in this irresponsible manner might do considerable harm. So in Paris, on April 2, he wrote her a frank but friendly letter. In it he said that he did not think she should continue to be a member of a Society which she thought flourished by trickery and false representation.

He reminded her, however, that there was no use in her trying to convince him that the supernormal phenomena were brought about by H.P.B.'s chicanery—"for many of us have seen phenomena when Madame B. was far away from us, and these very letters received from Adyar [from members of the Council there] testify to letters having been phenomenally received by Sreenevas Row and others, and other phenomena taking place just as they did before H.P.B. left."

He pointed out also that the strength and value of The Theosophical Society did not rest on "miraculous" phenomena. Even if all of it *could* be proved a fraud, it would not change his opinion "one iota as to the benefit to be derived by the world from our Society's work."

On the whole it was a kindly letter, making an appeal to her common sense and decency. It concludes: "So now I have said my say in my usual plain but honest way, let us be friends and allies, as we have hitherto been, and with sincere regards to Mons. Coulomb, I am, faithfully yours, H. S. Olcott."

But to return to the problem that lay immediately ahead of him in London, this arose out of a clash of two strong, dominant personalities with opposing outlooks on Theosophy. Each was a potential leader of the lodge, and each had a following.

One of these was Mrs. Anna Kingsford, a woman of intellectual power and broad culture, but with a strange character. She had no love for her own child, but lavished excessive affection on her pet guinea pig. She believed herself to be the reincarnation of Hermes, Joan of Arc, and other well-known historical characters. Self-confident and ambitious, she thought she was the angel of a new religious epoch. Mrs. Kingsford had not been to India but was a deep student of the Christo-Egyptian teachings which she considered superior to those of the Indian Mahatmas.

The competitor for leadership in London was Mr. Alfred P. Sinnett who had recently returned from India. His books, *The Occult World* and *Esoteric Buddhism*, had aroused tremendous interest in Theosophy among the general public. It was known that he had for years been receiving direct instruction in the ancient wisdom by means of the letters from the Masters. And Sinnett had, judging by the letters the Colonel received in reply to his recent circular, by far the larger following.

But the Kingsford faction was strong, active, and very vocal. Misunderstandings were increasing, and if the situation were not handled properly, disharmony would certainly disrupt the London Lodge. This would be a great pity, and the irony of it was, the Colonel thought, that the Hindu and the Christo-Egyptian teachings were fundamentally exactly the same—both based firmly on the perennial philosophy, which he called the Ancient Wisdom, or Theosophy.

The meeting of the lodge for the election of officers was held in the chambers of one of the members at Lincoln's Inn. Dr. Archibald Keightley, who was present, describes the scene: "Colonel Olcott was in the chair and endeavored to adjust the differences of opinion without success. By him were seated the contending parties, Mohini Chatterjee and one or two others, facing a long narrow room which was nearly filled with members of the Society."

As the dispute waxed warm, a stout lady arrived, very much out of breath, and took the seat next to Archibald Keightley. He did not know her, but as she sat down, someone alluded to an action of Madame Blavatsky's; the stout lady remarked loudly: "That's so."

Archibald writes: "At this point the meeting broke up in confusion, everybody ran anyhow to the stout lady, while Mohini arrived at her feet on his knees. Finally she was taken up to the end where the 'high gods' had been enthroned. . ."

The Colonel tried to continue the proceedings, but it was

impossible. Everybody was too interested in H.P.B., who had suddenly arrived from Paris and, as she said, "followed her occult nose" from the railway station to Lincoln's Inn. The meeting was adjourned and never reassembled.

The Colonel, however, finally solved the London problem by issuing a charter to Mrs. Kingsford for the formation of a separate lodge. This was called the "Hermetic Lodge of The Theosophical Society." Soon, however, it became a separate society known as the "Hermetic Society," with Mrs. Kingsford as President and Mr. Edwin Maitland as Vice-President. The Colonel made a friendly address at the first meeting of the new society and established good relations with this, the first splinter group of his beloved Theosophical Society.

Alfred Sinnett, now the acknowledged leader of The Theosophical Society in England, was not very happy about the presence of H.P.B. and the Colonel in London. Many intellectuals, and members of the higher social circles of the "capital of the world," had been attracted to this odd, interesting movement, and were attending meetings in the Sinnetts' drawing room. There was, as Sinnett and Bertram Keightley have both written, something of a boom in Theosophy in Europe at this juncture.

Despite his many fine qualities, Sinnett was something of a snob. He wanted desperately to establish Theosophy in the "best circles," and felt that the founders would be a hindrance rather than a help in this. They were such a blunt, forthright pair. Olcott was a Yankee, inclined to do and say things that would, Sinnett thought, put the cultured English "teeth on edge." H.P.B. was a tempestuous Russian. Though of noble birth, she had none of the well-bred English restraint and decorum. Sinnett remembered scenes at Simla and Allahabad, and mentally held his breath while she was in London.

Unaware of such feelings in their old friend, the founders took immense delight in the rising tide of this great movement, born nine years earlier in their New York apartment. In the drawing rooms of the great, the talk was all Theosophy. "At Mrs. Bloomfield Moore's . . . met Robert Browning, and talked Theosophy with that master of verse,"

writes Henry. At other gatherings he met other members
of the *literati* of the day, including Matthew Arnold. Sir
Edwin Arnold invited him to lunch and presented him with
some pages of the manuscript of the *Light of Asia*—"a
precious gift." Young Earl Russell had the Colonel up to
Oxford for a night, and Lord Borthwick—a member of
The Theosophical Society—took him for a vacation on his
estate in Scotland.

Olcott's representations for the Buddhists to the Secretary
of State for the Colonies went well, and as a result all the
grievances of the Ceylon Buddhists were eventually removed.
In fact the Colonel's efforts in London for the cause seemed,
on the face of things, to be a tremendous success in every way.

Something else, also quite promising at first sight, began
to take shape. Two years earlier, in 1882, a society had been
formed in London for the investigation of psychic phenomena. It was called the Society for Psychical Research, or
briefly the S.P.R. Its aims were to study all forms of apparently paranormal phenomena, to test their genuineness, and
to attempt to find a satisfactory rationale for any truly extrasensory experiences.

The S.P.R.'s founders and leading members, some of whom
were classical scholars and others scientists, meant to apply
the methodology of modern science to their chosen field of
research. The folklore tales of ghosts, second sight, mind
reading, foretelling the future and so on were to be put
to the objective, cold-blooded tests of the laboratory. Science
was slaughtering the old church dogmas, so let science determine the truth of psychic phenomena; let scientific method
determine what were man's latent powers, if any, and whether
or not he survived death.

By "science" the S.P.R. meant the developing physical
sciences of the West. They knew nothing whatever of ancient Eastern science, and looked with skepticism on the
old saying, *Ex Oriente Lux* (Light from the East). The
S.P.R. founders were all Britons, largely conditioned by
the fact that they belonged to a people who had proved their
"superiority" over the natives of the East. Unlike the two
founders of The Theosophical Society, the S.P.R. men had
received no training in occult science—or Raja Yoga—which

throws light on man's true nature and provides a rationale for his extrasensory powers.

Nevertheless, among them were men of high attainment and character. Henry Sidgwick, the President of the S.P.R., was Praelector in Moral and Political Philosophy at Trinity College, Cambridge. Frederick Myers was a brilliant classical scholar and a poet. Edmund Gurney was another classical scholar and a doctor of medicine. These three were the nucleus, but around them were other men of distinction: Lord Rayleigh, the great physicist, Arthur Balfour, later to be Prime Minister of England; Sir William Barrett, Professor of Physics at the Royal College of Science in Dublin.

It was inevitable that this young society should become interested in the reports of theosophical phenomena—especially as the founders of the Society were in Europe, near at hand for discussions. Meetings between the two parties were easily arranged. Mrs. Tennant, at whose house the Colonel met many of the notables of Victorian England, was the mother-in-law of Frederick Myers. And Myers himself had been a member of The Theosophical Society for almost a year.

So it was not long before Henry Olcott was dining with the S.P.R. leaders at their homes or clubs. His first host had an appropriately inauspicious name—Mr. Coffin. But Henry had no thoughts of bad omens as he enjoyed Coffin's good dinner at the Junior Atheneum Club, where he met Professor Barrett, E. Gurney, Frank Podmore and others of the S.P.R. "Truly a brilliant company of scholars and literati," he confided to his diary.

They invited him to give evidence before an S.P.R. committee about the psychic phenomena he had experienced since meeting H.P.B. Well, why not? he asked himself. There was nothing to hide—though some of the experiences were rather personal and very precious. But if he refused, it would throw suspicion on the authenticity of the wondrous stories that had stemmed from the center of Theosophy. Besides, he should give what help he could to this group of earnest searchers and aid the cause of spiritual science. Moreover, through the approval of these men—all leading lights in their own fields—the theosophical phenomena would gain in prestige and acceptability to the general public. In this way, surely, Theosophy would be helped forward.

Ruminating thus, Henry became eager to cooperate with the S.P.R. investigators, so much so that later H.P.B. accused him of thrusting the phenomena before them. Following the example of their President, Mohini and Padshah agreed to be questioned. Sinnett, too, who had given the skeptics more than enough to digest in his *Occult World*, was quite willing to meet an S.P.R. committee of inquiry.

On a sunny morning early in May 1884, Henry sat in conclave with two members of the S.P.R. Committee, Frederick Myers and Herbert Stack. Olcott considered the latter to be "a man of high culture and of scientific tastes." A stenographer was also present to record in full the questions and answers.

Henry told the committee about his guru's first visit to the New York apartment, at that time the headquarters of The Theosophical Society. He told them about Damodar's astral journeys, about the visits of Master K.H. to his tent at Lahore, and of the recent letter that fell in the railway carriage between Paris and Calais. To a question from Myers, he replied that he had seen his guru in the flesh more than four times, and had seen him in astral form "fifteen to twenty times."

Sixteen days later, that is on May 27, the Colonel was questioned by the full Committee of Investigation: Myers, Stack, Gurney and Frank Podmore, the latter an archskeptic whose openly expressed creed was that, in such investigations into paranormal phenomena, one should always assume abnormal dishonesty rather than abnormal psychic powers. On this occasion the evidence was mainly concerned with the abnormal delivery of Mahatma letters, the precipitation of handwriting, phenomena in the shrine-room at Adyar, and the Adepts' telepathic powers. There was a good deal of cross-examination from members of the committee, whose legitimate business it was, of course, to be skeptical until they obtained circumstantial proof beyond "reasonable doubt."

But Henry felt that all had gone well. Everything he had told them, incredible though it may seem, was quite true and, being intelligent men, they must surely come to accept it as such—especially when supported by the evidence of Mohini, Sinnett, and Padshah, who came before the committee on other days. The Society for Psychical Research would publish a favorable report. H.P.B. would be accepted as the messenger of the Great Brotherhood of Adepts by more and more people, who would thus rediscover the ancient wisdom! The spread of the soul-destroying, materialistic philosophy would be stemmed in time to save mankind from disaster.

At the end of June H.P.B. came over from Paris, and the founders spent some time together in England before Henry left for Germany on July 23. He was to be a guest at the home of the Gebhards at Elberfeld in the Ruhr.

Herr G. Gebhard was a manufacturer, banker, and consul. His wife, Mary, was a deep student of the occult, and had been one of the late Eliphas Levi's two pupils (Baron Spedalieri was the other). After Levi died, Mary heard of The Theosophical Society, wrote to the Colonel, and eventually became a member.

Henry says of her: "A sweeter or more loyal character I never met. She was one of those women who spread about them an atmosphere of love and virtue, fill their homes with sunshine, make themselves indispensable to their husbands and adored by their children."

Her children living at this time numbered five, four of them sons. They were all grown up. Herr Gebhard was away in America when the Colonel arrived, but the house was filled with the sunshine of warm hospitality.

Groups of interested visitors came to talk of Theosophy, and three days after the Colonel's arrival the first German branch of The Theosophical Society was formed—"The beginning," writes Olcott, "of the movement in the most intellectual country of Europe. . ."

The weeks passed pleasantly. About the middle of August H.P.B. arrived from England bringing with her a large party: Mohini, Bertram Keightley, Mrs. and Miss Arundale, and Mrs. Laura Holloway.

H.P.B.'s presence in the Gebhard mansion brought a spate of occult phenomena, to the delight of all present. It also brought a number of foreign visitors, some of whom were destined to play a part, for good or ill, in the unfolding theosophical drama. Among them was a Russian journalist named Solovioff, and an American, Professor Elliott Coues of the Smithsonian Institution—a man with hidden ambitions for position and power.

On August 31 Frederick Myers and his brother arrived at Elberfeld, apparently to see what strange things were taking place in the theosophical camp. The Colonel's diary for September 2 reports that Myers was working on H.P.B.'s manuscript. He does not say which manuscript. Two days later he writes that Myers and his brother left after "a valuable conference with H.P.B."

So everything in the theosophical garden seemed to be splendid, and the golden days of late summer passed pleasantly among intelligent, congenial friends. But the distant rumblings from a storm gathering over India were getting louder. Henry writes that on September 10 they "received from Adyar a lugubrious letter from Damodar, intimating that the missionaries were hatching a plot, evidently with the help of Mme. Coulomb."

Damodar was not particularly cheerful by nature, but from this ultradismal letter it seemed certain that a really serious crisis was developing. Yet what could the founders do about it, except write letters? By the time they personally could reach Adyar, the situation would have either mended or gone beyond repair. Yet they must return as soon as possible!

Then, before they could leave Germany, the storm broke. On September 20, the *London Times* published a sensational article about H.P.B. and her phenomena. The story had been cabled from the *Times* Calcutta correspondent and gave, in substance, an article appearing in the September number of the Madras *Christian College Magazine,* the organ of the Protestant missionaries who had ever been enemies of the Society.

The article quoted letters from H.P.B. to Emma Coulomb which, if genuine, showed that, with the assistance of the Coulomb couple, H.P.B. had been cleverly faking her supernormal phenomena. Evidently the Coulombs were prepared to sell their own reputations, as well as that of H.P.B. Through the *Times* article, the "exposé" would very soon be known throughout the whole civilized world.

The Colonel did not, of course, believe that the letters were genuine. He knew too well how dedicated his old chum was to the cause. Like himself, she gave all her time and energy to it, and would be prepared, if necessary, to give her life for it. Even if she *herself* told him that her "miracles" were a fraud, he would not believe her. He would conclude that she was indulging in such crazy talk to test him or for some other reason. Since he had first met her ten years ago, he, an experienced investigator, had seen too much, under conditions where trickery and jugglery were impossible, to accept the theory of fraudulence.

And as for the Mahatmas, being H.P.B.'s invention—as the story claimed—had he not met several of them in flesh and blood a number of times? Had he not seen the illustrious Master Morya ride up to the old Bombay residence on a horse, had he not walked and talked with Master K.H. near Lahore, sat and talked with Hilarion and others in other places? They were as solid and real as his family and friends. More real, actually, because they had the power to lift high his heart and raise his consciousness, to leave an indelible stamp on his memory, life and character!

Still, this scandal could deal a shattering blow to the promising blooms of the theosophical tree. Many of those who did not have the advantage of his own intimate acquaintance with H.P.B. would undoubtedly believe the story. Imposture was always so much easier to swallow than the fact of the existence of yogic powers—to men of the West, anyway.

And the S.P.R. Committee of Investigation, whose interest was in phenomena only—not in the esoteric teachings—how would the great scandal affect them? There was only one thing to do—get back to Adyar, study *all* the facts of the situation, and decide what action to take.

H.P.B., who had been suffering unbearable mental torture during the days of rumor and malicious innuendo, was now ablaze. She wrote a letter to the *London Times,* denouncing the letters allegedly from herself to Emma Coulomb as forgeries. In press interviews published in the *Pall Mall* and other journals she stated her intention of returning to India forthwith, and prosecuting the Coulombs and the missionaries concerned for libel.

The memorable house party at Elberfeld broke up. The Colonel left for India via Paris and Marseilles. H.P.B. set off for the same destination by way of London and Cairo.

Chapter 15

"INGENIOUS IMPOSTER"
1884 - 1885

Arriving back at Adyar about the middle of November 1884, the Colonel was told in detail of the events leading up to the press "explosion" that had echoed around the world.

Briefly, what he learned was this: Madame Coulomb, who as housekeeper held the keys of H.P.B.'s upstairs rooms, had refused to let Dr. Hartmann, Damodar, or anyone else enter the rooms. This upset Hartmann particularly, because H.P.B. had given him permission—verbally before leaving— to make use of her rooms for any private work he had to do.

Husband Alexis had the run of the roof because he was in charge—officially by the Colonel's orders—of some new construction work there. Consequently, as Damodar was at this time sleeping and working downstairs, the whole upstairs area was virtually isolated. It was exclusively Coulomb territory, and they guarded it jealously.

The devilish plot behind all this was apparently not suspected until Emma Coulomb's public remarks and innuendos about "trap doors" and "secret panels" began to be heard, and it looked as though Alexis might be carrying out some unofficial alterations of his own on the upper floor.

Members of the Board of Control decided to impeach the mischief-making couple. Sworn affidavits from a number of responsible people declared that Madame Coulomb was guilty of many offenses, including attempts to extort money from members of the Society, wasting the funds of the Society, slandering H.P.B., circulating rumors that the object of The Theosophical Society was to overthrow the British Empire, and stating that the occult phenomena were either frauds or the work of the devil.

A strongly-worded letter from the Master Morya to Dr. Hartmann spurred the board members to cable the founders for permission to expel the couple from the Society headquarters. This obtained, the Coulombs were given orders to quit. But they refused to go immediately, lingering on to suit their own convenience and plans.

Emma tried to blackmail the Society leaders at Adyar, asking for three thousand rupees for her silence about "things she could tell" the world—but it is significant that at this time she made no mention of incriminating letters from H.P.B. which might be marketable in the right quarters. Alexis told Dr. Hartmann—apparently to help open the well-filled wallet of his confederate, Mr. Lane-Fox—that ten thousand rupees were being offered to them for the ruin of The Theosophical Society. The insinuation was that this handsome offer came from enemies of the Society (presumably the missionaries), but that the noble Coulombs would accept a lower sum in order to save the Society from ruin, even though they regarded it as anti-British, anti-Christian and based on fraud.

At about the same time Alexis asked Damodar pointedly if he knew of secret passages in the shrine room. Then finally, on May 25, the Coulombs were driven off the premises. They went to lodge with some of missionary Rev. Mr. Patterson's church members. But just before leaving, when handing over the keys of the upper rooms, Alexis showed the "secret contrivances" to the board members. These contrivances included a hole in one partition of the two-partition wall dividing H.P.B.'s room from the shrine room. It was opposite the back of the hanging shrine cabinet, and gave access from H.P.B.'s room to a narrow wall space. But there was no opening through the second partition to the back of the shrine itself.

The hole, thus revealed by handy man Coulomb, would therefore be of no use as a secret entrance to the shrine cupboard—even presuming that the latter had a sliding panel in its back. It seemed pretty obvious to the board that Alexis had not been able to complete his diabolical work of making the secret opening before he was forced to quit the premises. Coulomb declared that there *had* been a hole through the second wall partition to the shrine room, but that he had blocked it up. What his motive could be in blocking up one hole and leaving the other to "expose" the frauds, the Society leaders could not fathom. It seemed like balderdash. Obviously he had planned to complete the hole-making but had run out of time.

Those who examined the other contrivances—sliding panels in the back of a wardrobe, and in the wall leading from the stairway into another cupboard in the shrine room—decided that they were of quite recent origin. None worked smoothly and silently; in fact they made a great deal of noise and would be of no use whatever for carrying out trick phenomena. Clearly they had been constructed after H.P.B. left for Europe as part of the Coulomb plot for obtaining money, either through blackmail, or by selling information to the missionaries. In either case Emma would have avenged the imaginary wrongs she had suffered from H.P.B.

On August 9 the Coulombs made contact with the *Christian College Magazine* with the package of letters meant to shatter the foundations of the hated Society. They would also ruin for ever the reputation of that quick-tempered Blavatsky woman who, in their opinion, was obviously in league with old Nick himself. The Colonel would suffer too, which was a pity in a way because they liked him. He was honest and a thorough gentleman. But he should not have been so gullible.

A question that springs to mind is, why did the Coulombs waste nearly three months after their leaving Adyar before launching their deadly missile? The critics answer that it probably took them that long to sort out the scraps of H.P.B.'s writing—which Emma had been collecting over the years—and to concoct the letters, or appropriate insertions in letters, which they put forward as written to them by H.P.B. The incriminating parts of the letters were written in vulgar phraseology, quite unlike the cultured French style of the aristocratic Helena Blavatsky.

It is said that the handwriting of Alexis Coulomb was similar to that of H.P.B.. Moreover, he was a good draftsman and "could copy anything." So probably the forging of the letters was *his* particular job.

After a fortnight at Adyar the Colonel sailed for Ceylon. He wanted to report to his Buddhist friends there on the results of his mission to London on their behalf, and to meet his much-maligned chum in Colombo. She herself was sailing triumphantly from Cairo, where she had dined with the Egyptian Prime Minister and collected from the police a dossier on the Coulomb couple. In her investigations she had been helped by a young English scholar and educationist, Mr. A. J. Cooper-Oakley who, with his wife Isabel, was accompanying H.P.B. to India. Another theosophist coming from England was an English curate named Charles Webster Leadbeater. He had joined H.P.B. in Egypt. From Cairo H.P.B. had sent Olcott the following cable: "Success complete. Outlaws. Legal proofs. Sail Colombo, *Navarino*."

Some of the revelations unearthed in Egypt were published later by the Rev. Charles W. Leadbeater in the *Indian Mirror*. Apparently Emma Cutting, before her marriage to Alexis Coulomb, had worked as a governess in the family of a certain Egyptian Pasha, but was expelled because of the vicious ideas she was teaching her young charges. She had met Alexis' mother, Madame Edward Coulomb, and soon got herself invited to the Coulomb hotel in Cairo. Alexis at this period was fancying himself as a mesmerizer, and he found in Emma a willing subject for his experiments.

Monsieur Fortune, who had been manager of the Coulomb hotel at the time Emma was there, told the investigators that she was "more mischievous than mischief itself." One of her favorite gimmicks at that time was to give out that she could discover hidden treasure through her clairvoyant powers. In this way she talked a few fools into giving her the money for the expenses of making searches in clairvoyantly-divined spots, and digging up the treasure. But no booty was ever found.

In due course the couple, Alexis and Emma, inherited the hotel, but it was not long before they had lost the business through bad management. About this time they made friends with a runaway Indian servant who had stolen the jewels of his master, a raja. He told them that he had buried most of the jewels in India, but was afraid to return there. If the Coulombs would go, he would give them directions for finding the loot, and a good share of it for themselves.

They went; but even with Emma's wonderful clairvoyance, they were not able to find any jewels in the place indicated by the Indian thief. Maybe he did not trust them enough when it came to the point. Anyway he fooled them. Then they tried various ways of making money, including another attempt at the hotel business. But they failed in everything, and were living on their wits in Ceylon when they read of Madame Blavatsky's arrival in Bombay and her association with The Theosophical Society.

The news was like a ray of sunshine on their dark cloud. Madame Blavatsky was an old acquaintance whom Emma had once helped with a loan when the Russian lady was in temporary financial difficulties in Cairo. Emma recalled that she had some interesting psychic powers and, of more importance, a very soft heart. So the Coulombs came to H.P.B. at Bombay in March 1880, as told earlier.

*   *   *

Now, on December 21, 1884, the Colonel, H.P.B. and party arrived back in Madras, after spending a short time in Colombo. A tumultuous reception was given to them by members of The Theosophical Society and hundreds of students from the very Christian College whose professors had been attacking H.P.B. in their journal. She was garlanded by the students at the pier, and escorted in procession to a public hall which was filled with her supporters.

The Colonel writes that as H.P.B. entered the hall, "they rose to their feet and gave vent to their feelings in roars and cheers and *vivas* as she slowly walked through the press to the platform, her hand nervously gripping my arm, her mouth set like iron, her eyes full of a glad light and almost swimming in tears of joy."

To the students, and the Indians generally, she represented the rebirth of their own *sanathana dharma*. She stood for their age-old belief in the power of yoga and the existence of Mahatmas. In trying to discredit her, the Christian missionaries were slapping the face of *Bharata;* and that day the Indians showed unequivocally on which side they stood.

Back at Adyar a dispute arose. H.P.B. had brought writ-

ten statements from witnesses in Cairo which she regarded
as legal proofs that the Coulombs had fled Egypt to escape
arrest for fraudulent bankruptcy. But the Colonel knew
from his legal experience that the statements were not in a
form for production in court. H.P.B. was anxious to be
taken immediately to a judge, or barrister, to file her suit for
slander against the Coulombs. She insisted on it. The Colonel refused to take her. "Then I'll go by myself—and have
this stain wiped from my character," she declared, finally.

"If you do, I'll resign my office, and let the convention
decide between us," he replied.

The annual convention was due to meet in a few days.
At Henry's threat H.P.B. yielded, and agreed to be guided
by a special committee of legal advisers drawn from members
of the convention.

The committee in due course, after much deliberation,
decided unanimously that H.P.B. should *not* prosecute her
defamers in a court of law. There were several reasons for
this decision. The names of the Mahatmas would be irrev-
erently bandied about in such a trial, and this went very
much against the grain of the Indian members. Moreover,
it would be difficult to prove in court that the letters were
forgeries, and even if there were a verdict in favor of H.P.B.,
the skeptics, unacquainted with the facts and philosophy of
yoga and Theosophy, would not have their opinions changed
by the judicial verdict. Also, and perhaps most important,
it was well known that the Bench in Madras was strongly
anti-Theosophical Society, and reports of conversations over-
heard in Madras City suggested that the case had already been
decided by the Anglo-Indians with prejudice against H.P.B.
The legal men on the committee knew that she would not
have a chance of justice from the judge before whom the
case would come.

Said S. Subramania Iyer, a committee member who was
later a high court judge and Vice-President of The Theosophical Society: "We cannot bind Madame Blavatsky, but
as a member of our Society I do not think it is the proper
course for us to give the world the spectacle of a spiteful
cross-examination. . ." He pointed out that every reasonable
man could form an opinion on the evidence "without going

Group at Adyar convention, 1884. H. S. Olcott is standing at back on right. Others seated on verandah include: W. T. Brown (second from left), T. Subba Row (third from left), Damodar K. Mavalankar (fourth from left), H. P. Blavatsky (fifth from left), Dr. Franz Hartmann (sixth from left).

into a court of justice in which results are very often contrary to the truth."

The Colonel thought the decision of the committee a wise one, and H.P.B. bowed to it. But she was not happy about it. Dropping her threatened action against the Coulombs and the missionaries looked like weakness and left the stain on her character, she felt. Moreover, she had won a court case before—in New York, taking a line quite against the instructions of her legal counsel. She had never regarded discretion as the better part of valor.

* * *

When the founders were being garlanded and cheered by the Christian College students on December 21, 1884, a special investigator of the Society for Psychical Research was already in Madras. This was Richard Hodgson, a lean, sharp-eyed young Australian, a graduate of St. John's College, Cambridge, England. He was plunging for the first time into the deep, secret life of mystic India, but he lacked nothing in self-assurance and an imperial contempt for the "natives."

After their interrogations of the leading theosophists in the summer of '84, the S.P.R. Committee had come to the cautious conclusion that there was a *"prima facie* case for part at least of the claims made."* But the committee was badly shaken by the publication of the Coulomb letters and the press stories of trap doors and fake phenomena. It decided to send an investigator to India to check the genuineness of the vital letters, and to examine people and places connected with the psychic phenomena reported by the Colonel and other witnesses. In this way they hoped to estimate the value of the testimony received.

The committee chose Richard Hodgson as special investigator. Not that he had any special qualifications for the job; he was even less experienced in psychic research than his principals!

Hodgson's reception and treatment at Adyar were somewhat mixed. Damodar, T. Subba Row, and other Indians were non-cooperative. In fact, the former two tended to mislead rather than to help him; they were both *chelas* of the Mahatmas, and both resented a Westerner poking his nose into Eastern esoteric matters that were none of his business. Further, they had no sympathy with Hodgson's brash police detective methods of probing into things which they knew themselves to be true, and sacred—things which he was obviously not equipped to understand.

H.P.B. had a bad presentiment about Hodgson and the role he was destined to play. Perhaps she felt as Caesar had felt when looking at a potential enemy—"Yon Cassius hath a lean and hungry look; such men as he are dangerous." At any rate she felt no sympathy for Hodgson and showed him no phenomena, though he very much wanted a sample.

The Colonel, on the other hand, did all he could to help the young investigator. Still interested in psychic research, and with full faith in the theosophic phenomena, Henry hoped that the S.P.R. might yet prove a good ally of The Theosophical Society in the big fight against materialism. So he made all important and relevant documents— including diaries—available for the investigator's scrutiny, and as Hodgson, himself, wrote: "he [Olcott] rendered me every assistance in his power in the way of my acquiring the evidence of the native witnesses . . . he desired me not to hesitate in taking the witnesses apart for my private examination, and he made special arrangements for my convenience."

But Hodgson did not give much time to investigations at the headquarters. He examined the rooms upstairs, but he could not inspect the shrine (cupboard) itself, because it had vanished. He suspected Babula, who had arrived back at Adyar just before Hodgson came, of doing away with it, on H.P.B.'s orders. But, in fact, several Theosophists, considering the shrine desecrated by the Coulombs, had burned it in the society compound. This was done sometime in September, long before any one knew that an S.P.R. investigator would be coming.

In the Colonel's diary for January 3, 1885, we read, "Hodgson left for Madras to take up the Coulomb side of the story." Olcott, the honest old Civil War sleuth, felt that the young Cambridge graduate would soon find the obvious holes in the Coulomb evidence.

Hodgson also traveled to Bombay to have a look at the

"Crow's Nest," scene of some of the miraculous happenings reported to the S.P.R. Committee. The incredible events he was investigating had all taken place from one to four years prior to his arrival. In such a length of time features of localities often change a little, and people forget more than a little. The Indian mentality is never very strong on exact factual details anyway, and after such a period Hodgson had no difficulty in cross-examining the Indian witnesses into several inconsistencies. He made much of this in his report, inferring that their evidence was thus proved totally unreliable.

Finally, with a few of the letters allegedly written by H.P.B. to the Coulombs, and some samples of Master K.H.'s handwriting in his pocket, he headed for home. He arrived back in England in April 1885. But he had apparently made up his mind about the phenomena connected with The Theosophical Society before he left India.

In June the S.P.R. Committee published some of its conclusions on the Hodgson Report. But not till December 1885 did it publish the full notorious report—with an addition by Mrs. Henry Sidgwick who had just become a committee member; she made some incredible statements about events and phenomena she had never witnessed.

The Committee of Investigation agreed with its sleuth Richard Hodgson that the incriminating letters to the Coulombs were in fact written by Madame Blavatsky, and that the shrine phenomena were totally fraudulent. Furthermore, there was, it said, a strong presumption that all the narratives (known to them) of supernormal events were due to either, (a) deception by H.P.B., or (b) illusion or unconscious misrepresentation by witnesses.

To anyone who studies *all* the known events and phenomena through the dispassionate eye of time—as distinct from Hodgson's hasty investigation of a small fraction of the data —it is hard to escape the conclusion that there was more than poor judgment in the way the committee—on such obviously inadequate foundations—maligned a defenseless woman's character. In fact it is difficult to believe that a group of supposedly cultured and honorable people, representing a young organization that hoped to be classed as a "learned Society," could have ended its report with the following defamatory conclusion:

"For our part we regard her [H.P.B.] neither as a mouthpiece of hidden seers, nor as a mere vulgar adventuress; we think that she has achieved a title to permanent remembrance as one of the most accomplished, ingenious and interesting imposters in history."

The committee had discounted Hodgson's spy theory, but never supplied an alternative satisfactory motive. H.P.B. was evidently an imposter merely for the sake of imposture.

What the report stated publicly of Henry Olcott was almost as bad, and even more illogical. It concluded that this experienced criminal investigator and successful lawyer was the dupe of Madame Blavatsky—dupe enough not to have seen through her imposture during his ten years of close association, to say nothing of his own personal experiences of paranormal events when Madame Blavatsky was far away!

From what was written at the time it seems clear that the Society for Psychical Research (or some leading members of it) expected to ruin its elder sister, The Theosophical Society, through this report. But what those S.P.R. members did not understand was that—unlike their own organization—The Theosophical Society was concerned with much more than paranormal phenomena. The "miracles" of the Masters and their *chela* H.P.B. were a beating of drums and a ringing of bells to stir people from their age-old lethargy, and bring them to centers of brotherhood where matters of great moment to the future of mankind could be discussed, where foundations could be laid for a new outlook, a new philosophy of life.

Chapter 16

THE WAKE OF THE STORM
1885

The concerted attacks of the Coulombs and the missionaries, together with the frustration of not being permitted to
prosecute her slanderers, and frequent bazaar rumors of
more missionary plots afoot, proved too much for Madame
Blavatsky's health.

"The condition of her heart renders perfect quiet and a
suitable climate essential. I therefore recommend that she
should at once proceed to Europe, and remain in a temperate
climate—in some quiet spot," wrote her medical attendant,
Dr. Mary Scharlieb. Several physicians "expressed the opinion that under any sudden excitement death might be in-
stantaneous."

On March 29, H.P.B. therefore resigned her office as
Corresponding Secretary of The Theosophical Society and
gave Babula orders to pack her trunks. The Colonel and
Dr. Hartmann went into Madras and bought tickets for
the French steamer *Timbre*, sailing to Europe in two days.
Four tickets were procured, as Dr. Hartmann, Miss Mary
Flynn of Bombay, and an Indian known as "Bawaji," or
sometimes "Babaji," were traveling with her. Bawaji had
worked for some time at the Society headquarters, and
wanted very much to make the trip with H.P.B. In fact,
according to the Colonel's diary, his Guru had *ordered* him
to go.

Too ill to walk or be wheeled up the gangway, H.P.B. was
seated in a hospital chair on the wharf and lifted aboard
by a hoisting tackle. On March 31 she left her beloved
India for the last time, sailing for Naples and the cooler
climes of Italy.

"Poor dear old chum of ten years' collaboration, thus we part. . ." wrote Henry. His loss was greater, he said, than if she had been "wife, or sweetheart, or sister," for now he must carry the heavy burden alone.

He awoke on the morning of April 1 to the usual Adyar sounds of cawing crows and the fishermen loudly slapping the river to drive fish into their nets. Walking out on the roof, Henry watched them below him, circles of dark figures standing in the shallow water, and slowly closing in to form smaller circles. The rising sun was spraying a mist of red over the bay and sky. It was a peaceful scene, but somehow empty and lonely. There was a strange feeling of desolation, as if the spirit of the place had gone—the turbulent but vital spirit of H.P.B.!

As the days passed, reports and letters began to show that this dispirited, unhappy feeling was not only in his own heart, but everywhere throughout the Indian branches and abroad. Why, it was being asked, had not H.P.B. prosecuted her slanderers, and why had she left India? A rumor was spreading, launched by her enemies, that she had been finally exposed as a Russian spy, and was on the run to avoid arrest. What was the truth about it all? people were asking. Some members resigned from the Society; others waited though their minds were troubled by doubts and unanswered questions. A blight of gloom and apathy spread over the sick body of The Theosophical Society.

The Colonel was aware of all this and began, himself, to wonder if the whole experiment, for which he had given up so much, was after all a failure. One blow upon another had hammered the Society since its inception. Its first alliance—that with the Arya Samaj—had eventually blown up in their faces. Swami Dayanand had not agreed with the eclectic platform of The Theosophical Society embracing the fundamental teachings of Buddhism and the Parsi (Zoroastrian) faith—both of which, he said, were false religions. According to the Swami there was but one God of authority, the word of the Vedas, and he was its prophet or interpreter.

Disruption with The Theosophical Society was thus inevitable. It came. "The Swami, losing his temper, tried to repudiate his own words and acts, and finally turned upon us with abuse and denunciation, and put forth a circular to the public and posted handbills in Bombay to call us charlatans and I do not know what else," wrote the Colonel.

But Dayanand, admired by the Colonel in spite of his shortcoming, did not live very long after the disruption. Olcott thought that he was one of the two undesignated enemies whose deaths were "prophesied" by the Master K.H. at the camp near Lahore. But if so, the Master was stating a *fact*, not a *prophecy,* on the night of November 19, 1883. Swami Dayanand had died twenty days before the Master's visit to Lahore. At Ajmere in Rajasthan on October 30 he had been poisoned, rumor said, by a Maharaja's concubine whom he had displeased. The Colonel, traveling and lecturing in the north at the time, had not heard of the death, but presumably the Master knew of it.

No blow, however, had equaled this last one. It was almost a knockout and the Society was tottering. Could he, the Colonel, save it? He and his old chum had always worked better together—despite their frequent quarrels. But now the "Twins" were permanently asunder. H.P.B. was far away and near to death. She could no longer inspire him with her extrasensory knowledge, great insight and power. He was irretrievably alone for whatever work of reconstruction could be done.

"But whatever a man really WILLS, that he has," Henry had written a few years earlier. Now, at the age of 53, this was still his motto. But he flavored it with the humility born of hard experience; "Master, Father—with Thy help I shall conquer!" he wrote in his diary.

Some of those around him thought he should wait quietly at Adyar until the clouds rolled by. But this was not his way. He must go out and meet the challenge, must try to repair as soon as possible the damage that had been done. He planned a long lecture tour of the far-away lodges in the north and west of India.

At about this time some friends told the Colonel of their meeting with a Telugu Brahmin astrologer who possessed a palm leaf copy of the famous old Indian book of prophecies known as the *Bhima Grantham* or the *Nadigrantham.* They said that in checking prophecies about themselves, they had discovered that the book contained much about The Theosophical Society.

The Colonel was very interested. Prophecy had always intrigued him, and now especially he felt the need of oracles and soothsayers to help him. With two Telugu-speaking companions he went to the astrologer with the palm leaf volume, which had Telugu characters etched on its leaves with a stylus. The prophet told Henry many things about himself and the Society, both past and future. Some of the incidents of the past had been known only to himself, yet his companions confirmed that the astrologer's words were actually written on the old palm leaves. So Henry began to have confidence in the prophecies.

The Society, said the astrologer, was "passing through a dark cycle, which began seven months and fourteen days ago, and will last nine months and sixteen days more, making for the whole period seventeen months exactly."

All the sevens and multiples thereof rather pleased the Colonel's fancy. He felt that the dark days were numbered and brighter skies lay not too far ahead for the Society. At any rate the palm leaf reading cheered him greatly at a time of gloom, and, he says, "no doubt helped to give me the courage to go forth on my public tours of that year."

In *Old Diary Leaves** he writes his ideas and theories about these mysterious, ancient leaves of prophecy, some of which contained accurate statements about living people and current affairs. Other statements, however, proved to be worthless.

Quite apart from H.P.B.'s leaving India and all connected with it, one thing that depressed the Colonel and made him feel very much alone on the battlefield, was the mysterious departure of young Damodar. This had happened before H.P.B. left Adyar, and while the Colonel himself was on a tour of Burma.

On February 23, 1885, Damodar had sailed for Calcutta from Madras on the S.S. *Clan Graham*. The Colonel writes: "Four persons on this side of the Himalayas had voices in this matter, of whom three were H.P.B., T. Subba

------

* Vol. 3, p. 237 et seq.

Row and Maji of Benares. . . The name of the fourth party
I shall not mention, but merely say that he is equally well
known on both sides of the mountains, and makes frequent
religious journeys between India and Tibet. Damodar hoped
to be allowed to go with him on his return to Lhassa. . ."

Damodar's real destination was his Master's ashrama somewhere in Tibet, which he had often visited in his astral
body, but never before in his frail flesh. Through overwork
and worry in the last few months, connected mainly with
the Coulomb crisis, "consumptive tendencies had shown
themselves and he had had some hemorrhage."

The question now was—what had happened to him? Had
he ever reached the ashrama?

On June 3 the Colonel sailed for Calcutta and his formidable lecture tour of the north. The first public lecture was
programmed to take place at the hill station of Darjeeling—
a very good place to be in the heat of June, and also a point
from which he might, perchance, hear something of the fate
of Damodar. Disquieting rumors had been circulating about
the young man since he had left Darjeeling for Tibet a couple
of months earlier on April 13—rumors that he had perished
in the snows while trying to cross the mountains. So at
Darjeeling Olcott had a long talk with the chief of the
coolies who had accompanied Damodar through Sikkim toward Tibet, and then brought back his superfluous luggage
and a pocket diary. The final entry in Damodar's diary read:
"April 23rd—took bhat (rice) in the morning and proceeded
on from Kabi alone, sending back my things with the coolies
to Darjeeling."

Their last sight of Damodar, the chief said, was trudging
alone up the mountain road toward the Tibetan frontier
and disappearing around a turning. On their way back the
coolies passed the personage who was following after, and was
due to rendezvous with Damodar at some point a little further on from where the coolies had left him. The personage
and Damodar needed to travel separately through Sikkim
to the rendezvous point. The chief of the coolies had heard
—through the coolie "grapevine," perhaps—that the meeting
had been effected, and Damodar had traveled on with the
caravan of the personage. Presumably he crossed the Tibet-

an frontier dressed as a Tibetan.

From Darjeeling the Colonel, feeling a little happier, plunged back again into the heat of the Ganges plain, and proceeded with his tour of the Society branches there. At Benares he went to see Maji in her *gupha* (cave) on the bank of the Ganges. Damodar had visited her several times just before going to Tibet, and now the Colonel asked her about him.

She explained many things about how a Mahatma over-shadows—partly or completely—the body of a *chela,* such as H.P.B.; she gave her blessings to Babula who was with Ol-cott; but she would not say anything about the fate and future of Damodar. Perhaps she did not know. The Colonel had found by now that her prophecies were not very reliable. But then who *can* see the future, wholly and truly?

The subjects of the Colonel's lectures varied according to the requirements of his gatherings. In fact, he usually let the local committees suggest the subjects. Sometimes this landed him in an awkward predicament, as at Lucknow, where he was startled to find, on arrival, that he was pro-grammed to lecture on the subject of "Islam." "I had then," he writes, "no more than the slight knowledge of the subject which one gets in the course of his general reading, and I felt very reluctant to speak before so critical an audience as awaited me." But there was no escape; the handbills had been distributed, the lecture was to be given next day, and the whole of the Moslem public was expected to be present.

So Henry borrowed a copy of the *Koran* and another Mos-lem book, and sat up all night to read them. Theosophy, he found, gave him the key to the deeper meanings between the lines of the exoteric teachings in this as in other religions.

Thus, when he stood before his huge audience in the Royal Pleasure Hall of Lucknow, he treated his subject as an impartial theosophist, his chief desire being to get to the truth beneath the surface of religious practices, and to announce that truth without fear or favor. "Some good genius must have inspired me," he writes, "for, as I pro-ceeded, I seemed to be able to put myself in Mohammed's place, to translate his thoughts and depict his ideal, as though I were 'a native here, and to the manner born' . . . The audience was certainly aroused to a pitch of enthusiasm, for they gave it tumultuous expression, and the next day a committee waited on me with an address of thanks, in which every blessing of Allah was invoked for me and the wish was expressed that their children knew 'one tenth as much about their religion' as I did." Later the Colonel was asked to join the Islamic Faith as he was considered a natural-born Moslem—"one of the sons of the Prophet."

But Henry said "No" to the invitation. He loved all religions—or rather the deep theosophical truths at their base—but earlier he had officially embraced Buddhism as the religion of his choice.

At Lucknow, as at most centers, he was put through a searching inquiry into the pros and cons of the Coulomb case. In some centers—where busybodies had been fomenting suspicion and unrest—the inquiries were extremely exhaustive—and exhausting. The missionaries added to Olcott's troubles by creating disturbances while he was there.

But the fact was he had an intimate knowledge of the Coulomb case: the events, the people, and what lay behind the scenes. Furthermore, he had boundless faith in the objects and the teachings of The Theosophical Society. He was patently honest and sincere; he rang true like a genuine coin. Thus he was able to remove all doubts and fears from the members of the various lodges. Their spirits were raised; their belief in the good faith and noble ideals of the Society renewed. Indeed many who had come to the Colonel's lectures out of idle curiosity, titillated by stories of the great scandal, joined up as new members of The Theosophical Society.

As he moved toward the west of India, the dark distrust and wavering courage he had encountered in the northern plains gave place to friendly welcomes and kind words on his arrival at each center. At Nagpur he lectured on "The Aryan Rishis and Hindu Philosophy" to an enormous audience. At the beginning his chairman and host, Nagpur's principal pleader, laid over Henry's shoulders, after the ancient Hindu fashion, a crimson embroidered *chadda* (shawl), a symbol of honor.

In the middle of the lecture an epileptic in the audience

fell down in a convulsive fit. The Colonel sprang from the platform and hastened to render aid. His old magnetic power suddenly returning, he was able to bring the patient quickly back to normal, and in less than two minutes he was back on the platform talking again of the powers of India's ancient rishis. The audience responded enthusiastically to his words and demonstration. A new branch, the Nagpur Lodge, was formed on the spot.

At Bombay he found many members still loyal to the cause, among them Tookaram Tatya, an intelligent man of the lower caste and a great worker for Theosophy. Henry lectured at Framji Cowasji Hall, scene of his maiden theosophical address in India. Then he moved on to Poona where he stayed with a Jewish family of Theosophists and Kabbalists. From Poona he traveled to Hyderabad, the Nizam's capital, giving public talks there and also at the adjacent British military station in Secunderabad.

Thence he worked his way southward to Anantapur. To reach this city he had to travel all night in a bullock cart, but it revived him to find the place decked with flags of welcome, and a band of musicians out to greet him. At Anantapur he gave his fifty-sixth, and last, lecture of this tour; it was on "Modern Scepticism and the *Brahma Vidya*" (knowledge of God).

Returning to "green and lovely Adyar" after the long campaign he felt that he had successfully repulsed the attacks of his enemies and confounded their prophecies. The Society in India, far from expiring, was now stronger than ever. Many new members had been admitted into the thirty-one branches he had visited, and seventeen new branches had been formed. Faith, belief, and loyalty had been re-established. The Society—his Rock of Truth—had weathered its first great tempest, but what did the dark forces have in store for the future?

Chapter 17

THE EXPOSURE EXPOSED

The great exposé of H.P.B. and her partner in the *Proceedings of the Society for Psychical Research*, December 1885, has been itself exposed by a number of thoroughgoing analyses of the case, and there are many books and pamphlets on the subject. Anyone interested in reading the original report should do so in conjunction with these critical analyses.*

The first thing that becomes obvious in any unbiased study of the Hodgson Report and the events of the early days of The Theosophical Society is that the investigator is not trying to find the truth, which is supposed to be his function, but to make out a good case for the prosecution. Facts are of importance only as they help to strengthen his brief.

As his critics point out, he condemns all the witnesses as totally unreliable, except his own "prosecution witnesses", namely the Coulombs; their word alone is credited with any value as evidence. Those he condemns include not only the Indians—for whom he shows tremendous contempt—but also any Western witnesses for the defense. He casts aspersions on the whole of Sinnett's evidence simply because of the latter's minor discrepancies in estimating time intervals. Colonel Olcott is written off as a totally unreliable witness because of "peculiar lapses of memory or extreme deficiency in the faculty of observation." He suggests, too, that Olcott manufactured evidence to support certain Blavatsky fabrications under pressure from her, or from the Masters (which in Hodgson's opinion amounted to the same thing as he considered she had invented the Masters).

* See, for instance, (1) Appendix of *The Real H. P. Blavatsky* by William Kingsland, 1928.
(2) *Obituary: "The Hodgson Report" on Madame Blavatsky,* 1885-1960 by Adlai E. Waterman, 1963.
(3) *Defense of Madame Blavatsky* by Beatrice Hastings, 1937.
(4) *The Hall of Magic Mirrors* by Victor A. Endersby, 1969.

The committee decided, however, that the Colonel was honest and no fraud, but merely a dupe and a fool. A study of Henry Olcott's life reveals that his memory was, in fact, sometimes at fault, especially in his later years. But no part of his career suggests that he suffered from deficiency in powers of observation or was easily duped. His contemporaries, including C. C. Massey, a fellow lawyer, regarded him as a shrewd man with a realistic outlook on human nature. And his earlier work—scientific agriculture, journalism, crime investigation, law practice—suggests that his powers of perception were at least normal and that he was wide awake to deception and knavery. After coming through the temptations to bribery and corruption as an investigator in the "Carnival of Fraud"—as attested by the heads of the government departments concerned—is it likely that he would condone fraud in the fabric of something for which he had forsaken all his worldly interests—that is, the Theosophical movement?

In the Coulomb evidence no flaws were revealed by Hodgson for the simple reason that he suppressed anything inconsistent or contradictory. Several examples of such suppression from the report are pointed out in the writings of his critics.

The report ignores the important fact that many things happened when H.P.B. was miles away from the locality. For instance, Mr. W. T. Brown, who was at Adyar at the time of the Coulomb crisis, writes in the *Religio-Philosophical Journal,* October 16, 1886:

"When the Coulombs had taken themselves off the premises, a letter came to Dr. Hartmann and Mr. Lane-Fox from the Master K.H. through the self-same desecrated shrine." This letter, he says, spoke of Damodar's faults and weaknesses, and his "self-esteem was considerably mortified thereby. Damodar and I had had a dispute and, as neither of us would yield, the Master evidently observed the psychic commotion, and thought right to interfere." This, Brown states, was only one of numerous examples of phenomena.

The Colonel, Damodar, and W. T. Brown all saw and talked with the Master K.H. in the flesh at Lahore. Another *chela,* Mr. S. Ramaswamier, District Register of Assurances at Tinnevelly, went to see his guru, the Master Morya, in Sikkim. They met there and conversed for some time in the morning sunshine. The Master was riding a horse, and neither man nor horse was phantasmic.

In order to explain such events, consistent with his theory that the Mahatmas were a hoax, Hodgson had to invent the existence of many confederates for H.P.B. In the latter incident, for example, he "saw no improbability in supposing" that 'Master M.,' a tall majestic figure, immediately recognized by his *chela* Ramaswamier, was in reality a confederate of H.P.B.; that this confederate had crossed the frontier to Sikkim in order to impersonate the Master, in case Ramaswamier happened to reach the spot. This in itself was an improbability considering the difficulty of crossing the border at that time.

What motive a man could have in doing such a troublesome and dangerous thing Hodgson's imagination alone knew. Furthermore, any such confederate would have needed to have the Master's extrasensory powers to carry out this operation. No one knew of Ramaswamier's intention to go to Sikkim, nor the route he would take.

Even Mr. A. O. Hume, skeptical and critical about all things, felt sure about one thing—the reality of the Mahatmas. He had some good reasons for this. Once he had received a note from the Master K.H. inside a letter on municipal business, coming from a person who had no connection with occult pursuits. The letter arrived through the post in a sealed envelope. Another time, when H.P.B. and her friends were a thousand miles away, a Mahatma letter was dropped on Hume's desk as he sat writing at home; it seemed to fall out of the empty air. Reporting a third phenomenal occurrence in a note to Sinnett, he writes: "Today a very long letter from K.H. and an envelope from Morya were deposited during the night in my flower shed. The phenomenon is very perfect—as there are no Olcott or Old Lady (H.P.B.) or anyone else here."*

To cover all the facts and events—even within Hodgson's narrow frame of reference—H.P.B. would have needed many

---

* See the collected manuscripts of the Mahatma Letters to A. P. Sinnett in the British Museum.

confederates in different parts of India. The S.P.R. men inferred that she had. Any substantial money payments by her being definitely out of the question, they decided that the confederates were her followers, somehow under her power and willing to assist her in hoodwinking their fellow theosophists.

What the S.P.R. investigators failed to realize was that those Indians who followed H.P.B. did so because they had faith in the *genuineness* of her yogic powers and spirituality. If they had been drawn into a network of fraud by her they would have lost interest in both her and her Society. Why should they have assisted her in chicanery for no personal gain, either material or spiritual?

Damodar was named as the number one fellow conspirator. Hodgson's theory was that, unable to face his family after discovering that the fabulous H.P.B. was an imposter, Damodar stayed on at headquarters to assist her in the dirty work. But even before the S.P.R. master detective had finished writing his exposé of the Mahatma hoax and other rogueries, Damodar had demonstrated by deeds his utter belief in the reality of the Mahatmas. As described earlier, he went off alone to Tibet to reside at his guru's ashrama, an idiotic, not to say highly dangerous, thing to do if the Mahatmas were figments of his and H.P.B.'s imagination.

It is more than strange, too, that a Mahatma invented by H.P.B. could have been seen in the early part of this century by the great Indian sage, Sri Aurobindo, who says: "Once when I was practising yoga, He whom the Theosophists call Master K.H. came and stood before me and watched my yoga. I requested him to accept me as his disciple; but he said, 'Your Master is different.' "

Aurobindo later wrote a poem called *The Mahatma Kuthumi*, a passage from which reads:

> "And I [i.e. Kuthumi] walk
> Amid men choosing my instruments,
> Testing, rejecting, confirming souls,
> Vessels of Spirit for the Golden Age (which) in Kali
> comes."*

---

* See *Mahayogi Sri Aurobindo*, by R. R. Diwaker, Appendix 111, pp. 248-9.

Babula, too, is branded by the report as a conspirator, assisting H.P.B. in her "trick phenomena." Hodgson bolsters this theory with the erroneous story that Babula had previously been in the employ of a French conjurer. But the French employer, whom Olcott met, was in fact a restaurateur.

There are many people who cannot keep a secret for two minutes, but Babula—if Hodgson was correct—kept this hot secret for the rest of his life. Why should he do so? For the sake of his job? He was not so fond of that, often being on the point of leaving it when H.P.B.'s tongue got too sharp for him. "Babula, driven to desperation, as he says, gave warning. It had better be taken, for no other such good boy can be found. H.P.B. cross enough to eat everybody's head off," writes the Colonel in his diary for January 16, 1881.

It is hardly likely that H.P.B. would have treated Babula so roughly if he had been an accomplice possessed of such good blackmail material. Also any threats from the servant himself would have been of a different nature, surely. After H.P.B. finally left India, the Colonel kept Babula on at Adyar, and there is no record of his ever telling Olcott, or anyone else, that he had helped H.P.B. in fraudulent phenomena. In fact any statements he ever made supported the genuineness of her yogic powers.

The letters on which the accusation of trickery was based —the letters supposedly written by H.P.B. to Emma Coulomb —were never shown to anyone connected with the defense of H.P.B. William Kingsland, who knew H.P.B. personally, writes: "This fact alone is quite sufficient from a judicial point of view to dismiss the whole case; but what can we say of the 'honourable' gentlemen of the S.P.R.? . . . We are, I think, entitled to assume that there were substantial reasons why these letters were withheld from the defence. . ."

Hodgson submitted some of them—perhaps not the incriminating ones—to a so-called handwriting expert in London, Mr. F. G. Netherclift. This gentleman said they were written by H.P.B. The parts he saw may have been, of course, as H.P.B. had written a number of letters to the Coulomb woman. On the other hand, they may *not* have been, for Netherclift proved the complete unreliability of his judgment later on in a famous British criminal court case.

Hoping for "expert" backing for his contention that H.P.B. had also written the Mahatma letters to A. P. Sinnett and to other people, Hodgson handed Netherclift a few samples of the "K.H." handwriting. Netherclift said at first that they were *not* written by H.P.B. This did not suit Hodgson's book at all, so he took along more samples, and under due persuasion or pressure, it would seem, the "expert" finally agreed with detective Hodgson that they *were* written by H.P.B.

As against this shaky decision by Netherclift, an opposite opinion came from the Caligraphist to the Court of the German Emperor. This gentleman, Herr Ernst Schutze, having been shown specimens of H.P.B. and K.H. handwriting by Herr G. Gebhard, stated that there was "not the remotest similarity" between them. His conclusion was corroborated in recent years (during the 1960's) by Dr. Paul L. Kirk, Professor of Criminology at Berkeley University, U.S.A., and considered one of America's leading criminologists. Dr. Kirk compared photographic specimens of the two handwritings, as shown in Hodgson's report—without any knowledge of the identities of the principals involved—and gave a decision against the Hodgson/Netherclift conclusion. Dr. Kirk's verdict was that the H.P.B. and K.H. handwritings were *not* by the same person.

The originals of the Mahatma letters to A. P. Sinnett are now in the British Museum where anyone can view them and form his own opinion. Better still, he can read them in book form, and judge by the contents, and the style, whether Madame Blavatsky could have been their author.

Beatrice Hastings, a great prose stylist and critic, says that not only is the style of the letters quite different from that of H.P.B.'s but each Master has a distinct and different style of his own. The ordinary reader—if he reads long enough—will perceive this fact for himself, and feel the personality of each Master behind his letters.

On the question of content, William Kingsland writes: "I do not see how anyone with any knowledge of the circumstances in general, or of Mme. Blavatsky's characteristics and resources, can possibly think that she could have written them herself, consciously, 'out of her own head.' There may have been exceptions in some of the letters, but in the great bulk of them the internal evidence is of such nature that it is impossible for me to think that Mme. Blavatsky could have been their original author."

In saying that H.P.B. wrote them "out of her own head," Hodgson was unwittingly giving her the credit of being a very great sage indeed. But of course he was not able to read the bulk of the letters which were published much later.

There is, however, one aspect of this question which may to some extent explain Hodgson's and Netherclift's conclusion. While some of the earliest letters were either written or "precipitated" *directly* by the Master himself, "precipitation" was soon stopped by order of the Chiefs of the Brotherhood, and letters had to be produced in some other way. Sinnett wrote, in his later years, that he thought most of the letters, from the time of the change, "were dictations to a competent clairaudient amanuensis, and Madame Blavatsky was generally the amanuensis in question." Master K.H. himself writes: "Very often our very letters—unless something very important and secret—are written in our handwritings by our *chelas*."*

But automatic writing, whether through clairaudience, possession, or partial possession, while resembling closely the handwriting of the communicator—incarnate or discarnate— also shows some features of that of the amanuensis or medium. At least that is usually the case.

So an "expert" examining a Mahatma script produced by H.P.B. as "clairaudient amanuensis," could easily be misled by certain Blavatsky idiosyncrasies in the writing, and conclude that she had written it consciously, from her own mind, trying to forge the Master's script, or rather the handwriting she had invented as the "Master's script."

One feels that if Richard Hodgson had known more, and understood more, about the occult techniques employed by the Mahatmas, he would not have gone so far astray on this and other points.

For every crime there must be a motive, and the detective-cum-prosecutor had great difficulty in finding one to fit this case. Why should H.P.B. renounce all the normal pleasures and pursuits and interests of her sex and class; why should she work like a slave for Masters and a cause spun from the

---

* See *The Mahatma Letters to A. P. Sinnett*, p. 291.

insubstantial web of her own imagination and imposture? There would have to be a strong, driving motivation behind this for it to be reasonable. Hodgson could not make any of the usual hidden motivations fit the character or the circumstances. It was not "pecuniary gain" certainly, nor was it "religious mania" or "morbid yearning for notoriety," decided the perplexed Hodgson. Then the great light dawned on him: she was a Russian spy!

The British government in India had, several years before, dropped this suspicion. But Hodgson resurrected it, and decided that she *must* be a spy. The poor fellow could find no other satisfactory basis for the great edifice of chicanery that his mind had constructed around her.

In what manner her "bogus phenomena" could help in the spy business he does not attempt to show. Nor has there ever been the slightest evidence, in the long years since then, to suggest that H.P.B. was a spy, or took any real interest in Russian affairs of state. In fact, the reverse was so.

Another of H.P.B.'s enemies and detractors, the Russian journalist, M. Solovioff, cuts this last piece of ground from under the Hodgson feet. On page 114 of his book, *A Modern Priestess of Isis,* Solovioff writes: "This [spy theory] he [Hodgson] had to prove . . . yet he has no evidence of any sort, for it is impossible to regard as evidence the fragments he quotes from her writings, from which no serious man could draw a conclusion of the sort. . . H. P. Blavatsky was not a spy."

Concerning Hodgson's report in general, Alvin Boyd Kuhn, an impartial observer as historian of the Theosophical movement, writes: "He rendered an *ex parte* judgment in that he acted as judge, accuser and jury, and gave no hearing to the defence. He ignored a mass of testimony of the witnesses to the phenomena, and accepted the words of the Coulombs, whose conduct had already put them under suspicion."*

It seems that Hodgson himself eventually became aware that he had gone wrong in this his first major project in psychic research. Many years later he remarked to Annie

---

* See *Theosophy: A Modern Revival of Ancient Learning* by Alvin Boyd Kuhn, New York, 1930.

Besant that he "would have given a very different report had he known in 1885 what he learned afterwards."*

There is no doubt that he *did* learn, in the many years he later devoted to psychic research, that there are forces and intelligences beyond those accepted by materialistic science. He who had scoffed at the Adyar shrine, calling it a "conjurer's box," set up a "shrine room" of his own in order to keep psychic conditions undisturbed. Having developed mediumistic powers, he believed he was receiving communications from his deceased childhood sweetheart.

Hodgson had the doubting, questioning mind that is certainly necessary for sound psychic research, but—like others of the S.P.R.—he bent so far over backwards in skepticism that he was inclined to lose his balance. And he does not seem to have been entirely impartial and disinterested in his investigations of The Theosophical Society. He desired, he says, demonstrations of occult powers and was greatly disappointed at not being shown any at Adyar. In a letter to Sinnett, Mahatma K.H. mentions this "personal disappointment he [Hodgson] felt which made him turn in a fury against the alleged authors of the 'gigantic swindle.' "

Hodgson's complete lack of any background understanding of India, and the resentment felt by key Indian *chelas* against one probing into their sacred preserves, were other contributory factors leading to the unfortunate verdict. In fact Mahatma K.H. blamed the attitude of T. Subba Row and Damodar for two-thirds of Hodgson's delusions.**

By no means did all members of the S.P.R. share the conclusions of the notorious report. It is on record that one of its founders, the famous scientist Sir William Barrett, F.R.S., expressed his feelings strongly on the matter to educationist Dr. J. H. Cousins. The latter wrote in *The Theosophist* for October 1925: "Shortly before my departure for India (1925) I found myself with Sir William in a Dublin tramcar. Talking over my future relationship with the T.S. at Adyar, he volunteered the opinion 'that a wrong had been done to Madame Blavatsky in the Report on the

---

* See *The Real and the Unreal*, Lecture 1 in a collection of Convention Lectures, given in 1922 by Dr. A. Besant, entitled *Your World and Ours*.
** See *Letters from H.P.B. to A.P. Sinnett*, 1925, p. 122.

Coulomb affair in the *Proceedings of the S.P.R.*' He expressed the hope that the Report which was 'a blot on the *Proceedings* would some day be withdrawn.' "

But when the S.P.R. is pressed by individuals or organizations to withdraw the report, the answer given is that the Society for Psychical Research is not responsible for the opinions of its members, or committees of members, that the S.P.R., as such, holds no corporate opinions, and cannot, therefore, be held responsible for the report—or words to that effect.*

This, no doubt, is technically true. But in reality the S.P.R.—and not a committee of so-called experts, long since dead and gone—has always been held responsible for the report. Scores of encyclopedias and books in the libraries of the world state that Madame H. P. Blavatsky was exposed as an imposter by the Society for Psychical Research—and the popular press repeats this every so often. Therefore it can reasonably be assumed that hundreds of thousands of people have, throughout the decades, read such statements, and assuming the verdict to come from some kind of "scientific body," accepted it as true. The S.P.R. is, therefore, morally responsible for this spread of error and injustice.

Those members of the S.P.R. who, as self-appointed judges and jury, damned H.P.B. as an "ingenious, accomplished and interesting imposter," predicted that the Society which she had founded on fraudulence would soon fall to pieces.

---

* As an example of this, the following letter was written by the Hon. Secretary of the Society for Psychical Research in London to the Editor of *Time*, dated 25th July, 1968:

We would like to make a correction to the article on Religion published in the issue of 'Time' dated July 19th, 1968.

In this feature, under Theosophy, it is stated in connection with Madame Blavatsky quote Controversial wherever she went, she was accused in 1885 by the Society for Psychical Research in London of fraud, forgery and even of spying for the Czar unquote.

We would point out that, as stated in all copies of the Proceedings of this Society, "Responsibility for both the facts and the reasonings in papers published in the Proceedings rests entirely with their authors."

Comments on Madame Blavatsky were contained in a report by Richard Hodgson in Part IX of Proceedings dated December 1885 and any accusations therein contained are the responsibility of the author and not of this organization.

This letter was never published by *Time*.

The report of 1885 certainly did shake the ten-year old Society to its foundations. But now many Theosophists, seeing the event through a longer perspective, feel that, like many catastrophes, it was really a blessing in disguise. The blast of it separated the chaff of mere miracle-hunters from the grain of true potential occultists.

Most important, the teachings propounded by H.P.B., and their effects, give the lie to the cruel, unjust S.P.R. verdict. Her writings, particularly such works as *The Secret Doctrine,** *The Key to Theosophy** and *The Voice of the Silence,** belong not to one generation or two, but to the centuries. They are still selling steadily on all continents, and being studied today, not only by theosophists, but by university professors, students, and research scientists. Scientific theories are in many respects just catching up and coinciding with the doctrines revealed by H.P.B. and her Masters.

And the Theosophical movement, far from crumbling beneath the Hodgson hammer, is still a strong international force. Despite its faults and failures, the movement has done a tremendous amount of work—much of it beneath the surface—toward uplifting the thoughts of men and changing their attitude toward their fellow men. It should do much more yet, for it holds the key to the perennial philosophy, the elixir of life for a lost and bewildered humanity. Could such a great power for good come through the mind and heart of a charlatan?

*   *   *   *   *

NOTE: In 1968 the Secretary of the S.P.R. in England wrote *Time* magazine dissociating that society from any responsibility for the Hodgson report. In April, 1986, the *Journal of the Society for Psychic Research*, Vol. 53, No. 803, published an article by Dr. Vernon Harrison, a member of the S.P.R. and an expert on forgery. After studying the Hodgson report, he concluded that Hodgson was prejudiced and ignored evidence in H.P.B.'s favor, that his case against her was not proved, and that an apology is owed her. Thus 100 years after the investigation, H.P.B.'s name was cleared from the accusations of the S.P.R.—Ed

---

* Published by The Theosophical Publishing House.

Chapter 18

TROUBLE IN EUROPE
1886 - 1888

The Colonel believed that he and his chum H.P.B. had worked together for humanity in former incarnations. At the deeper levels of their natures they were in perfect accord, and always worked well as close partners. But now they were like two divided heads of one body—heads far apart and out of touch. Misunderstandings and conflicts were inherent in the situation.

During the years 1885 and 1886 H.P.B. was engaged, despite the sickness of her body, in writing her *magnum opus, The Secret Doctrine.* She worked on this in southern Italy, at Würzburg in Bavaria, while with the Gebhards for a time at Elberfeld, and then at Ostend in Belgium.

At Adyar, after the turmoils of the great "exposure," relative peace reigned—except for an occasional growl echoing from the "wounded lion" in Europe, as Olcott described his old chum. He was, himself, pursuing a new line. Paranormal phenomena, on which he had been so keen in the past, had backfired on him and The Theosophical Society. The Western world and the westernized sections of India were obviously not yet ready for it. So he would play it down. There would be no more talk about Masters and "miracles"— at least not in public.

The theosophical teachings could stand alone without the support of *siddhis*; though the latter were certainly a demonstration of the truths contained in the former. The Society's main object—to form a nucleus of the Universal Brotherhood of Humanity—was in itself sufficient to keep the Theosophists well occupied. Then there was the bringing to light of the ancient treasures in the Sanskrit scrolls, and with that the study of comparative religion, philosophy, and science—ancient and modern.

The object for which the Society had originally been formed—the investigation of the hidden laws and powers in man and nature—now came last on the list. The emphasis must be put on the first two aims—establishing a nucleus for the true brotherhood of the human family, and the study of the deepest truths in the collective wisdom of the ages. Only those people who felt real brotherhood and understood the spiritual evolution of life, as taught in the perennial, unchanging philosophy, could accept, understand, and rightly use the realities of the third object. Only *they* could see that the yogic *siddhis,* the paranormal powers, were a logical step forward in man's evolution, and that the existence of supermen who had attained to some of those powers was not only credible but inevitable.

The Christ had pointed out that swine will not only ignore pearls, but turn and rend the givers. Well, that had been illustrated. Men had to be ready to receive certain knowledge, otherwise they would turn in fury against the benevolent teacher. Strange perhaps! But, anyway, no more of it. . .

"Olcott has become a Brahmin, a regular Subba Row for secrecy . . . he is mortally afraid to pronounce even the Masters' names, except in strict privacy," wrote the old "caged lion" who, far off in Europe, caught the scent on the breeze.

For Henry the occult highlight of 1886 took place on June 7. That morning the postman brought him a letter from Tookaram Tatya in Bombay. It expressed great concern for Damodar's fate, and asked if there had been any authentic messages about him. But there, on the back of Tookaram's very letter, was the answer to his question, written indubitably in the well-known handwriting of the Master K.H.

It was a message to the Colonel, and had most likely been "precipitated" on the back of the page during the letter's transit—a fairly common occurrence in the early experience of the Society leaders. Olcott smiled and felt himself wishing that Hodgson, Myers, or others of that proud, superior committee could be standing at his elbow.

The message said that Damodar had been through great suffering and severe trials. This was his karma for the "questionable doings in which he had over-zealously taken part, bringing disgrace upon the sacred science and its adepts . . . but he will recover in course of time." This perhaps meant that he had not acted wisely in the Coulomb-missionary-S.P.R. crisis. The letter told Olcott that: "This ought to be a warning to you all. . . To unlock the gates of the mystery you must not only lead a life of the strictest probity, but learn to discriminate truth from falsehood. . ."*

But, thought the Colonel, the boy is alive and with his Master, that's the main thing.

Apart from his work for The Theosophical Society and the Ceylon Buddhists, the Colonel devoted his energies during 1886 to several new projects. One of these was translating and annotating a 305-page French book on apparitions, by Adolphe d'Assier. This was published in English the next year as *Posthumous Humanity, a Story of Phantoms.*

Another project was the founding of the great Adyar Library. Back in April 1885, soon after H.P.B. left, he wrote in his diary: "decided to finish the new room upstairs [late shrine room] and convert it into a library."

It was apparently decided later to spread the library into H.P.B.'s old bed-sitting room as well. He writes in September 1886: "Began to move the Modern Library into the large room upstairs, until now occupied by Oakley in succession to H.P.B."

These were the small beginnings of the realization of a dream that was far from small—to revive the old Oriental learning and make it more and more available to the modern West and East alike. "We hope," he wrote, "to bring to light and publish much valuable knowledge now stored away in the ancient tongues. . ." The library would be a center at which many rare books and ancient Sanskrit manuscripts would be collected, and at which there would be a staff of pandits working. It would become a magnet to students, scholars, and sages from the whole civilized world.

To the opening ceremony of the library, at the annual convention in December 1886, he invited the priests of all

---

* See *Letters From the Masters of the Wisdom,* First series, Letter No. 29.

religions. All came except the Christians. "Blessings were invoked upon the enterprise by Hindu, Parsi, Buddhist, and Mahommedan Priests. Such a thing had never been seen in India as the religious teachers of the antipathetic Sects of the East uniting in a ceremony like this. . ."

Now, wherever Olcott traveled in India or abroad he kept his eyes and ears open for anything that might be of value to his library, which he hoped would eventually become "a second Alexandria . . . a new Serapeum."

By the end of 1906, just before his death, the library contained 12,562 valuable old manuscripts and 14,326 printed books. Since then it has continued to grow, and the Colonel's dream has come true in part—the staff of Sanskrit pandits is there, and students travel from many parts of the world to study the rare old books and manuscripts.

In 1967 the library was moved to its own spacious building at Adyar, as it had long outgrown the area it had occupied in the main headquarters building. Today the library's treasures include 17,400 manuscripts on palm leaf and paper, embracing about 40,000 works. There are about 100,000 printed books on the various philosophies, religions and cultures, as well as 350 Indological and 100 Theosophical journals, with all their back volumes, which are of great value for research. The library's own publications—the Adyar Library Series and Pamphlet Series, and the research journal *Brahmavidya*—cover a wide variety of fields. The library has won high international repute for its outstanding contribution to the renaissance of Indian culture and Indological studies.

The foreign mail arriving in November 1886 brought Henry two surprising documents from H.P.B. One was a manifesto attacking the Theosophical organization, written by two old friends: Arthur Gebhard of Germany, and Mohini Chatterji, the handsome Calcutta lawyer who was still stirring the feminine hearts of Europe.

The attack was against what the writers considered the arbitrary power vested in Adyar, particularly in the person of the President-Founder himself. Olcott was stunned to find his Adyar headquarters likened to a "papal institution," and read of himself as decked in the "purple of authority,"

New Adyar Library building, opened 1967.
There is a bust of Colonel Olcott erected on the grounds in front of the building.

and the "festive garments of pride and worldliness." He rubbed his eyes.

The second document received was H.P.B.'s long reply to this startling criticism of the President and the organization. Mohini and Gebhard's attack was dated September 23, and was apparently sent to H.P.B. for her approval and endorsement. She replied on October 3, and sent the manifesto, and a copy of her commentary on it, to the Colonel in India.

The attack on the Colonel was, she said, entirely unjust. His "Special Orders," of which much was made, simply showed his desire to give importance to the Society—not to himself. His love of display was like a mother dressing up her child, for which she would die any day. "The whole globe may be searched through and through," she wrote, "and no one found stauncher to his friends, truer to his word, or more devoted to real practical theosophy than the President-Founder; and these are the chief requisites in a leader of such a movement. . ."

The Theosophical organization was by no means perfect, she admitted, but the President-Founder had struggled for twelve years to make it as perfect as possible, and he was ever ready to listen to constructive criticism and advice. But the foolish philippic before her was carping, negative, and out-of-date, attacking rules that no longer existed. In her masterly style she completely annihilated the Colonel's two assailants.

Her defense was woven into a penetrating restatement of the *raison d'être* of the Theosophical movement, and when the document was published much later it was called "The Original Programme of The Theosophical Society."

The Colonel's first reaction to it was a smile. "A cannon to kill sparrows!" he wrote in the diary, and next day set off by bullock cart and rail to lecture at far centers and collect Sanskrit manuscripts for the library.

But he wisely took the attack as a straw in the wind, and began the series of adjustments and readjustments that brought more and more autonomy to the National Sections of the Society.

Hearing that H.P.B., now living in London, was founding a new magazine, he wrote to her and remonstrated against this "setting up of a rival competing magazine to hurt as much as possible the circulation and influence of our old-established organ, [*The Theosophist*] on the title-page of which her name still appeared."

Earlier, while she was still living in Ostend, H.P.B.'s guru had told her that she must go to London and establish there a group of earnest, sincere students of occultism. This, he said, was the only way to save the Society in Europe.

Around her in London gathered a number of intelligent, highly-educated young people of good families. Despite Hodgson, Myers and others, they believed in the existence of the Mahatmas and desired wholeheartedly to work for the spread of the esoteric philosophy. They felt that under Sinnett the ship of Theosophy was in the doldrums. It needed the sharp winds of H.P.B.'s presence to get it moving again. These new disciples were few in number, but quite genuine and, therefore, a power. They formed the Blavatsky Lodge, and their numbers steadily increased.

Bertram Keightley, one of these early few, writes in his *Reminiscences* that as *The Secret Doctrine* would take another year to prepare for the press, H.P.B. had urged that in the interim some sort of public propaganda for the wisdom religion was necessary. Dr. Archibald Keightley adds the point that H.P.B. had difficulty in getting her views expressed in *The Theosophist*. The Colonel was officially editor of that journal, but as he traveled a great deal most of the editorial work was actually done at Adyar by Mr. A. J. Cooper-Oakley, M.A. who had accompanied H.P.B. to India at the close of 1884. The "Old Lady" did not care for some of the editorial views expressed by Cooper-Oakley.

One way and another the London group around H.P.B. agreed that it was necessary for her to have a magazine of her own, where her views would get immediate and full expression. So despite the Colonel's strong objections, *Lucifer* (the Light-bringer) came into being in London.

Another unhappy note sounded in Olcott's ears in the fall of 1887. Mohini Chatterjee and Bawaji, spoiled by adulation of the Westerners—especially the women—and other features of European life, had, it seemed, grown too big for their turbans. After making various attacks on the founders they both resigned from the Society in October. "Foolish young men," writes the President sadly.

*   *   *

1888, the year of another crisis that threatened to split the Society, dawned inauspiciously. On January 7 the Colonel noted: "C-Oakley seems to have a very bitter and hostile feeling towards me, avoids me, and shuts himself up in his room. . ." A little later Cooper-Oakley threatened to establish a magazine himself "to be called *The Vedantin* for which the plans and money are ready—if H.P.B. exasperated him much more. Stuff!"

Then came a spell of bad health for Henry—persistent boils and a bad foot, probably gout. So, pressed by his old friends, General and Mrs. Morgan, he left on March 7, for a rest at Ootacamund in the Nilgiris.

Compared with his normal high-pressure life of traveling, lecturing, writing, organizing and administering, "Ooty" spelled tranquility. He read and joined in the social life of the British officials who made "Ooty" their summer headquarters.

These were the people who had in the past regarded the founders with much suspicion and hostility. But the climate was changing. Or could it be that the Colonel was a more comfortable and less frightening character than his former Russian companion? At any rate, Henry was invited to all the important functions—"Dined at Government House. . . Attended Lord and Lady Connemara's weekly reception (al fresco, with tennis, etc.) . . . To Lady Collins' to luncheon . . . Received Lady C's invitation to a dance . . . Attended the first ball of the season at Government House. . ."

The Colonel obviously enjoyed this high-level socializing, and felt glad that his Society was becoming "respectable." Imagine, for instance, being asked to lecture at the new Breeks School, which was under "very influential" patronage! His audience there was a mixture of Britishers and Hindus, but the subject chosen for him had a strong British flavor— "The Noble Army of Ghosts and their Mansions." He made it as theosophical as possible by comparing the Summerland of the spiritualists with the Eastern idea of Kamaloka; he was asked to lecture again next day to a fully European audience.

While at Ootacamund the Colonel bought a piece of land on which was built: "as a hot-weather retreat for H.P.B. and myself, and other European workers at Adyar, the cottage since known as 'Gulistan'—the Rose Garden." He evidently still hoped that H.P.B. would be able to return to India.

But over in foggy London trouble was brewing. Sharing a large house at Holland Park, London, with the Keightleys and the Countess Wachtmeister, H.P.B. was apparently very dissatisfied with the current rule from Adyar. She had complained in letters to Henry, and now things had almost reached a breaking point between them. She had a signboard ready, she said, to have painted on it one of two notices— either "European HQ of the T.S." or "Western Theosophical Society." If the Colonel did not agree with the various changes she demanded, the latter notice would go up outside the Holland Park house, and The Theosophical Society would be divided irrevocably into two halves, "*entirely independent of each other.*" If, on the other hand, he agreed to what she called "the inexorable evolution of things," Adyar and Europe would remain allies, and, "*to all appearance,* the latter will seem to be subject to the former. . ."

To Henry the most important thing was to keep the Society as one body so that its impact on world thought would not be impaired. The head of that body was the office of the President-Founder. If this headship was ignored, undermined or treated with disloyalty, how could the body continue to exist? As Abraham Lincoln had quoted from the Good Book: "If a house be divided against itself, that house cannot stand."

Henry reasoned thus with himself. But beneath the reasoning there was probably some personal pride involved. Having labored so long for the Society, building it up through struggles and self-sacrifice, he had come to identify himself to a large extent with the organization. It was his status symbol; it spelled out his own success or failure in life. Henry was not, of course, oblivious to the fact that H.P.B. was a much greater occultist than he. She had had direct training under the Masters in Tibet, he was convinced, and was their direct messenger. She would inevitably become the Theosophical center of gravity wherever she happened to be. Through her came the power and the teachings. Sincere students would sense this, and gather round her as the focal point of the movement.

That was as it should be, but his old chum always made a terrible hash of anything to do with organization or administration. She knew nothing about it, hated it, and yet would at every opportunity poke her finger into it. The outer organization was *his* province, and she should leave it to him. There was only one solution; he must go to England and see her personally. "Body" and "Soul" must get together again before the cause of the Great Ones was shattered by division and dissent.

* * *

The good ship *Shannon* sailed through the Ionian Sea toward the heel of Italy. A rough passage from Bombay lay behind her, and the Colonel, a seasoned sailor, had been seasick, but today the weather was fine and the seas calm. He strolled on the sunny deck, thinking of what lay behind and in front of him.

At Adyar an emergency meeting of the Society Council had given its President full discretionary powers to do what he thought best in Europe. But what would be best? Had his old friend and co-worker changed, or would she still be understanding and reasonable when discussing things, face to face? He hoped so. But he began to doubt it. There had been so many difficult letters from her. Could she be jealous of him, her old pupil? Would she break The Theosophical Society if she did not have her own way?

Tomorrow he would reach Brindisi. Then he would catch the train to Paris, traveling through the Swiss Alps, and the Mt. Cenis Tunnel, by daylight—if he were lucky. He went below to his cabin to dress for dinner.

While he was dressing an envelope dropped suddenly from the air onto the table before him. He picked it up, and his eye caught the familiar handwriting of the Master K.H. A warm thrill ran through him. The powers were still working, and he was not forgotten in this hour of need.

He slit open the envelope and drew out the letter. It was a long one and began by speaking of the misunderstanding that had grown up in Europe. Then it began to clarify H.P.B.'s position. "Just now on deck, your thoughts about her were dark and sinful, and so I find the moment a fitting one to put you on your guard. . ." Henry was startled, having momentarily forgotten the telepathic power of an Adept.

Further on, the letter said: "Of these [the Masters' agents] for the past thirty years the chief has been the personality known as H.P.B. to the world (but otherwise to us). Imperfect and very troublesome, no doubt, she proves to some, nevertheless, there is no likelihood of our finding a better one for years to come. . . Her fidelity to our work being constant, and her sufferings having come upon her thro' it, neither I nor either of my Brother associates, will desert or supplant her. . .

"To help you in your present perplexity: H.P.B. has next to no concern with administrative details, and should be kept clear of them, so far as her strong nature can be controlled. But this *you must tell to all: with occult matters she has everything to do.* . . In the adjustment of this European business, you will have two things to consider—the external and administrative, and the internal and psychical. Keep the former under your control, and that of your most prudent associates, jointly; *leave the latter to her.* You are left to devise the practical details with your usual ingenuity."

The letter closed with the warning to show it to no one— "not even to H.P.B. unless she speaks to you of it herself. . . It is merely given you, as a warning and a guide. . ." The Colonel folded the letter, put it in his pocket and went thoughtfully in to dinner.

He was still thinking about it next day as his train rolled through Italy and climbed into the Swiss mountains. It was one of several reminders he had had from the Great Ones that he did not always understand the inner work H.P.B. was doing, and was unjust to her. His *dharma* in this life, they pointed out, was to organize and keep alive the "body" through which the teachings could come to the world. Well, he accepted that role, though it did not leave the leisure and solitude necessary for the sustained spiritual exercises essential to his own progress. Sometimes he wondered if, in the fourteen years since he had been accepted as a neophyte of the Brotherhood, he had made one step toward adeptship. But perhaps that was wrong thinking, for the Masters assured him that *selfless* work for the Society was itself a spiritual exercise that would take him along the narrow way toward the shining goal.

Selfless work—no desire for fruits in praise, fame, or status: that was the key! And he must remember that H.P.B. worked from occult patterns that were sometimes quite enigmatic to him. He must stick to the exoteric side of things. But sometimes the exoteric and esoteric sides overlapped and intermixed; and that made things difficult.

On the evening of August 26, Henry reached 17 Lansdowne Road, a pleasant house standing opposite the green of Holland Park. Inside he was given a warm welcome by his old chum and a number of her new followers—the Keightleys, E. D. Fawcett, the scientist Carter Blake, H.P.B.'s sister Vera Zhelihovsky, and others.

There were many difficulties to be ironed out, but Henry found that the really big problem he had to solve was H.P.B.'s avowed and fixed intention to form an independent section for her students of esoteric philosophy and practice. Whatever the appearance of things had to be on the surface, she said, in reality this section must be free from the rules and regulations emanating from Adyar.

The Colonel hated from the depths of his nature the whole idea of this projected *imperium in imperio,* this empire within an empire, as he considered it. Furthermore, he disliked the secrecy and pledges she was proposing to introduce. They both had tried once, in the early days, to turn the whole Society into a closed body with secrecy and passwords. But the attempt had failed. At Adyar in 1884 H.P.B., Subba Row, Damodar, and others had endeavored to organize a secret group of members. That, too, had failed.

If this new attempt by H.P.B. succeeded, it must—with the two heads far apart—inevitably divide The Theosophical Society in spirit. With a secret body within its body would the Society be able to achieve the feeling of oneness that lay at the heart of brotherhood?

H. S. Olcott and H. P. Blavatsky in London, 1888

Nevertheless, esoteric considerations were obviously involved. And "with occult matters *she* has everything to do" the Master had reminded him firmly aboard the *Shannon*. If indeed—as H.P.B. informed him—their guru wanted this esoteric section formed for the purpose of reviving the sagging Theosophical movement, particularly in Europe, then of course he must agree. More than that, he must play his allotted role, he must help her to organize it on a sound basis. In this way he would help the Master's plan and, he hoped, assure that the least possible harm was done to the harmony and unity of the mother Society; he would endeavor to offset the harmful aspects of the new scheme.

So, in the large attractive study that overlooked Holland Park, the Twins came to an amicable agreement and worked together on the new plan. They even recaptured some of the old flavor and camaraderie of the New York days, for he found time to help her on the proofs of *The Secret Doctrine* and the magazine whose birth he had resented— *Lucifer*.

On October 9, 1888 the President issued an official order in council forming an "Esoteric Section of The Theosophical Society." The sole direction was vested in Madame H. P. Blavatsky as its head, and it had "no official or corporate connection with the Exoteric Society, save in the person of the President-Founder."

Then to dispel rumors about a split between them, they isued a joint communiqué which in effect said that, while differing sometimes in views as to methods of procedure and propaganda, they were yet of one mind, united in purpose and zeal, and "ready to sacrifice all, even life, for the promotion of Theosophical knowledge, to the saving of mankind from the miseries which spring from ignorance."

While in England the Colonel lunched with Professor Max Müller at Oxford, and spent much time with old friends, such as Stainton Moses and the Sinnetts. Officially, he organized the lodges of England, Scotland, and Ireland into a British Section, with its own constitution and a high degree of autonomy.

Late in October he left for Naples to embark on the *Arcadia* for India. The overland journey took him to

Rome for his first visit there. From his hotel he wrote a warm, friendly letter to H.P.B.: "Well, I have seen St. Peter's . . . it beats everything I have seen; it takes the cake. . . I saw the gilded, worldly soul of Catholicism there. . ." Further on he writes that he had had "the most unexpected and splendid visit from M [Master Morya] in the train. I felt so rejoiced I could almost have jumped out of the window. He was so kind, so loving and compassionate; despite all my faults and shortcomings, he bears with me and holds to me because of the useful work I have now and then done, and of my fervent desire to do my duty.

"If he has not told you already, he will; so I shall not flog my tired brain to describe how he came, talked, looked and went. Goodnight, Chum—to you and to all. Yours, Maloney."

Chapter 19

"IN THE MIDST OF LIFE. . . . ."

1889 - 1891

On a rainy day in early September 1889, a woman journalist from America drove in a two-wheeled cab along Lansdowne Road and stopped at No. 17. She was ushered into the large room at the left by a maidservant, and sat waiting for Madame Blavatsky—the fascinating, mysterious character about whom she wished to write a story for her paper, *The Commercial Gazette* of Cincinnati, Ohio, U.S.A.

She waited only a few moments; then "the folding doors were thrown open and I stood face to face with a gentleman of grand physique, of genial face, of wonderful beard, a gentleman so unique in manner and appearance that at once involuntarily I exclaimed: 'Colonel Olcott.'

" 'The same, and you are my countrywoman. Be seated.' "

A few minutes later H.P.B. hobbled rheumatically into the room and joined them. The journalist, sitting at the large, book-bestrewn table with the two founders, easily got her story. It was about the incredible literary output of this sick but indomitable lady. The monumental work, *The Secret Doctrine,* had been published only the year before, and now she had two new books almost completed—*The Key to Theosophy* and *The Voice of the Silence.*

But what was Henry Olcott doing in London less than a year after he had gone off, leaving Theosophical Society affairs here—he thought—as calm as an English millpond? He had received a cable asking him to come and make a two-months' lecture tour of Great Britain, and that, ostensibly, was why he was here. But beneath the surface there was a more impelling reason.

The set-up of the Esoteric Section was not working out as well as hoped. Stresses and strains between Adyar and London continued. He felt that H.P.B. interfered too much in *his* province—executive matters. But, he conceded, perhaps he did not always perceive that esoteric questions were frequently involved. It was a fact, though, that H.P.B. now wanted to have full Presidential powers as his representative in her area. Her London followers wanted her to have those powers, too. They regarded the "old man at Adyar" as a "bottleneck" and made merry over his "fustian Executive Orders," she informed him.

It was geographical division and third parties that always caused such misunderstandings. Now that the Twins were together "on the ground" again, they could talk things over, and their deep common purpose united them as of yore. They would work out the problem somehow between them before he left.

Meantime he helped her with her literary work when he was not out of London, lecturing somewhere in the provinces, or busy with old friends and new. Among the new friends was a well-known social worker and freethinker who had recently joined H.P.B.'s group of pupils—Mrs. Annie Besant. Of her he writes in his diary: "Mrs. Besant I find to be a natural Theosophist; her adhesion to us was inevitable from the attraction of her nature towards the mystical. She is the most important gain to us since Sinnett." Then hearing her speak on theosophical subjects at public gatherings, he commented: "very able and facile discourse. She is a power indeed." "A magnificent lecture, and a chivalrous defence of H.P.B."

Among the old friends was his dear sister, Belle, who had come from New York to see him. They had not met since he left his native shores in 1878—eleven years before. In 1886 he had been delighted to hear about the publication of her first book, entitled *The Kitchen, John and I*. Perhaps this had helped her finance the present journey.

It was a joyful reunion. He took her to see some of England's attractions, including the Tower of London, pointing out there—he writes—"my old quarters in the Salt Tower, where I lived in 1858." They went together to a "splendid organ recital," to meet Henry's new friends, and out shopping—"Bought her a mantle, which she sadly needed, poor thing." In less than a month she had gone again, back to New York.

Christmas came, bringing him "a variety of cards" and a "splendid silk rug from Countess Wachtmeister." With H.P.B. he went to the home of a Mrs. Hunt for Christmas dinner. All made merry together, the Colonel contributing some of his much-appreciated comic songs. He did not know it, but this was to be his last Christmas dinner with his chum. He left next day for India, and never saw her alive again.

But before going he gave her the Christmas present she really wanted. It came in the form of one of his "fustian Executive Orders," appointing H.P.B. as Chairman of an Appellate Board, to be known as "The President's Commissioners" for Great Britain and Ireland. Other Commissioners appointed to the Appellate Board were: Annie Besant, William Kingsland, and Herbert Burrows. To this body he delegated his executive powers, making its members his personal representatives for the territory named—"Provided, however, that all executive orders and decisions made on my behalf by the said Commissioners shall be unanimously agreed to and signed by the four Commissioners above designated."

He selected the other three Commissioners for their practical good sense and steadfastness of will, "believing that they would suffer nothing very revolutionary to be done to upset the steady working of the Society."

Because he had legally wrapped it up in this way, putting a bridle on H.P.B.'s impetuosity, the "Christmas gift" looked larger than it really was.

*   *   *

One would like to be able to say that all went well and amicably between the Twins from that Christmas on, but it was not so.

Early in July, 1890, the Colonel received a letter from H.P.B., backed by some of her friends, demanding that he reorganize the movement in Europe with her as permanent president there. At the end of the month came an official copy of a resolution which had been passed by the British Section, "vesting permanently the Presidential authority for the whole of Europe in H. P. Blavatsky." The resolution was signed by W. R. Old, as General Secretary of the British Section. It was—London thought—a *fait accompli*.

On receipt of this document in India, the Colonel drove his carriage to the printers who were busy getting out the Supplement of *The Theosophist* for August. Three hundred and fifty copies had already come off the press.

"Destroy them," said the Colonel, "and start again. Here is an Executive Notice to be inserted." It read:

> The following Resolution of the Council of the British Section of July 2nd, 1890, is hereby cancelled, as contrary to the Constitution and By-laws of the Theosophical Society, a usurpation of the Presidential prerogative, and beyond the competence of any Section or other fragment of the Society to enact.
>
> H. S. Olcott, P.T.S.   Adyar, 29th July, 1890"

Below the notice was printed the British Resolution.

In his diary that evening Henry commented: "That may mean a split but it does not mean I shall be a slave." Then he sat by the darkening waters of the Adyar River, musing. In happier days he had taught H.P.B. and Damodar to swim here, had laughed at Damodar's pencil legs and taunted him for his terror of the water, saying that he would never make an Adept without more courage—until the lad finally set his lantern jaws grimly and took the plunge. Plump Helena had enjoyed the sparkling waters, the teasing and the fun, hugely.

Had it now come to a final break between them? He owed her loyalty as his former teacher and inspiration, certainly. But there was a superior, higher loyalty. *That* he owed to those who had chosen him to play a key part in their plans for the betterment of humanity. They had often told him what his part was—to be a faithful custodian of a sound, workable organization or mechanism for the dissemination of the theosophical philosophy. It was his duty to fight for *that* above all.

But then he asked himself if his action had been motivated

Henry Olcott's brother, George Potts Olcott

purely by his sense of duty, or was there some personal pride, some masked love of power, mixed up in it? If so, the Masters would—as often before—rap his knuckles sharply. But by then it would perhaps be too late. The break would have come. He was very worried when he went to bed that night and slept uneasily.

The year 1890 was having some highlights as well as shadows. One of the highlights was a letter from his eldest son Richard Morgan, with a recent photograph showing a fine, open-faced young man. Now 29, he was apparently doing well in the export business, with big plans for new commercial ventures. But he was very much a man of the world, a club man—as his father had been at that age. It would be nice to see him again.

A dark note had been the recent death of one whom Henry had loved like a son—T. Subba Row. What a strange death it was! The learned occultist was covered with boils and blisters from crown to toe as a result of blood poisoning from some mysterious cause. Subba Row thought, himself, that it was due to the malevolent action of elementals whose animosity he had aroused. Henry agreed with this when he visited the sick man to try magnetic healing. As he approached, he felt an "uncanny influence" about Subba Row.

The magnetic healing brought the patient renewed strength, and he appeared to be getting better. But then a relapse came. "At noon on June 24th, 1890, he told those about him that his guru called him to come, he was going to die, he was now about beginning his *tapas* [mystical invocations], and he did not wish to be disturbed." He died during that night.

T. Subba Row was one of the few who had received a letter from Damodar in Tibet, and he spoke of this again to the Colonel on his sickbed. A brilliant luminary of Indian esoteric philosophy, he had been admired and loved by H.P.B., Damodar, and many others. Unfortunately, he had resigned from The Theosophical Society in April 1888, owing to a dispute—"due in a measure to third parties—which widened into a breach between H.P.B. and himself about certain philosophical questions," writes the Colonel. "But to the last he spoke of her . . . in the old friendly way."

T. Subba Row (1856-1890)

These good feelings were reciprocal: in her letters H.P.B. always wrote of him with admiration and friendship. She says in her correspondence that T. Subba Row objected strongly to her giving out so many esoteric secrets to the profane in her *Secret Doctrine.* He apparently chose to overlook the fact that she was doing this under the direction of her guru. This, she said, was the chief factor in the breach that came between them.

Two men from H.P.B.'s group were now in India helping at Adyar—author and metaphysician E. D. Fawcett, and journalist Richard Harte who had come to help edit *The Theosophist.* They seemed to be loyal to the President, but news of the projected arrival of a third London member increased the Colonel's apprehensions about the problems in London. In September, after the August *Theosophist* bearing his Executive Notice must have reached London, Henry heard that Mr. Bertram Keightley M.A. (Cantab.) was on his way to India.

He drew the conclusion—through a disturbing message from a third party—that Keightley was on a secret mission from H.P.B. of which he, Olcott, knew nothing. "She is plainly scheming to undermine my authority even in India," he notes in his diary. This growing conviction was supported by an "abominably revolutionary manifesto" she had published in *Lucifer,* subverting his presidential dignity.

The Colonel evidently decided that he must change his tactics. No doubt he remembered the vehement protests that had issued from his chum when he had wanted to resign the Presidency in order to work for the Buddhist League a year earlier.

Late in September 1890 his diary tells us that he wrote a letter to Mead—one of H.P.B.'s disciples and her current private secretary—saying that he "wished to retire and leave H.P.B. to muddle T.S. affairs as she chose." This preliminary shot was followed a couple of weeks later by "a very long letter to H.P.B. defining our relations and telling her I meant to retire."

H.P.B.'s reply was that she would make *any* sacrifice if he would stay in office. She added that the Masters disapproved of his resignation. Henry answered that he would remain

at the helm for the present, provided she would alter the
pledge which the Esoteric Candidates were then taking.
It was then "worded so as to exact perfect obedience to her
in all their relations with the T.S.; in short, giving her
quasi-dictatorial powers. . ." It had been the cause of much
of the trouble between them, the Colonel felt. H.P.B. agreed
to his terms and altered the pledge to a form which he found
more discreet and acceptable. "Had we been together," he
writes, "the mistake would not have been made."

He was glad that this threat of resignation had silenced
for the time being the popping of guns in London. He had
quite enough traveling on his program without going to
England. Soon he would be off on a long journey to
Australia—not to mention a visit to Burma as well.

* * *

One day in early April 1891 the Colonel arrived in Toowoomba, Queensland—six hours journey by rail from the
capital, Brisbane. It was a pleasant country of rolling
meadows and winding, willow-marked creeks against a background of blue hills. But the human situation in which he
found himself was far from pleasant.

This trip to Australia had been in connection with a bequest made to him for The Theosophical Society by a
Queensland member, a botanist and horticulturist named
Mr. C. H. Hartmann. The legacy was a substantial one,
consisting of 42 acres of beautiful gardens, plantations, con-
servatories of rare plants, and a country house. In addition
there were shares in productive mines and a nice sum of
money in the bank. The will had been contested by the
Hartmann family but the Colonel's title was "declared perfect by the highest judicial tribunal."

The family, a brother, two sons, and a daughter of the
dead man, not having received a cent in the will, looked
upon Olcott as their enemy. They had been going about the
town complaining of the wrongs done to them and exciting
prejudice against Olcott and his Society which, they said,
had robbed them of their inheritance. Henry, who was
staying at the Imperial Hotel, felt that it would not take
much to incite the mob to stone him out of town. When

he went to make his first call on the family, he was received with icy hostility.

But having learned all the circumstances, Henry himself felt that these struggling, hard-working pioneers had been treated unjustly by the deceased man. He decided to give the property back to them, keeping only a thousand pounds for The Theosophical Society. This sum would, in a way, be carrying out the late Mr. Hartmann's wish to help the theosophical cause. Olcott would take also, he told them, the expense of his journey to Australia. (He had traveled first-class for the first time in his theosophical life, on the strength of the expected legacy.)

With this renunciation of his legal right to the property, public opinion in the town, and beyond, underwent an immediate change. The heirs now went about singing his praises. He was invited to give a public lecture on "Theosophy and Buddhism" in Toowoomba at which the chairman was a member of Parliament. "So it happened," he writes, "in every town I visited . . . my rooms at the hotels were thronged by ladies and gentlemen of the highest social position, anxious to question me and join the Society. . ." Even "Christian clergymen of orthodox repute and much influence joined the Society."

Through the press this good feeling, born of his generous act in Toowoomba, spread through the continent of Australia, and wherever he went he met with warm feelings and packed audiences. Before his arrival in the antipodes there had been three weak Society branches in that part of the world, one in Melbourne, one in Wellington (New Zealand), and one in Hobart, Tasmania. When he left there were seven good ones—"among whose members were thoroughgoing Mystics and Theosophists, from whom I then expected much, and who have not disappointed me."

On May 8, the *Sydney Morning Herald* carried a friendly paragraph on his visit to Sydney where, incidentally, Henry was hobnobbing with the Governor, The Earl of Jersey, whom he had met in England and found sympathetic to the theosophical work. On the same day of crowded activities the Colonel organized a Sydney Branch of The Theosophical Society with 23 members. But also on that day, twelve thousand miles away, something unexpected, sad and terrible, had happened. His deeper self knew about it, but the knowing did not get through to his consciousness until the evening of the next day, the 9th. It came as a deep feeling of sorrow, loss, emptiness. . . He could not describe it, but his intuition told him what it meant. In his diary that night he wrote: "Had an uneasy foreboding of H.P.B.'s death."

On the following day, the 10th, he wrote: "This a.m. I feel as though H.P.B. were dead; the third warning." He tried to shake off the cloud of depression because that evening he had to give a public lecture. About 600 people came. As he was leaving the platform, a newspaper reporter stepped up to him and spoke quietly. A press cablegram had come, he said, from London. It announced the death—on the 8th of May—of Madame Helena Petrovna Blavatsky.

Henry canceled his programmed tours of New Zealand and Tasmania and took the first available ship to London.

Bertram Keightley, who had been staying at Adyar, joined him at Colombo. Rheumatism was back in Henry's legs, and he did not go ashore at Aden.

From Marseilles they traveled overland and reached London in two days, on July 4th. William Q. Judge, who had come from America, was on the railway platform to meet them and took them by cab to No. 19 Avenue Road, St. John's Wood. This was the house to which H.P.B. had moved during the previous year, and where she died. It was the Colonel's first visit there. He was greeted affectionately by Annie Besant and the other residents.

In the room where Helena Petrovna had died less than two months earlier, Henry sat alone remembering the years they had spent together; the early years when she had been "Jack"; the happy, laughing years when she was "Mrs. Mulligan"; the comradely years when she was "Chum" or "Old Horse"; the luminous, elevating periods of her great teachings, when she was the vehicle of one or another of the Masters. Then, of course, there had been the difficult times, too, when he had disagreed with her. . .

"Surrounded by the objects she had left," he writes, "the latest books that she had been reading, the big chair she had sat in, and the dresses she had worn. . . I felt the full force of our irreparable loss. . . I never expected that she would leave me so abruptly. . . It seemed almost that, instead of having gone on the long journey to the higher spheres, she must have just taken temporary leave of us. . ."

Only a few months earlier they had both been caught in the coils of *maya*—a stupid kind of power struggle. Instead of struggling against her, he should have tried harder to understand her problems, her work, and her point of view. But now it was too late. The form of the one he had known and loved as a true friend was nought but a handful of ashes in a silver urn. How true and significant were those simple words: "In the midst of life we are in death."

Now *his* was the only hand on the helm of the sensitive ship of Theosophy. Would the Masters continue to guide him? Did he really deserve it?

He felt a light touch on his arm. It was Annie Besant, the greatest of H.P.B.'s London disciples. The two of them sat in silence, meditating. Then, there in H.P.B.'s room, they made a solemn pledge to be true to the great cause and to each other.

Henry realized that it was a critical time for the Society. History showed that the unity of organizations always broke down when the real leader died. He must do his best to hold this one—the vehicle of the Masters—together. He must personally tour England and the Continent, visiting France, Germany, Denmark and Sweden. He must give all the strength he could to the forth-coming *first* European convention. Then he must cross the Atlantic to long-neglected America, where William Judge had been carrying on and doing great work in the last few years. But that birthplace of The Theosophical Society now felt it was out on a limb, forgotten. It must be brought firmly back to the center of things.

From America he planned to cross the Pacific to complete his Buddhist mission in Japan. But he must be back in India in time for the annual convention in December. India, too, needed some reassurance now after the passing of the vital head of the movement. He would be taking a third of H.P.B.'s ashes for burial in the "sacred soil," as she had long ago requested. The other two-thirds were for Europe and America.

It was a big program of arduous journeys, demanding health and vitality. At the age of 59 he still seemed to have a sufficiency of these—his gouty leg notwithstanding. Anyway it was his duty, his *dharma,* to carry the standard onward, against whatever opposition still lay hidden in the closed hand of time.

Chapter 20

SHOCK FROM AN OLD FRIEND
1891 - 1893

At about seven in the evening of September 23, 1891, Henry's ship drew close to his native shore in New York harbor. It was over twelve years since he had sailed away on the great venture with H.P.B., and his eye noted a number of changes. Then, as the crowd on the wharf separated into individuals, he saw awaiting him with upturned faces Belle, Emmett Robinson (Bob), Alexander Fullerton, and other members of the Society.

Belle, who was almost like his twin soul, threw her arms around him before his feet had fairly touched the wharf. Brother Bob shook hands warmly, and the others welcomed him like a returning hero. Belle took him off to stay at her home.

The next few days were spent in visiting friends and relatives. With his sister he went to see an old acquaintance of Lamasery days, Laura Holloway. On the 25th he wrote: "George drove me about Orange. Consulted Bob about family matters. Family dinner—Emily present." George was his youngest brother, now only 41, and Emily his youngest sister.

By the first week in October he was in San Francisco staying at the home of a Society member, Dr. Anderson. There to see him, within a few days of his arrival, came his mother's brothers, Isaac, George, and Edgar Steel. Henry was overjoyed to see these three uncles who long ago in Ohio had awakened his interest in spiritualism which had led eventually to H.P.B. and the Path. Now they were big ranch owners in the golden West.

From San Francisco Henry took ship to Japan, where he collected the signatures for his Buddhist platform and was back in India in time for the annual convention of December 1891.

His diary for January 16, 1892 states: "Began a series of historical reminiscences of the T.S. and H.P.B. for *The Theosophist,* under the title, *Old Diary Leaves.*" This, compiled from his daily diaries and old documents, and brought to life by personal memories, was to become his *magnum opus.* Later printed in book form, it runs to six volumes spiced with anecdotes of his thaumaturgic chum and the fascinating lore of India.

His object in writing this work was not only to provide material for future historians, but to "combat a growing tendency within the Society to deify Madame Blavatsky." There were disturbing signs that a new sect was springing up around her memory—a sect of people who, when challenged on the intrinsic reasonableness of one of their statements, would answer with restrained breath, "But you know she said so. . ." as if that closed all debate.

This raised the Colonel's bristles. To him *no* person should be taken as final authority on matters occult and spiritual. In this he was true to the teachings of his Master and his late colleague. For this freedom of thought, this absence of authoritarianism, he had continually fought.

"It was but too evident," he writes in the foreword of *Old Diary Leaves,* vol. 1, "that unless I spoke out what I alone knew, the true history of our movement could never be written, nor the actual merit of my wonderful colleague become known." He loved H.P.B. as he knew her—warmhearted, generous, difficult, tempestuous, unique, and one of the greatest occultists of modern times—and he wanted no false image of her to sully the annals of truth.

Three days after starting on *Old Diary Leaves,* on January 19, he writes in his diary: "F. T. Sturdy arrived from London with fateful message about which we talked nearly all day." The message, which was signed by W. Q. Judge, had been considered—by Judge and by Annie Besant—too important to risk sending by post. Sturdy had traveled to India especially to bring it to the hand of the President.

Exactly what that message was is not known. It apparently concerned something which Henry was supposed to have done when last in London, during 1891. Whatever the "something" was, Annie did not approve of it, and discussed it with Judge. Together they decided to send the message by special courier to Olcott. Evidently it was an accusation and either requested, or demanded, the President's resignation.

For two whole days the Colonel talked over the matter with Sturdy and one or two colleagues at Adyar. From Sturdy he learned of strong rumors abroad that the Masters had abandoned Olcott and that the real head was now W. Q. Judge. Many written Mahatma messages had apparently come through the latter, bearing—it was said—the seal of Master Morya. At Avenue Road, London and other places, Judge was now looked upon as a great mystic. A scheme had been devised to send one of the leading London members to Australia to persuade branches there to come "entirely under Judge's control." Some members in England and America apparently wanted to reduce the "old man at Adyar" to the position of a mere figurehead.

In a depressed frame of mind, Henry could not sleep for thinking about the turn events had taken. It was true, he admitted, that he had not heard directly from his guru for some time. Perhaps the Mahatmas had really withdrawn their help and protection. Perhaps all that was being said was true, and Judge would be a better leader for the Society now at this stage. With H.P.B. gone, perhaps Judge was the better channel for the great Mahatmic influence.

At the convention of 1888 the Colonel had appointed Mr. Judge as the International Vice-President of The Theosophical Society. A year later this appointment had been ratified by election among convention members. So if Olcott resigned Judge would automatically become the President of the Society. Maybe that would be best.

Some misgivings haunted the Colonel's mind, however. He was not altogether sure that the "Mahatma letters" which had been issuing from wherever Judge happened to be at the time, were genuine. For one thing the Master's seal on the letters looked bogus, and some of the messages did not ring

William Q. Judge and Henry S. Olcott

true to Henry's mind.

But these were vague suspicions, and he repressed them. After all, who was he to sit in judgment on the little Irishman he had known so long? Judge had always had occult potentialities and seemed to have developed a great deal in recent years.

Since the mid-eighties the President had been reorganizing the Society into autonomous Sections. Now, instead of a quasi-autocracy, it was a constitutional federation, and the President's office was like that of a constitutional monarch. So perhaps a strong hand was not needed any more at the helm. If it were the Masters' will, as it seemed to be from their long silence, he would resign and let Judge take over.

Henry made this decision with some sadness, remembering all the struggles he had gone through to build up this worldwide, dynamic vehicle for the spread of the sacred science. Now it was to be taken from him, and he would be left unwanted.

He would move up to the beautiful "Gulistan" in the Nilgiris, and devote the rest of his life to his literary labors. There would be time for reading the many books he wanted to read, time for meditation, contemplation, the inner search. "Old age has yet its honor and its toil, death closes all." Well, his health had not been the best for some time; he needed a rest from travel and talking.

On January 21, he wrote to inform Judge of his resignation, sending a copy of the letter to Annie Besant who had taken over the reins of The Theosophical Society in England. He followed this with a "circular letter to all Sections."

The first protests over his resignation came from the Indian Section, several leading members threatening to resign from the Society if he left. He was, it seemed, popular in India, while Judge was not.

Then two practical difficulties arose with regard to immediate retirement: it would take some months to effect a legal transfer to the Society of certain securities held in his own name, and Judge could not become President while still holding his present position of General Secretary of the American Section, as this would give him three votes out of a possible five in the General Council. Henry wrote

Judge to this effect, and told him that in view of the legal difficulties about property transfer, the date of his resignation must be deferred for a few months.

But there was another factor—more nebulous, and yet actually more powerful than the others—which made him hesitate. His extrasensory perception was not in the same class as that of his late colleague H.P.B.—nor, it would seem, equal to that of Mr. Judge—but it did appear to work on occasion. Just before daybreak on the morning of February 10, 1892, as he lay in a state between sleeping and waking, he heard clairaudiently the voice of Master Morya. The voice told him a number of things, some of which surprised him.

Among other matters, the Master said that he must stay at his post until given permission to resign. He assured Henry that their relationship was unbreakable and that the stories about the Mahatmas having withdrawn their protection were false. In fact they kept constant watch over his work for the cause and would never desert him. The Master's voice further encouraged him by saying that a messenger of the Brotherhood would be coming to help him in his great task.

This gave a tremendous lift to the Colonel's morale. He felt quite sure that the experience was a genuine one and not just a mental projection. But he could not expect others to accept it as proof that the Masters were ordering him to remain in office. So he did not immediately revoke his resignation.

Henry and many others jumped to the conclusion that the promised "messenger" would be Damodar, returning from Tibet—and there was great excitement. But the weeks and months passed by with no more signs, and eventually hope faded. Yet, as Olcott tells in *Old Diary Leaves,* the predicted messenger *did* come—though not in the way expected.

Judge was one of the people the Colonel informed about the clairaudient message. But William Quan chose to ignore it. At the time he was rather busy, it seemed, with Mahatma messages of his own. He agreed that Olcott should defer his resignation, both for the practical reasons given and also because Judge himself had, he said, received a message from the Masters telling him that it was not the right time for the

President-Founder to resign.

But the soft-eyed, bearded Irish-American lawyer, who had for some years been employed in Emmett Olcott's law firm, Olcott, Mestre & Gonzalez, 35 Broadway, New York, seemed to Henry to be acting in strange and devious ways. Why had he, for instance, said nothing about the Colonel's clairaudient message and then written to Henry about a similar "Mahatma communication," of his own, received some time after the Colonel's information must have reached him? Then, when he attended the European convention in London in July 1892, why did he keep silent about the "wishes of the Master"—which he claimed to have received himself directly—allowing the convention to accept Olcott's resignation, and vote for Judge as succeeding President?

The European members got their first intimation of the change of Olcott's policy about the resignation well after the convention, from the President-Founder's Executive Notice of August 21, 1892. In this he announced that he was revoking his resignation and resuming active duty.

At Adyar the Colonel was getting a good deal of help from Bertram Keightley and from Sidney Edge, an English lawyer who had earlier abandoned his legal career to work with H.P.B. in London. After her death he had come out to India to join the headquarters staff.

Then, on December 22, 1892, while preparations were being made for the convention, another member arrived from London with a collection of documents that appalled the sixty-year-old President. The new arrival was Walter R. Old, a professional astrologer whose writings were well known in Europe under the name "Sepharial." He had been General Secretary of the Society in England during 1890 and 1891, and was one of those who had "held H.P.B.'s hands as she died, sitting in her great chair." Now he was going to be an assistant editor of *The Theosophist* at Adyar.

The documents Old brought, and his allegations, were so serious that both Edge and Keightley were called into consultation. In the main they were written messages in the script of Master Morya. Some bore his signature and the seal that purported to be his cryptograph. Walter Old felt sure that these were spurious messages, that Mr. Judge was writing them himself—forging the script and using a false seal. Edge and Keightley were inclined to agree with him.

The Colonel's former vague suspicions were now strengthened. The messages certainly did *not* sound like the words of his great guru; they showed ignorance of facts, were often trivial and foolish, and usually slanted in a manner to bring direct benefits to Mr. Judge.

An alleged communication from the Master in the previous October, for instance, ordered Annie Besant not to go to India, and suggested that there was a great risk in her going—that her life would be in danger at the hands of Henry Olcott. His adored Teacher would never write such a thing; it was not only cruel; it was absurd nonsense. Henry had a tremendous admiration for Mrs. Besant and high hopes for the part she might play in the future of the Society. In fact, she was perhaps better fitted than Judge for the leading role as President. William Quan knew Olcott's thoughts on this; so here perhaps was a motive for keeping her away from India.

Then there was the seal. The Colonel had little doubt that this was the same seal he had himself obtained back in 1883. He had gone at that time to an old Moslem seal maker named Badarrodin in Chandi Chowk Street, Old Delhi; had sketched his guru's cryptograph from memory, and asked the old man to engrave it on a brass ring. This was done for the price of half a rupee.

Returning to Adyar he had given the ring to H.P.B., saying; "Send this as a present to 'Father;' he can wear it on his watchchain."

H.P.B. examined it. "Badly drawn—the 'M' looks more like a 'W'—how can I send him that!" She threw it into a box with other junk.

In London five years later Bertram Keightley had found it when she asked him to clear out an old box for her.

"What's this?" he asked.

"Oh it's only a flapdoodle of Olcott's."

Henry had intended it all for a lark, but realized afterwards that it was really a silly one.

Normally, in H.P.B.'s time, letters from the Master M. did

not bear his seal. But this badly-drawn one was now appearing on alleged messages from him, coming through Judge. It seemed to Olcott and others that William Quan might have got possession of the seal during one of his visits to H.P.B. in Europe toward the end of her life.

During the convention, soon after Old's arrival, the papers were shown to an old Society member, Judge Khandalavala, who advised the Colonel to prosecute the case against W. Q. Judge, "as it was too serious a menace to the Society's prosperity to allow it to go on."

One day at the end of January 1893, the Colonel, with Sidney Edge and Rai B. K. Lahiri, a Notary Public, walked along the street called Chandi Chowk in Old Delhi looking for seal maker Badarrodin. After considerable search they located a small shop of a seal maker named Allah Banda, and inquired about Badarrodin.

"He was my brother. Alas, he is dead from cholera—only eight months ago."

The Colonel showed Banda some impressions of the seal engraving that was appearing on the Judge "Mahatma letters," and asked him to comment.

"It's the work of my brother," Banda said, after a moment's examination.

"How can you recognize it?"

"Just as you would know your brother's handwriting, I can recognize my brother's seal making by the peculiarities of its workmanship."

He went on to say that they had both learned the craft from the same teacher, their father. Allah Banda was quite willing to sign a statement before the Notary Public to the effect that the impressions on the paper before him were from a seal made by his brother Badarrodin.

Six months later, in July of 1893, Walter Old and Sidney Edge published, with the Colonel's consent, an article in *The Theosophist* attacking William Q. Judge's ideas as revealed in his magazine *The Path*. The article was restrained, considering the views of these two gentlemen about the part Judge was playing.

The main point of their criticism was that Judge was setting up a creed or dogma within the Society. This dogma was that a belief in the Mahatmas' existence was essential to the progress of the Society and the belief must be accepted on faith by those who had no personal proofs of it. It was enough that those in high standing and authority had the personal proofs. Furthermore, truisms uttered by Masters became something more than truisms, and "letters received from a Mahatma will not permit of the usual tests of identification."

Such doctrines went hard against the eclectic platform on which the Society stood. They could certainly not be accepted by the Colonel, Old, Edge and a great many other members. The article by Old and Edge said nothing about their suspicions of fraudulence—unless Judge could read between the lines.

William Judge and his followers in America took strong exception to the article and threatened to withdraw the Section's financial support to Adyar unless Old and Edge were removed from the headquarters staff. This threat the Colonel ignored.

In September 1893 Henry wrote privately to Judge, frankly expressing disbelief in his "pretended intimacy with the Mahatmas." Nevertheless he felt—and Bertram Keightley, who was also a lawyer, agreed—that the evidence against Judge was not strong enough for prosecution. So the matter remained in abeyance while stories continued to circulate, and the anti-Judge section increased in size and discontent.

Toward the end of the year 1893 the Colonel received word that Mrs. Annie Besant was coming to India. Her visit had been planned to take place earlier, but was postponed for various reasons,* including Judge's alleged "message from the Mahatmas."

But now she was definitely coming and would tour India to lecture at many centers. Remembering her eloquence in

* W. Q. Judge wrote in a letter to Olcott during 1892 that Annie Besant was going to do a lecture tour in America at the end of that year for payment. She needed the money, he said, to settle old debts "growing out of the Freethought Co.", and because of a recent loss by the "failure of a debtor and a bank" . . . "She can make plenty here," whereas, "in India she cannot make a cent." Judge stated that he, himself, was organizing through an agent an America-wide tour for Mrs. Besant during the next December and January.

England, and the reports of how she had triumphed at the Parliament of Religions in Chicago this year, the Colonel felt excited at the prospect of what her visit could mean for the cause in India. Something was needed to stir his Indian brothers out of their lethargy.

"Mrs. Besant put her foot on Indian soil for the first time at the hour of 10:24 a.m. on 16th November, 1893," wrote the Colonel. He sensed the significance of the event, but could not foresee what indelible footsteps she was destined to leave in that land.

Short in stature, Annie dressed at the time in late-Victorian fashion—skirts touching the ground and shoulders puffed out with what were called leg-o'-mutton sleeves. Her face was strong and determined, the light of a noble soul shone through her serious eyes. She might not always be right, reflected Henry, but she would always do what she *thought* was right, whatever the cost. With her came the Countess Wachtmeister.

Mrs. Besant's first lecture in India was given at Tinnevelly in the South on the subject of "Life after Death." The audience was large and the reception good. She gave another lecture the next evening on "Materialism," and the following day had to hold an improvised durbar for her many visitors. "At the close of it eleven persons joined our Society, of whom five were materialists whose beliefs had been quite upset by Mrs. Besant's lecture," wrote Olcott.

The lecture tour continued through Madura and on to Trichinopoly. It was here that she lectured on "India, Past and Present" in a style so eloquent and with such pathos that it made the whole audience weep. "I was so moved by her discourse," writes Henry who was chairman, "that I could hardly command my voice for closing the meeting."

It was at Trichinopoly that he received an unexpected solution to the mystery of the promised "messenger from the Masters." Again the E.S.P. experience came in the early morning while he lay between sleeping and waking. The familiar voice of his guru came across the astral currents and sounded in the Colonel's ear. The voice said: "This is the messenger whom I told you to be ready to go and meet: now do your duty."

Annie Besant

The President writes: "The surprise and delight were such as to drag me at once into a state of waking physical consciousness, and I rejoiced to think that I had once more received proof of the possibility of getting trustworthy communications from my Teacher at times when I could not suspect them of being the result of auto-suggestion." He had certainly not expected Annie Besant to be the agent selected by the Mahatmas to help with the work in India.

As the tour continued, and the tremendous response to Mrs. Besant's eloquence rose to a crescendo, the Colonel became even more convinced that she was indeed the promised messenger. And time confirmed the early impression. He writes much later, in *Old Diary Leaves,* vol. 5, that Annie Besant's work in India "is the best possible evidence that she is, indeed, the agent selected to fructify the seeds which had been planted by H.P.B. and myself during the previous fifteen years." He goes on to say that with her deep love of Hinduism she was able to sweep away all vestiges of the mistrust that had grown up among orthodox Brahmins. For, despite all the Colonel had been able to say to the contrary, many of the dyed-in-the-wool Brahmins had looked upon the founders as "secret agents for Buddhist propaganda, and would-be destroyers of Hinduism." Annie Besant changed all that.

But before the big lecture tour to the north got under way, there were some conferences at Adyar between the Colonel, Annie Besant, the Countess, and Messrs. Edge, Old, and Sturdy. Together they went over the documents that had been gathered with regard to Mr. Judge's activities. Referring to these private conferences, Mrs. Besant writes: "I looked into the mass of evidence which was in the hands of Colonel Olcott, but which, taken by itself, while arousing the gravest suspicion, was not sufficiently clear, definite and conclusive to justify Colonel Olcott, or Mr. Keightley, the Secretary of the Indian Section, in taking action which would commit the Society. But it happened that within my knowledge there were other facts unknown both to Colonel Olcott and Mr. [B]. Keightley, which made the evidence which was in their hands complete, and so rendered it, to my mind at least, convincing. . .

"All put together made so strong a body of evidence that it became a duty to the Society that it should be placed before it, and that Mr. Judge, as its Vice-President, should be given an opportunity of definitely meeting the charges if he could, so that an end might be put to a position so painful to all concerned, and so dangerous to the reputation and honor of the Society."

The Colonel and his colleagues agreed with this point of view. He asked Mrs. Besant to draw up the formal charges against the Vice-President. This she did in the form of a prosecutor's brief, presenting six charges with supporting evidence. In the main the charges covered: deception in the use of a seal and in other matters; untruthfulness with regard to communications with the Masters; and the sending out of messages and orders as if sent and written by Masters, such messages and orders being proved to be non-genuine by (a) error in matter of fact, (b) threat based on mistake, and (c) triviality. The probability of such messages being fraudulent was further enhanced by the facts that (i) they occurred only in letters from, or within the reach of, Mr. Judge, (ii) the knowledge displayed in them was limited to that possessed by Mr. Judge, and (iii) they were calculated to bring personal advantage to Mr. Judge, in some cases directly, and in all indirectly, because of his being the only person through whom such written messages were received.

Without the Colonel's permission, Mrs. Besant sent a copy of her brief to Mr. Judge. Olcott wrote a letter giving Judge the option of resigning his office or submitting the case to trial. He had in mind that if his old friend were guilty, he might wish to retire quietly from the offices he held in the Society, in which case the unpleasant details of the case would not be made public. Only a general public explanation would be made by the President.

Mr. Judge cabled back a blunt denial of any guilt, stating that he would not resign.

The President felt then forced to convene a judicial committee to try his old friend and colleague. The trial was scheduled to take place in London on June 27, 1894, before a jury of twelve leading members from various sections.

Chapter 21

THE STRUGGLE WITH MR. JUDGE
1894 - 1895

Within half a mile of Henry's home and offices at Adyar stood the village of Urur. Early in May 1894 he heard that there was a piece of land for sale there, and one morning walked down the road to inspect it. Most of the residents knew him well and greeted him warmly as he moved among their mud-walled, thatched houses; the village was primitive but clean.

The piece of land, facing the main road from Madras, was adequate to his purpose, so he decided to buy it. The project he had in mind was no official concern of the Society. Money for the costs involved would, therefore, have to come out of his own meager personal resources, but he felt that the great possibilities were worth the sacrifice.

His heart had long bled for the people of the village. Not only did they suffer great poverty but something worse—they were untouchables, pariahs, outcastes. High-caste Indians would not employ them as domestic servants, and many would even cross a street rather than come near an untouchable. Their lot in life was to do the worst, most unclean type of work for very little pay. They had no privileges, no rights, and no chance of ever rising to a higher social status. They were born outcastes and must die outcastes.

Their leprous untouchability was not due to any physical disease or contamination. It was simply because they did not belong to any of the castes in the social system decreed long ago by Manu, and later corrupted by man. Therefore, superstition, prejudice, and self-pride had built the psychical wall that kept the poor pariahs in a nether world of their

own. It was enough to freeze the genial currents of any
soul.

And the people of Urur were representative of many millions more throughout India. So, though there must have
been some enlightened souls who saw the evil of it all,
nothing had been done about it. The problem seemed too
gigantic, perhaps, for any one man to tackle. It would be
like taking a hammer to break up a mountain. Foolish!
Quixotic!

But the Colonel knew that one man must strike the first
blow. He also knew that mountains can be moved by a hammer—and faith. That was, in fact, the job he had been
engaged in for nearly twenty years now. His Society was a
very tiny hammer compared with the great mountain of materialism against which it labored. Yet in only two decades
some fissures had been made that were letting in the light,
and in the fullness of time the mountain would crumble.

His first dent into his lesser mountain—untouchability—
would be a school for the untouchables—the first of its kind
in India. Into the darkness of complete illiteracy would come
the early rays of the dawn of learning. Thus in time the
pariah would become a more useful citizen, he would have
more pride in himself, a higher social status, a fuller life. . .
Besides, the Colonel felt that if he himself dared to set the
example, other hammers would be lifted and more blows
struck against this mountain of injustice.

Before sailing off toward the unpleasant task awaiting him
in England, Henry gave instructions for the erection of a
mud-walled school building, and for the management of the
school itself until his return later in the year.

It was in June 1894, while the Colonel was in London,
that the first forty-five of India's outcaste illiterate millions
began their formal education at the "Olcott Free School."

*   *   *

The Colonel reached England on June 14, 1894, but for
some reason the meeting of the Judicial Committee was
postponed until July 10. It took place on that date at 19
Avenue Road, London, the committee consisting of: Colonel Olcott, in the chair; Messrs. B. Keightley and G. R. S.

Mead (General Secretaries of the Indian and European Sections, respectively) ; Messrs. A. P. Sinnett and E. T. Sturdy (delegates of the Indian Section) ; Messrs. H. Burrows and W. Kingsland (delegates of the European Section) ; Dr. J. D. Buck and Dr. Archibald Keightley (delegates of the American Section) ; Messrs. Oliver Firth, E. T. Hargrove and J. M. Pryse (special delegates of Mr. Judge from America). Mrs. Besant and Mr. Judge were also present.

The Colonel made an opening address in which he outlined the circumstances leading up to the meeting. He then stated that certain protests had been made by the accused which were later carefully considered by himself and members of the General Council.

The main point in the protests was that the present tribunal could only try the Vice-President on charges which implied on his part acts of misfeasance and malfeasance as an official, "whereas the pending charges accuse him of acts which are not those of an official, but of a simple member; hence only triable by his own Branch or Lodge (*vide* Section 3 of Article XIII), at a special meeting called to consider the facts."

Another important point made by Mr. Judge was that the principal charge against him could not be tried without breach of the constitutional neutrality of The Theosophical Society in matters of private belief. In other words, to try him on the charge of forging the handwriting of certain Masters, sending out fraudulent messages in their names, and so on, was to imply that the Society officially accepted the existence of Mahatmas or Masters as a creed or dogma.

After deliberation, the Judicial Committee resolved that "the charges are not such as relate to the conduct of the Vice-President in his official capacity, and therefore are not subject to this jurisdiction." It also expressed the opinion that a statement made by it "as to the truth or otherwise of at least one of the charges as formulated against Mr. Judge would involve a declaration as to the existence or non-existence of the Mahatmas which would be a violation of the neutrality and unsectarian nature of the Society."

The Colonel put the matter this way: "Nobody, for example, knows better than myself the fact of the existence of the Masters, yet I would resign my office unhesitatingly if the Constitution were amended so as to erect such a belief as a dogma: everyone in our membership is as free to disbelieve and deny their existence as I am to believe and affirm it."

So the trial of Mr. Judge fell through. There was some talk of laying the charges before a Committee of Honor, but this also came to nothing.

Then two days later, on July 12, two statements were read to the members of the European convention. One was by Mrs. Besant. It gave in essence the history of the circumstances of the Judge case from her point of view. It was purposely lenient, overlooking his use of the seal and certain other aspects of the case. The crux of her statement was that she believed Judge to be an occultist, often receiving messages from the Masters, or their *chelas,* in various ways, but *not* by direct writing by the Master, *nor* by direct precipitation. Where Mr. Judge had erred, she maintained, was in letting people assume that written Mahatmic messages, issued to them by the Vice-President, had been actually written or precipitated directly by the Master himself. This procedure she regarded as illegitimate. Anything written by the receiver's own hand, whether automatically or consciously, should be proclaimed as such in order to leave no false impressions. She herself, she declared, had gained false impressions from Mr. Judge in this way.

The second statement to the convention was by Mr. Judge himself. The gist of it was that he denied the charges of forging the names and handwritings of the Mahatmas or of misusing the same. Whatever messages from the Mahatmas he had delivered he declared were genuine, so far as his knowledge extended. "They were obtained through me," he said, "but as to how they were obtained or produced I cannot state." Further on he said: "I have done my best to report—in the few instances when I have done it at all—correctly and truthfully such messages as I think I have received for transmission. . . ."

With these two statements, and the private conversations that went on around them, it was hoped that the whole unpleasant business would be closed. Mr. Judge's friends, and people who felt that he should not be required to make any explanation, were pleased with the outcome. But other members felt that his escape had been through a technicality and he should clear the air by giving a full explanation. So the Society throughout the world remained split into two factions—anti-Judge and pro-Judge. There was still anger and indignation on both sides. Nothing had really been settled by the abortive meeting of the Judicial Committee and the two public statements.

*   *   *

After a trip to Berlin and a tour of branches in Britain, the Colonel was back in "charming Adyar" by September 19. There he found a very angry man—the tall, angular Walter Old who held the two important positions of Treasurer and Recording Secretary. He listened contemptuously to a detailed account of what had gone on in London and promptly resigned as "unable to accept the official statement with regard to the enquiries held upon the charges proferred against the Vice-President of the T.S."

He had a perfect right to do this, the Colonel said, but not the shadow of a right to his next action. He had earlier made copies of the documentary evidence in the Judge case —to which he had official access as Recording Secretary—and these private and confidential documents he took to England and put "into the hands of one of the most unsympathetic and caustic literary experts on the London press."

It was not long before they began to appear in the *Westminster Gazette*. The Colonel's diary for November 20, 1894 says: "Foreign mail in. Old has published 8 chapters of a series in which the entire private papers of the Judge case are included. A caddish act." Six days later he wrote: "Old's series of attacks and exposures of Judge case are completed. Beastly caddishness!" So the trial by press and public opinion was on. This was an ill-informed, caustic and abusive trial not only of Judge, but also of the leaders of The Theosophical Society who, it was declared, had hushed up and condoned the Vice-President's misdemeanors. Pandora's box was open, and what ensued was marked more by emotionalism than by calm good sense and sagacity. Misunderstandings, bitterness, antagonism—in fact, all that jungle of emotions which the true theosophist works to subdue—were soon on public display.

"Judge informs me that Mahatma Morya has made him sole Head of the E.S.T. (Esoteric Section of Theosophy) and Annie is turned out! A nice mess cooking!" writes Olcott early in December. The "mess" was that Judge had issued a circular called *By Master's Direction*. It was supposed to be addressed to members of the Esoteric Section only, but somehow found its way into the public press.

Up to this time, following H.P.B.'s death, Judge and Annie Besant had shared the Headship of the E.S.T., he in America and she in Europe. Now Judge wrote: "Under the authority given me by the Master and H.P.B. and under Master's direction, I declare Mrs. Annie Besant's headship in the E.S.T. at an end." The reason he gave was that Mrs. Besant had become, unknown to herself, a vehicle of the dark forces that were plotting to overthrow the Society. In order to do this, these forces had influenced certain Brahmins in India—working through racial pride, religious prejudice, and personal ambitions. The chief living agent in use among the Brahmins, Judge declared, was Gyanendra N. Chakravarti of Allahabad who had spoken on Brahminism very successfully at the Parliament of Religions in Chicago, 1893. Annie Besant, he said, had come under Chakravarti's hypnotic influence.

Dr. Archibald Keightley, who was now very much of the Judge faction, backed up this idea that Mrs. Besant was under the domination of Chakravarti. He had seen the process taking place at the London headquarters, he said, when Chakravarti was there in 1893. The Brahmin used to make magnetic passes over Mrs. Besant, ostensibly for the purpose of coordinating her subtle bodies. But A. Keightley gave as his opinion, as a physician, "that the magnetism of a woman advanced in the critical age of mid-life, a vegetarian, an ascetic, by a man, a meat eater, one of full habit, large appetite and of another and dark race, is not wise. The latter magnetism will assuredly overcome the former, however excellent the intentions of both persons." He went on to say that he had seen an entire change of view in Mrs.

Besant as a result of this magnetism.

The Colonel was very indignant about such accusations concerning "an unselfish, loyal friend" and a "sister of the distressed and the oppressed." He was almost equally appalled that Professor Chakravarti, "one of the most brilliant scholars of modern India, whose private career is without a stain and whose life has been lived in sight of the whole world," should be thus publicly impeached as a tool of invisible dark forces.

While this attack on Annie Besant was being made through private circulars and public press, she was far away on a lecture tour, stirring Australian and New Zealand audiences with her eloquence. Reporters of the leading Australian metropolitan newspapers wrote enthusiastic pieces about her public lectures: "Probably the most eloquent discourse ever delivered from a platform in this city. . ." "One of the extraordinary features of Mrs. Besant's charm and force as an orator is that . . . she always manages to deal with her subject in an attractive light, gripping the attention of her audience at the start, and by force of her oratory, the perspicuity of her reasoning, and the instructiveness of her matter, never releasing that hold until the end."

She was in New Zealand when she received word of Judge's attack "exposing" her as a false teacher, a vehicle of the dark forces, and expelling her from the Esoteric Section of the Society. Not knowing what had really occurred, and feeling that there must be some mistake, she withheld her reply until she returned to India at the end of the year.

Mrs. Besant resigned her office as President of the Blavatsky Lodge in order not to involve that body in the public charges made against her. The lodge, however, unanimously re-elected her to the office. When she reached India from Australasia she replied to the charges against her through the Indian and British press and a pamphlet, of which 20,000 copies were circulated to Theosophical Society members throughout the world.

At the convention at Adyar in December 1894 the President read his address and then a debate on the Judge affair ensued. Following a fair-minded exposition of matters as she saw them, Mrs. Besant moved a resolution that the President be requested to call upon Mr. W. Q. Judge to resign the office of Vice-President, "it being of course open to Mr. Judge, if he so wishes, to submit himself for re-election, so that the Society may pass its judgement on his position."

It was, she declared, the immemorial custom for every honorable man holding a representative office in any society to tender his resignation under such circumstances as existed (she had done so herself). Mr. Judge should be ready to resign, particularly as he held the office for life, or rather during the life of Colonel Olcott, the President-Founder.

Mr. Bertram Keightley seconded the resolution. There was considerable debate, some members wanting the Vice-President to be expelled from the Society. Mrs. Besant spoke strongly against this proposal of expulsion; it would put "another stigma on him in the face of the world," she said.

Her whole speech concerning Mr. Judge was "full of kindly compassion, free from even a tinge of malice," observed the Colonel. Amendments for more drastic action against Mr. Judge being finally withdrawn or defeated, Mrs. Besant's resolution was put to the vote and carried, *nem. con.*

"This means secession of the American Section," prophesied Olcott unhappily in his diary for that Christmas Day.

Judge refused to resign, and there followed a bitter, most untheosophical war of words in the theosophical journals of the day, such as *Lucifer* in London and *The Path* (Mr. Judge's journal) in America. Spearheading the attack on the anti-Judge side was George Mead, M.A., classical scholar of Cambridge and General Secretary of the British Section of The Theosophical Society. Of the pro-Judge faction Dr. Archibald Keightley seems to have wielded the most prolific and most sarcastic pen. He was also a Cambridge man and a year older than his uncle Bertram who belonged to the opposite camp. Others joined the verbal battle as misunderstandings multiplied, feelings flamed, and the ethics of true Theosophy were laid aside.

The supporters of Judge contended that he was correct in not resigning because, if he did so, it would be taken in America as an admission of guilt. To attack Judge on the grounds that he had himself written the Mahatma messages was to show ignorance of occult matters, they claimed. And, as proof, they quoted something H.P.B. had written in *Lucifer*:

> It is hardly one of a hundred 'occult' letters that is ever written by the hand of the Master in whose name and on whose behalf they are sent, as the Masters have neither need nor leisure to write them; when a Master says, 'I wrote that letter,' it means only that every word in it was dictated by him and impressed under his direct supervision. Generally they make their *chela,* whether near or far away, write (or precipitate) them, by impressing upon his mind the ideas they wish expressed and if necessary aiding him in the picture-printing processes.*

Those who believed Mr. Judge innocent, and supported his actions, quoted H.P.B. as saying in 1888 that Judge was then "a *chela* of 14 years standing." In 1874 he had, like Henry Olcott, begun his occult education under H.P.B. and had become a *chela* of the Masters. The assumption was that it was legitimate for him as a *chela* to write down in the Master's script any messages received through his *psi* faculty from the Master.

The Colonel and Annie Besant show in their writings that they, along with many other Theosophists, knew this fact about Mahatmic communications well enough. But they considered that in delivering the messages to other people, Judge intentionally gave the impression that letters were actually precipitated, or written, by one of the Masters. Judge's accusers also suspected that lower forces, masquerading as Masters, could be the influence behind some of the messages.

The scribes of the pro-Judge faction countered by supporting Judge's accusations that Mrs. Besant had come under the hypnotic influence of Professor Chakravarti, who was himself an agent of the dark forces; they quoted from a Mahatma letter to Sinnett in which some of the rigidly orthodox Brahmins of Allahabad are criticized.* Chakravarti belonged to this group of Brahmins which, according to the Judge supporters, was very much against The Theosophical

---

* See "Lodges of Magic", Lucifer, III, 93.
* See *The Mahatma Letters to A. P. Sinnett,* Appendix, Letter No. 134.

Society's practice of giving the precious esoteric teachings of India to all and sundry. Behind this pride of caste were the "dark powers" which were working against the spread of enlightenment.

The anti-Judge party considered this a very weak story. They pointed out that earlier in the year, when Judge made his accusations *against* Chakravarti—that is, 1894—he had written to Chakravarti offering support if the latter would consent to be the next President of The Theosophical Society. "If I cannot get you to look with favor on it [the idea of being President] then my next idea will be to keep thinking of your coming to work here [America], and keep wishing that Olcott may live for twenty years, so that I could work here with you and for you."

These overtures to the Brahmin Professor, thought some, were part of Judge's tactics to keep Mrs. Besant out of the position he coveted for himself.

Nonsense! countered their opponents. Judge knew nothing about the machinations of the Allahabad Brahmins and dark forces when he wrote that letter; he was then a great admirer of Chakravarti. It was Master who had enlightened Judge on the situation when later, in 1894, he gave the message entitled: "By Master's Direction."

Can anyone really know what the facts were behind all this thrust and parry? What were Judge's real motives, and what did he actually believe about the source of his controversial "messages?"

Alice Cleather, a fervent Judge follower, wrote years after the latter had died that his only fault in this matter was in "permitting himself to come under the powerful hypnotic influence of a professional psychic and trance medium, named Katherine Tingley." Alice Cleather knew this lady personally and states: "She had intended and planned—probably from the first—to obtain control of the American Section of the T.S. . . . . I discovered that most—if not all—of those [the Mahatma messages] which Judge gave out as having been received by him had come through Mrs. Tingley. . ."

The paper "By Master's Direction" was, said Alice Cleather, "written by Mr. Judge, but dictated by Mrs. Tingley."

However, Mrs. Tingley denied being a medium and testified in court that she was not.

Dr. J. D. Buck, an ardent follower of Judge, expressed what must have been the attitude of many people in America at that time. "I do not know," he said, "and have no means of knowing, the source or methods of Mr. Judge's communications with the Masters, but have supported Mr. Judge solely on my own knowledge of his work and character, deeming the matters involved in the said communications incapable of proof or disproof."

The Colonel himself thought that the demon called personal ambition had got the upper hand of his old co-worker, W. Q. Judge; that in consequence he had carried on a campaign to make himself the sole successor of H.P.B. as head of the Esoteric Section, and secure himself as the heir apparent to the Presidency of The Theosophical Society. Judge had escaped trial by his peers through the loophole of a technicality and had refused any explanation that would allay world-wide suspicions. Then, thought the Colonel, on the principle that attack is the best form of defense, he had brought the cruel charges against Mrs. Besant.

In the early months of 1895, letters and circulars from the outside world began to reach Olcott at "Gulistan" where he was working on *Old Diary Leaves*. On April 1 he wrote in his diary: "The Judge party are very active and aggressive, and assuredly we are at a crisis in the United States."

On May 10 he left India for Europe where he planned to tour Spain and other parts of the Continent and England on theosophical work. The case of the Vice-Presidency, from which Mr. Judge had refused to resign, was due to be considered at a General Council meeting at the headquarters of the European Section, 19 Avenue Road, London, on July 7. Henry had been invited to reside personally at Avenue Road while in London.

But when he landed at Marseilles on May 30 he received the news, not altogether unexpected, that W. Q. Judge was no longer a part of the Society. He had seceded, taking most of the lodges in the American Section with him.

Later the President learned that the secession of the American Section had been officially declared at a convention at

Boston on April 28. Dr. Buck had earlier circularized members and lodges of the Section giving reasons why he considered that the Theosophical organization should no longer be one society, but that sections should manage their own affairs entirely, as "No executive or general officer can exercise jurisdiction all over the globe." He urged the American Section "to pass unanimously a vote of secession and declare their entire autonomy. . ."

This the delegates did at the convention, but not quite unanimously. There were a few dissenters, the chief one being Mr. Alexander Fullerton, the man who had once come to Adyar to help the Colonel, but unable to bear the tranquility of the place after the bustle of New York in the 1880's, had returned in a few days. Now he made a speech in which he declared bluntly that there was "no occasion for the proposed Secession except to relieve Mr. Judge from replying to the charges against him."

But such words fell on deaf ears among the delegates, nearly all of whom were staunch Judge followers. Resolutions for secession and for appointing Mr. Judge Perpetual President of the "Theosophical Society, the Western Hemisphere" were passed by an overwhelming majority.

So it had come about—the disintegration Henry had feared since the death of H.P.B. He had always believed that a unified world-wide organization was the best vehicle for the teachings of the Masters. Theosophy should be able to speak with one voice. A powerful, unified bastion of truth was necessary in the swirling ocean of materialism.

But now the bastion was split in two. Henry felt at first that his work had been faulty, that he had failed the Masters. But at the age of 63 he was an old seasoned campaigner. He did not waste much time bewailing the loss. After all, there were still ten lodges in America loyal to the international flag. They were asking his leadership, asking to be incorporated officially as the new American Section of the world organization. Alexander Fullerton was acting as their General Secretary *pro tem.*

So all was not lost. There remained a sturdy, well-tried foundation on which he could build a bigger, stronger section—loyal to the basic truths and aims of the original So-

ciety. The storms of passion and personality had merely
carried away that which was somehow faulty in its structure.

As for Judge's new independent "Theosophical Society,
the Western Hemisphere"—that had no existence in the
Colonel's mind.*

<hr />

* The story relating to Mr. Judge is of course given as seen through the
eyes of Colonel Olcott in this biography, which is not the way Mr. Judge and
those supporting him saw it. There are many people today who greatly respect the memory of William Quan Judge, and his writings are still being
published and widely read.

Chapter 22

"GREEN OLD AGE"
1896 · 1906

One morning early in the year 1896 Count Louis Hamon —better known as Cheiro, famous prophet to kings and emperors—found awaiting him in his New York rooms a short, bearded man and a "remarkably handsome woman." They had come for a reading.

Looking into the man's palm, Cheiro told him bluntly: "You have reached the last chapter of your life."

Later the man asked him: "What do you see in the lady's future?"

"She has reached the most important year of her life. If she is connected with your career, she will take your place and carry on after you have gone. She will achieve some fame. . ."

Greatly interested in the woman's powerful personality, Cheiro asked if he could take impressions of her hands. She agreed, and after the impressions were made, signed them: "Katherine A. Tingley." Her companion then introduced himself as William Q. Judge, President of the Theosophical Society, Western Hemisphere.*

A few months after this, on March 21, 1896, W. Q. Judge died. Mrs. Katherine Tingley became his successor as President, and most of his followers accepted her leadership.

But what of the rump that was left to Olcott after Judge had sliced away the main body of Americans? It did not wither away as expected by its opponents. The Colonel was prompt to document it as the official American Section. Alexander Fullerton—a Princeton man, lawyer, and Episcopalian priest—was confirmed as its General Secretary.

---

* See *Mysteries and Romances of the World's Greatest Occultists,* by Cheiro.

The Colonel dispatched two of his lieutenants to assist Fullerton in building up the shattered American Section. In a six-months lecture tour of America the intrepid Annie Besant formed twenty-three new branches. The other lieutenant, Countess Wachtmeister, who despite "her age and growing infirmities" traveled over most of the country, was able to establish fourteen new branches.

The President, who himself toured Australia that year, wrote later in *Old Diary Leaves*: "The phenomenal growth of our Society during the year 1897 had no parallel in our previous history. Sixty-four new branches were added to the list. . . Deducting branches seceded, we had 402 living charters and recognized Centers remaining".

*　　*　　*

THE COLONEL

A merry man—they tell—whose Jove-like beard,
True to conceit, masked to the very end
A jovial youth-in-age; high Wisdom's friend,
E'en as old friends should be—by use endeared,
Familiar, warm and hearty; one that feared
But to be feared; whose lavish heart would lend
Its gold unasked for weaker hearts to spend,
Nor interest seek, save that they should be cheered.
A merry man—why not? True Wisdom's wage
Is counted not in coinage of sad looks:
She hath another reckoning for her books,
And pays in gladness. He is on her roll
As one that blithely bore to green old age
Burdens that would have crushed a sadder soul.

E. A. WODEHOUSE.

(The writer of this sonnet was a brother of the famous P. G. Wodehouse and Professor of English Literature at Elphinstone College, Bombay, in 1905. He knew the Colonel well.)

As the years wore on toward the close of the century, the Colonel kept busy as usual, despite some bouts of suffering and semi-invalidism through his gouty foot. One project he continued to work on during these years was the betterment of the lot of the Pariahs.

His educational movement for them, started modestly with the one school in 1894, had proved popular, and new centers were in demand. In 1898 he opened a second suburban school, calling it after his old chum "The H.P.B. Memorial School." Next year he started the third school, "The Damodar Free School." Two more appeared during the next few years.

Funds to help in these pioneer efforts came largely from the United States, Alexander Fullerton being one of the "fairy godfathers." Miss Sarah E. Palmer, B.S., of Wisconsin, and other teachers, came from abroad to help in this humanitarian work. Miss Palmer introduced the ideals of kindergarten, hitherto unknown in Madras, and it was not long before teachers from the caste schools were visiting Olcott's outcaste schools to study the new methods.

Then as Henry had dreamed, more hammers were raised. Sir Arthur Havelock, Governor of Madras, visited the Olcott Free School. Recognition and financial aid followed. The Madras Corporation opened more schools for Pariahs, and in 1925 took over responsibility for three of the five schools started by Olcott. In 1933 the H.P.B. School was handed over to the Madras government. The original school was left to be run by a Board of Management, whose Chairman must be the President of the international Theosophical Society.*

There was a tradition among the Pariahs that they had long years before been Buddhists, but through force of arms had lost their religion and been made outcastes. Many wanted to return to the shelter and dignity of the Buddhist faith, and the Colonel did his best to help them. He took several of their representatives to Ceylon where they received Pansil from the High Priest. Others followed this lead and became Buddhists. But the movement did not go forward as expected, and today most of these casteless people still worship on traditional Hindu lines.

---

* Today the Olcott Memorial School, located at the original site where Col. Olcott established the first school in 1894, and a primary school at the fishing village of Olcott Kuppam, on the beach adjoining The Theosophical Society's estate, continue to be run by this Board of Management. There are more than 1,000 pupils attending these schools, which are supported by funds from all over the world.

Olcott Memorial School at Adyar

But the Colonel's hammer on the mountain—symbolic of his whole theosophical work—set loose the rocks that started an inexorable landslide. The very names by which these people were known have vanished. We no longer hear of Untouchables, Outcastes, Pariahs. The first name change was to Panchamas, and then through the compassionate vision of Mahatma Gandhi they were called Harijans (Children of God). What a difference! The new name represents a new outlook, a new social conscience toward these people.

And though the mountain of prejudice still remains, who shall say that Olcott's brave hammer and mustard seed of faith did not start a disintegration that will eventually wash it away to the all-leveling seas?

The Colonel's work for education was not confined to his efforts for the underprivileged. Right from the beginning of his time in India he encouraged the foundation of Sanskrit colleges under the auspices of the Society. Also during his long lecture tours through the country he formed a number of boys' clubs and societies. In 1884 he formed the Aryan League of Honor for teenage boys. Some of its aims were to break down the artificial exclusiveness of caste that he found everywhere; also to stimulate pride in the great cultural heritage of India's past and encourage the youths to live up to the high moral standards of that heritage. Youths of the Hindu, Parsi (Zoroastrian), Buddhist, and Jain religions could become members.

This work for the rising generation was part of Olcott's great love for Mother India, the land of his Master, the fountainhead of the world's spiritual life. Mother India was suffering a temporary eclipse—an eclipse a few centuries old —but the day was coming when she would rise phoenix-like from her ashes. He was working hard to hasten that day.*

The President was glad that Annie Besant, relatively young and vital, was there to carry on the work. She un-

---

* Educationist, Dr. Kewal Motwani, writes in a biographical sketch of the Colonel: "As a result of his fervent appeal to the patriotic instincts of the people, seventeen of those present at the annual Convention of the T.S., 1884, formed the Indian National Union, changed to the Indian National Congress the following year, 'to serve the Motherland'. Strictly speaking, Olcott was the Father of the Indian National Congress, though the title was given to Mr. A. O. Hume . . ."

derstood and could expound the profound subtleties of Hinduism better than he. Nevertheless he had himself reached down to the luminous heart of the Hindu religion. This heart was the perennial philosophy, the esoteric truths taught him first by H.P.B. On this The Theosophical Society was founded. On this he lectured. For the rebirth, the fuller understanding and realization of this, he had traveled the burning leagues of India in jolting trains and springless bullock carts.

There were some—the narrower variety of Hindus—who thought the President leaned too far toward Buddhism. Yet there were many more balanced ones who appreciated the dedicated work he was doing for the Aryavarta of old, the spiritual India.

One of these latter was the learned pundit lexicographer, Taranath Tarka Vachaspati. This gentleman of Calcutta, author of a well-known Sanskrit dictionary, paid Henry an honor rarely, if ever, received by a Westerner; the pundit invested him with the sacred thread of the Brahmin caste and adopted him into his own *gothra* (family tree).

The Colonel accepted the honor with deep pleasure. He had always felt a blood-brotherhood with the Indians, whatever their caste. In many ways he felt closer to them than to his own American people. Unlike the British in India, Henry seldom dressed in a way that marked him out as different from the Indians. He adopted the native dress which he felt was much more appropriate to the climate than the tight hot clothes, tight shoes, stifling collars, and ridiculous ties in which the Westerners tortured themselves to be superior.

Indian photographs usually show him in the wide, loose, native-style cotton trousers, and the long, collarless shirt known as a *kurtha*; on his feet are mostly *chappals* (sandals), while a black round cap often crowns his snowy locks.

Henry Olcott was one who always tried to practice in his daily life the first object of his child, The Theosophical Society, that is, brotherhood toward all, without distinction of race, creed, sex, caste or color.

A half century after Henry's death, one old pupil of the Olcott Free School wrote about how the elderly President

Olcott in Indian Dress

The Theosophical Society headquarters building at Adyar today. The Adyar Library formerly occupied right wing.

used to take the school boys swimming in the Adyar river and perform comic acts to amuse them—things like "floating on his back on the water while he smoked a cigar and read a newspaper." The fishermen, poor and quite untouchable to Henry's Brahmin brothers, would come around to see the fun. After his swim and bath, the President would call the fishermen to his room and give them presents of sweetmeats, rice, and money.

Another of his old admirers recalled how once a dirty, ragged *jutkawallah* was driving his primitive cart in front of the big hall during a convention. Large, well-dressed crowds were standing about talking on the lawns in front of the building.

The pony got into some tangle with its harness, and the old driver went to free it. Suddenly the pony kicked him in the stomach and the man fell in a heap. Before the people nearby could make a move to help the prostrate man, the Colonel had rushed from the verandah some distance away, where he had been talking to friends, gathered the grimy *jutkawallah* into his arms, and carried him to a safe place. There he administered first aid and magnetic healing until the driver recovered. Then Olcott, an expert in such matters, fixed the pony's harness, and the old *jutkawallah* drove off, showering his blessings on the President.

The years near the turn of the century saw the President consolidating his Society gains and expanding into new areas. At Adyar there was plenty of building work to be done—enlarging the library, extending and decorating the Convention Hall, and other projects for making the world headquarters a place of serenity and beauty. To him this was important work, for: " 'Adyar' is not a place only, it is a principle. It is a name which ought to carry with it a power far greater than that conveyed by the name 'Rome.' "

Any spare moments were devoted to writing *Old Diary Leaves*, which continued as installments in *The Theosophist*. The early part of the series was now out in book form, and he notes in his diary that royalties on its sale had brought him £22 for a six months period in 1899.

The Colonel spent much time supervising the modeling of a statue of H.P.B. This was done by a sculptor of the

Statues of H. P. Blavatsky and H. S. Olcott
in Headquarters Hall at Adyar

School of Arts in Madras. In May 1899 H.P.B.'s statue came home to Adyar and was placed on its pedestal at the head of the Convention Hall. It was there just in time to be unveiled on White Lotus Day, when Theosophists throughout the world celebrate, at her own request, H.P.B.'s passing from her body. "*May 8th, 1899*: At noon 300 fisher-people and Pariahs were fed, and received copper coins. . . At 5:30 p.m. meeting held . . . statue unveiled.* Enthusiasm. I pinned a Blavatsky statue medal on breast of Govinda Pillay, the sculptor."

*   *   *

The first year of the new century brought another journey to Europe, his ninth since founding the Society, and a long lecture tour. In Italy he met Mary and Lucy Olcott, wife and daughter of his brother Bob. The charming young Lucy was the next year married to Frederick Mason Perkins, a well-known American art critic living in Italy. Later, in Germany, Olcott's favorite niece, Louise Mitchell—Belle's daughter—joined him on the tour and went with him to London.

The Colonel was on board ship at Hong Kong in January 1901 when the Victorian Age merged in the Edwardian. News of the old Queen's death "was signalled to us at the Lighthouse. Half-masteded flag. Grief of passengers; ladies cried. . ."

He was at the time on his way to the West Coast of America via Honolulu at which place he stopped off, was received officially by Queen Liliuokalani, and started a branch of The Theosophical Society.

At San Francisco brother Bob called to visit him, and he set off on an extensive tour of the States, lecturing at over thirty centers. One of the places visited was Elyria, Ohio, where half a century earlier he had made his life's start as a young farmer. "All changed and people nearly all dead," he notes.

After the American tour he broke new ground by going to Buenos Aires in the Argentine. In this stronghold of

---

* Later, after his death, a statue of Olcott was placed alongside that of his colleague, his arm resting on her shoulder.

Spanish Catholicism a Theosophical Center was struggling into birth, and the Colonel went to act as its midwife and nurse. He gave lectures at several centers, including the public library in the Government Palace at La Plata. "Very distinguished audience of 400 Senators, Deputies, Judges of High Court, Ministers of Cabinet, Professors, etc., and many ladies. Spoke over an hour in French fluently. Much praise and applause."

In addition to his travels in the new world, Henry toured a few places in Europe, and was back at Adyar on November 21: "Rest after 46,000 miles of tour. Home looks lovely in the monsoon. . ."

Sliding into his 70's, the Colonel was hale and hearty except for one trouble. The rheumatic complaint, known in his day as gout, came back to him again and again. At its worst it affected his feet, legs and arms. Sometimes it immobilized him completely or forced him onto crutches. In 1902, the worst year, he suffered for 77 days at a stretch.

Nevertheless, as soon as the crippling bouts were over, the Colonel was again a dynamo of energy: playing tennis at seven in the morning for exercise, writing, organizing, lecturing, and traveling. And now not only the kings and cabinet ministers of foreign lands, but even the British elite were accepting this venerable, white-bearded old man. Time had somehow made him and his odd mission respectable.

This reached a high in 1906 when the Prince and Princess of Wales visited India. On January 24 the President of The Theosophical Society "attended a levee of the Prince of Wales and was presented." Two days later he went to a State reception and was delighted that the Prince and Princess talked with him. "Prince knew my name and asked why I came to India."

Evidently Prince George—later George V—had no notion that the old American Colonel, by reviving India's pride in herself and her culture, was indirectly—but surely—undermining imperial power in this jewel of empire.

Henry himself was no longer the poor man that he had been since bidding goodbye to his law office in New York, living frugally and keeping a tight rein on personal expenses; his only standby had been the profit from the publication of

The Theosophist, and a few books—an income averaging about 2,500 rupees a year. This he had shared for some years with H.P.B.

Out of such a small sum, he could not, of course, finance his many long journeys abroad, but these were usually paid for by the organizations inviting him—the Buddhist groups or Theosophical Sections concerned. For this very reason he kept an even closer watch on his traveling expenses, staying at the cheaper hotels, when not a guest in a private home, and traveling second-class on ships.

Then in 1903 he received the heartening news that an old friend and member of the Society, living in Havana, Cuba, had left him a legacy. Owing to many legal complications, this involved a six-months sojourn in Europe. Then, in September 1903, he went to Havana and spent about a month there. The legal matters concerning the legacy seemed to be settled by the time he returned to India early in December 1903.

But there were further problems and delays, extending throughout most of the following year, and it was not until the end of 1904 that he finally received the money. On January 7, 1905 he states in his diary that he had acknowledged the settlement of the affair with the receipt of Rs. 125,370 as his share of his deceased friend's estate. It was a tidy sum then, and he wondered how much more time was left for the enjoyment of such affluence. His own desires were practically nil, beyond the bare necessities for living, but he looked forward to the prospect of spending the money on the cause he held so dear.

During 1905 he transferred the proprietorship of his small publishing business and his "Gulistan" property to The Theosophical Society, which had by then been registered as a legal entity.

The year that had begun so rosily with royal levees and receptions—1906—was to see the end of the Colonel's long period of relative tranquility. This, his last full year on earth, was to be a very eventful one.

It brought first a temblor that threatened to shake down a few theosophical edifices. The center of trouble was Charles Webster Leadbeater. In the twenty-two years since he landed in India with H.P.B., at the height of the Coulomb-missionary troubles, C.W.L. (as he was called) had served the theosophical cause faithfully and well in many capacities. He had helped promote Buddhist interests and education, edited *The Theosophist,* acted as Recording Secretary at headquarters, lectured, administered, and developed his great faculty as a clairvoyant investigator.

The Colonel had a high opinion of Charles as a reliable young man who put the cause before his own interests; he was a seer and a prolific writer on theosophical themes. And yes, he was even a potential future President of the Society.

Then came a thunderclap out of the clear blue. At the time C.W.L. was acting as tutor to some boys, sons of theosophical families in America. One youth, who had reached the age of puberty, was obsessed with overpowering sex urges and their attendant frustrations and fantasies. He asked his tutor for advice.

It was a special case and C.W.L. studied it as such, even employing his clairvoyant powers to detect associated forces and influences on other planes. Eventually, it was alleged, he advised masturbation.

The boy told his parents, and soon the theosophical seismograph was registering shocks around the world. Ex-churchman, theosophical lecturer, teacher and tutor, *chela* of the Mahatmas, C. W. Leadbeater was teaching unnatural and dangerous sex practices to boys!

Annie Besant was appalled at the news of the teachings and expressed her feelings strongly to friends. Later, however, she wrote a statement to say that she had accepted the allegations against Leadbeater without hearing the facts directly from him. These were in essence that Mr. Leadbeater had not encouraged the practice of masturbation, but since the boy could not stop it immediately, he was advised to lessen the frequency of his self-indulgence, gradually lengthening the intervals until it might at last be entirely renounced. Nowadays, with more liberal views on sex education, reactions to this advice would probably not result in such an outcry.

Olcott's diary shows that he, too, certainly did not approve of the alleged teachings, but he expressed no strong emotions

H. S. Olcott, Annie Besant and C. W. Leadbeater
at Adyar convention, 1905

on the question. Perhaps this was because the Colonel had lived long and mixed with peoples of many cultures, and nothing surprised him any more. His own attitude toward sex was that of the practical occultist who must come to good terms with this powerful biological force or be sabotaged by it. There is nothing in the records to show that sex played any active part in Henry's life after he became a *chela* of the secret Brotherhood. He seems to have sublimated it in his all-absorbing work.

As for the age-old problem of unmarried, highly-sexed youths, he—like his contemporaries—had no answer. Is it to be tortured frustrations, free love, promiscuity, brothels, early marriage? All have been tried at some time and place in history, and each has its drawbacks—economic, social, or psychological.

The exaggerated rumors continued. The written protests, the letters of disgust and indignation began to pour in. The hounds were baying for theosophical blood. It looked as if C.W.L. would have to go if reports were true. What a pity, thought Olcott; he had been such a promising member!

This was one of several problems, certainly the most unpleasant one, that the President-Founder had to face when he sailed westward for Europe and America in March 1906.

Chapter 23

"LITTLE MOTHER"

1906

The Colonel sat on deck feeling rather worried. England was drawing close; in fact they were due at Southampton tomorrow, four days ahead of his scheduled time of arrival. No one was expecting him; he had no idea where he was supposed to stay and, to make matters worse, tomorrow was Easter Monday. If he knew the English—and he did—everyone would be away from home and office, enjoying the holiday.

Back in Genoa he had been alarmed when informed that the ship on which he had come from India en route to England was to be quarantined because of an infection among the steerage passengers. Then he thought it a great stroke of luck when the Captain, an old friend, had quietly transferred him to another ship just leaving for Southampton. There had been no chance to send word to his friends in England about the change in his time and port of arrival.

Well, it was better than still being stuck back in Genoa. He knew London, and would find some digs somewhere.

Early the next morning his ship docked at Southampton. Henry had finished breakfast and was about to pack his few things when a knock came on his cabin door. Opening it, he beheld an elegantly dressed, attractive woman of about forty. Her eyes searched his face: "Are you Colonel Olcott?"

"I am—but who in the world might you be? No one in all England knew I was arriving on this ship."

"My father sent me to meet you. I told you about my father when I wrote to you earlier this year about joining your Society. My name is Marie Russak. You have forgotten. . ."

"No, I have not. But, come in and sit down."

Now it was ringing a bell in Henry's memory. Marie Russak—yes, the young lady who had intrigued him with her letter about how her father had appeared to her soon after death, and told her to study some books on Theosophy because these would solve many problems of life then troubling her. He had told her not to use spiritualistic mediums for contacting him, but to learn to meditate as taught in Theosophy; by that means she would reach him in her deep sleep state, and in time learn to remember the meetings.

Marie had obeyed, studying all the books available on Theosophy, living in seclusion as much as possible, and practicing meditation. Soon she was able to remember being with her father during the nights . . . remembering the advice and help he gave, leading her to the study of comparative philosophy in addition to Theosophy.

After about six years of such study and meditation practice, her spirit father told her to join The Theosophical Society. Marie was delighted at this prospect. It would surely be wonderful to join such "a company of truth-seekers, where peace and happiness reigned!" And so she had written to the President.

Now in the cabin she explained to him that a few days earlier while she was staying in Dresden, Germany, she awoke with the clear memory that her father had told her to go to Southampton, England, to meet Colonel Olcott who would be arriving on a ship from India during the Easter weekend. As further instructed by her father, she had booked hotel accommodation for the Colonel in London and then come on to Southampton.

"Wonderful . . . wonderful!" the Colonel nodded thoughtfully. "Just at the time I need you, too—in more ways than one." Then, slapping his half-packed trunk, he said: "Well let's pack up and be off to London, little Mother!"

Marie Russak writes in her "Memories of Colonel Olcott" how from that day on he always addressed her as "Little Mother." She believed that, in fact, she had been his mother in an earlier incarnation.

On the boat-train to London they sat at a little table having luncheon. The Colonel, she writes, accepted each

Marie Russak (1867-1937)

course of the *table d'hôte* as it came. But Marie refused the meats.

"Are you one of those 'hay-eaters' then?" joked Olcott. Then he laughed heartily at her obvious amazement in finding that the President-Founder of The Theosophical Society was a flesh-eater. He told her of his long struggle on the matter of diet.

Soon after going to India he gave vegetarianism a trial, he said, and kept it up for five years. Then, during 1887, his health and vitality had got so low that the doctors ordered him back onto a meat diet, beginning with chicken broth.

A couple of years later, being told that it would relieve his hereditary gout, he gave up meat again. But his way of life—shipboard travel, living in hotels, guest houses, homes of friends—made it difficult, if not quite impossible, to remain a strict vegetarian. It caused too much fuss and bother to other people, and he frankly did not consider the question of food that important. So he went back to eating whatever was available.

Marie Russak had booked a suite of rooms for the Colonel at the first-class Grosvenor Hotel, while she and a friend, Margaret Clifford, occupied another suite there. They had some fine talks on Theosophy and The Theosophical Society before the London members returning from their Easter holidays learned of the Colonel's presence in London.

Then Marie gave an afternoon tea at the hotel for some of the Colonel's friends. Among them, she recalls, were Mr. and Mrs. Sinnett, Bertram Keightley, William (later Sir William) and Lady Crookes.

Day by day, after that, visitors were pouring into the hotel suite, and there were many discussions on theosophical matters. Marie, sitting away in a corner, was amazed at all she heard. "Heated discussions and arguments centered around a great crisis in the Society occurring at the time, and those present overwhelmed the Colonel with their different critical opinions," she writes. The crisis was of course the C. W. Leadbeater question.

When Marie saw how the natural joyous radiance left the Colonel's face, and how after all the guests had gone he would sink into a chair, completely exhausted and sorrowful, she was greatly troubled. She began to ask herself: "Is *this* the Society of love, peace and brotherhood that I have for years dreamed of joining?"

One night she went to bed with a very heavy heart, but on awakening next morning remembered something her father had said to her during the night: "Base your theosophic life on the *principles* of Theosophy, not on the conduct of the *personalities.*"

"Very wise advice," the Colonel assured her when she related her experience. "The storms are always centered around some personality, and then the principles are forgotten. The trouble is that people will idolize some leader or teacher, then when they find the 'feet of clay' they are greatly disillusioned and condemn Theosophy. We must take as axiomatic the fact that all personalities are imperfect, we must *not* hero-worship *any one.*"

The crisis gathered momentum. People arrived from the Continent and America to discuss it, often keeping the Colonel talking till past midnight. Leadbeater was cabled to come from America and meet the charges.

Finally, on May 16, the entire Executive Committee of the British Section, with delegates from America and France, met to decide the fate of the theosophical teacher around whom the tempest raged. The sitting lasted three and one-half hours, during which the accused was called on to reply to the charges.

This was a critical moment, for if he denied them there would only be the boy's word against his. But C. W. Leadbeater did not deny them; he stated frankly, and without any signs of shame, that the charge was quite true. He had advised the boy as related.

The Colonel's diary for that day states: "The Committee adopted Resolution accepting his [C.W.L.'s] resignation in terms equivalent to expulsion."

Two days later Henry went to Paris where the members installed him "in a charming apartment, 36 rue du Collisee." From here he issued the Executive Notice about C. W. Leadbeater's resignation from the Society, fervently hoping that this would be the end of the whole painful matter.

In Paris the European Congress met in a fine hall, among

mirrors and crystals and walls of light-blue tint. There were several hundred delegates from fifteen different countries. On the second day the Colonel suddenly fell ill and was carried from the congress hall amid great consternation.

After a few days in bed he seemed fairly well recovered, however, and was able to attend a lecture by a promising member named Rudolph Steiner, and to sit for Mr. Taggart who was painting his portrait.

Henry spent 43 days in Paris on this, his last sojourn in a city he loved. Later, in Holland, gout and a general feeling of sickness came over him, and he spent his 74th birthday convalescent in Amsterdam, surrounded by "kind friends, lovely flowers and presents." When he was able to move about again he was taken by friends for his first ride in a motor car. But he did not enjoy it—"no autos for me, please."

About the middle of August he left Holland for Liverpool, where he was due to embark for America to attend the annual convention at Chicago—and, he thought, probably a new flare-up of the C.W.L. crisis.

Little Mother had spent as much time as possible with the Colonel in England, France and Holland. Before he left England he invited her to go to India with him later in the year as his permanent Honorary Private Secretary.

Marie Russak's heart really longed for this, but she was then at the beginning of a distinguished operatic career. A singing engagement at Bayreuth, Germany, later in the year, could not easily be broken—and several other obstacles stood in the way of going to India.

She explained this to the Colonel, saying that it would just not be possible to leave Europe in 1906.

He replied: "Make your preparations to join me in Italy in October, Little Mother. The obstacles will all be removed, and you will go home to India with me."

The Colonel disembarked from his ship at Boston. He was given the use of an apartment owned by one of the members, and his niece Louise Mitchell arrived from New York to be with him. Browsing through the Boston Public Library, he was delighted to find copies of all his books and pamphlets there, including his *Yale Agricultural Lecture* and his Theosophical Society *Inaugural Address* of November 17,

1875. He had no copy of the latter and was happy that the library typist made him one.

Moving on through Toledo to Chicago, he found the atmosphere warming up for the Convention. Many visitors called on him each day for discussions. The Leadbeater electric wire was still dangerously alive, and "the feeling very acute," both for and against C.W.L. The Colonel expected "rows at the Convention."

But, as often happens, the actual event proved much easier than anticipated. In his diary for September 16, he writes: "Opened Convention and managed things so that the acute crisis was averted. The Master's influence was strong with me."

After the Convention he went straight to New York, traveling in comfort with a "private room" on the train. He was still not well, living on broths with no solid food. But he kept going—lectures, letters, dialogue. He even let his companion, Louise, take him for a trolley ride to Grant's tomb. But he did not like the ride—"a most awful nuisance of noise and shaking. No more New York for me."

Some members of his family visited him, but he was disappointed in not seeing his brother Bob and he sadly missed Belle who had died since his last visit. One member of the old "Lamasery" group called to have a talk with him at his hotel. This was Laura Langford-Holloway, Belle's great friend. Much later she wrote a "Reminiscence" about this meeting for the New York Theosophical journal, *The Word*. It appears in the issue of October 1915.

After talking about Henry's late sister, who was the real link between them, and of other old friends, Laura prompted him to speak of William Quan Judge.

"Then, as he seemed lost in reverie, I laid my hand upon his arm, and said in a low tone: 'Henry, at such a time as this, and for the sake of the memory we shall both retain of this meeting—for me, whom you say you love for Belle's sake—will you not tell me that your old feeling for him survives? You know—'

" 'Yes, yes,' he interrupted, 'I know how you feel about him and always have felt. We learn much and outgrow much, and I have outlived much and learned more, particularly as regards Judge.'

" 'Yes, Henry,' I said eagerly.

" 'I know now, and it will comfort you to hear it, that I wronged Judge—not willfully or in malice; nevertheless I have done this and I regret it.'

" 'God bless you,' I said, and then I thanked him for his brave recantation."

Nowhere has the Colonel himself put in writing that he finally changed his opinion about Judge's actions and motives. But if Laura Langford-Holloway reported her last conversation with him faithfully, he *had* changed it.

Maybe, in the light of subsequent knowledge, he felt that Judge had not deceived him willfully and consciously, but had himself been the victim of deception by subconscious forces, or subtle entities, working either through his own mind or that of his adviser and helper, Katherine Tingley. Maybe he had decided, in the long view, that the whole matter was too deep and mysterious for human judgment, and agreed with the Irish theosophist and writer, George W. Russell (AE), who had written at the time of the Judge troubles: "Our only justice is compassion." But this is only speculation.

At the same New York meeting Henry remembered that Laura used to have good powers of precognition, and asked her to exercise them for him. He could never resist the chance of some fortune telling. She told him a few things about the future of the theosophical movement, including the fact that it would eventually regain its unity, then said:

"Written above your head is the word 'Come.' "

At this the old man jumped from his chair in great consternation. Then he confided to her that "Come" was the secret word agreed upon between H.P.B. and himself long ago. Whichever one of them died first would use it as a sign or password to show that any communication from the "other world" was genuine. Through the years the pact had gone from his mind, but when Laura pronounced the word, the memory of it came back vividly.

Laura writes that a depression seemed to settle over the old President as he wondered if her vision was a sign that his own death was not far off.

A few days later he was aboard the *Cretic* bound for Italy, where he planned to go on a lecture tour. The seas were calm. Henry was particularly careful about heights at this time because some soothsayer had told him that a fall would be the cause of his death. Nevertheless in mid-Atlantic on October 3, 1906, Destiny had its way.

About to descend a steep flight of stairs, he caught his toe on the edge of the first step and went tumbling to the lower deck, somersaulting on the way down. There were some eye-witnesses to the fall, and aid came immediately. The seventy-four year-old Colonel was carried to his bed, more shocked and injured than was at first apparent.

He was still an invalid when the ship reached Genoa six days later. Lowered to the wharf on a stretcher resting across the seats of one of the lifeboats, he was taken by friends to the Protestant Hospital.

Here he was kept by his medical advisers for 28 days. The Italian tour was canceled, but members of The Theosophical Society from different parts of the country came to see the President and, with the help of a temporary secretary, he carried on his official correspondence from his bed. He seems to have been quite happy and content in this hospital, noting in his diary that it was "homelike, clean and well-ordered." He also writes with evident pleasure that the Captain, First Officer, and Surgeon of the *Cretic* called to say good-bye to him before the ship left port.

But the most important of all who came to his bedside was Marie Russak. She had great news. While he was in America—she told him—his prophecy had come true: "The obstacles, one by one, *were* actually removed, and, strangely enough, without any efforts on my part." So the way to India was open for her. Now with her maid-companion, Miss Renda, she was ready to sail with the Colonel on the *Prinz Eitel Friedrich*. They left on November 7, 1906. Henry was able to walk aboard with the help of crutches. But using his leg made it swell again—"so back to bed and bandages." Little Mother made arrangements for one of the best stewards to devote his time exclusively to the invalid, who was soon able to sit out on deck. Here his meals were brought to him, and he enjoyed the sunshine while the deep blue Mediterranean glided past the ship's rail.

Marie Russak writes: "Colonel's helpless condition and genial presence made a strong appeal to officers and passengers alike, and in a sense he became the 'pet' of the ship. His deck chair was nearly always surrounded by people, and he would entertain them with stories of his world travels, especially of the mysteries of India. Seldom a day passed without his giving a talk on Theosophy."

At Port Said Marie took messages to his friends ashore, and some came aboard to see him. But in the Arabian Sea he caught a bronchial cold and for the next few days had difficulty in breathing. At Colombo, which they reached on November 24, many friends came out to the moored ship in Mr. Perara's steam launch to take the President ashore.

At his hotel in Colombo he began to feel very sick again, and the two doctors who examined him decided that he was in fact "dangerously ill with heart disease." He was put in a nursing home with two nurses in attendance. The doctors had grave fears that his heart would fail, and they would allow no one to see the patient except the nurses and Marie Russak. Gradually he improved, however, and on December 2 he was removed to the home of a Society member, Mr. A. Schwarz.

The Colonel loved Ceylon and its people but now, feeling that his life was drawing to a close, his one thought was to get home to Adyar. Thus, against the advice of his physicians, he sailed for Madras on December 8.

His diary, which had for weeks been written by other hands, now shows the Colonel's script again: "Stormy passage. Both ladies laid up" . . . "Ship and food execrable." Three days later after leaving Colombo they were inside the harbor at Madras. "Dr. Nanjanda Row came and helped me." The handwriting was shaky.

Describing the Colonel's last ride home, Marie Russak writes:

"It is about seven miles from the ship's landing to Adyar and I can say that practically the whole way was strewn with flowers thrown mostly by the hundreds of little outcaste children from the *panchama* schools which he alone had established for their education. On account of the Colonel's suffering, the carriage moved very slowly, and this enabled many of them to run alongside and in front of it. It was truly a beautiful sight to see their joy at the homecoming of their benefactor, and to see his loving response to them as they sang and called his name."

Chapter 24

LAST DAYS

December 1906 - February 1907

At the convention of December 1906 the President was not able to greet his guests personally—embracing old friends, looking after the comfort of everyone, presiding jovially at table—as was his wont. He was confined to bed, with his "left lung congested and heart dilated." Annie Besant had come down from Benares, now the headquarters of the Indian Section, to fill the role of Acting-President.

The Colonel was, however, carried downstairs to the great hall for the opening, and Mrs. Besant read for him his opening address. A few days later he was carried down again to close the convention. This was to be his last public address to an audience of Theosophists: for it he read his *first* speech to such an audience—his Inaugural Address in New York on November 17, 1875. He read from the typed copy given him at the Boston Public Library.

At the close he bade all the delegates farewell. The *Madras Mail* described the scene thus: "The delegates filed past the venerable old man—Hindus, Mohammedans, Christians, Parsees—some shaking hands, some bowing at his feet, some salaaming, according to their various customs, all united in one sentiment of love and reverence."

Henry noted in his diary that the Convention had been a "great success. . . 700 delegates—more than 100 over last year." His final sentence in the diary for the year reads: "Annie Besant says that Marie Russak had been sent to me (by the Masters) as she [A.B.] was to H.P.B. to serve her and make her declining years more comfortable and happy."

The Colonel's doctors warned him that he might pass away at any time. The thing that worried him most was the question of his successor. Annie Besant seemed to him most suitable as she was completely dedicated to the cause. But she had certain drawbacks. She was very involved in the work of the Esoteric School, and he felt she would not have sufficient time and energy to carry out the heavy presidential duties as well. He pointed this out, and asked her to find someone to take charge of the E.S., but she replied that this work had been placed in her care by H.P.B., and she could not be false to that trust.

Seeing how troubled the sick man was about this problem of his successor, Annie Besant "repeatedly suggested the name of a very old member who might be chosen," writes Marie Russak. But she does not give the name of the "old member;" it was probably Mr. Sinnett who had been Vice-President of the Society since Judge's secession. The Colonel, however, would have nothing to do with this suggestion. He wanted Annie as President, but she would not accept the necessary conditions. There seemed no way out of the impasse. "The Masters must settle it," he wrote in his diary on January 4.

During the next day he sent out fervent mental calls to the Great Ones beyond the Himalayas—and they responded. At 8:30 p.m. that day (according to the diary) Mahatma Morya and Mahatma K.H. appeared astrally in Henry's bedroom. Marie Russak and Miss Renda were both in the room at the time. They saw the two Masters quite clearly, and heard their conversation with the Colonel. Immediately after the two Mahatmas had vanished, Marie Russak wrote down an account of the meeting in the form of questions by the Colonel and answers from a Master. This account is still in the Adyar archives. Here is a relevant portion of it:

> *Question:* What is your Divine Will in reference to my successor—whom shall I appoint?
> *Answer:* (Master M.): Annie Besant.

> *Question:* She is so much in Esoteric work, will not that prevent her fulfilling properly the duties of President?
> *Answer:* We will overshadow her. . . .
> *Question:* Shall I appoint her with or without the conditions that I had in mind this P.M.?
> *Answer:* Conditions unwise, nothing binding.

There was further dialogue with the Colonel, and a little with Marie Russak, then "They disappeared, seeming to fade into the wall of the room. There were many people just outside the entrance to the Colonel's room, but none of them saw the Masters enter or depart."

So the matter was settled at last. Olcott appointed Annie Besant to succeed him as President. Of course the appointment would have to be ratified by a vote of the members, but the Colonel had very few fears on that score. Some old members certainly were against her, but she was on the whole very popular throughout the world. She would get the vote.

On the evening of January 11 the two Masters paid another astral visit to the bedroom of the dying President. This time it was to give guidance on another vital question. Marie Russak and Miss Renda were again present, and again the honorary secretary made a report for the records.

"We three," she writes, "had been discussing the question of whether or not Mrs. Besant and Mr. Leadbeater had been under a glamor when they had been studying together [apparently at the Master's feet].

"Suddenly we saw a light at the foot of Colonel Olcott's bed, which gradually took shape into a form, but very indistinctly.

"Colonel Olcott asked: 'Who is there?'

"Answer: 'Cashmere.'

"H.S.O.: 'Oh! That is the name I always gave K.H.'

"Answer: 'Yes, I am here—wait a few moments, the elements are troublesome.'

"After a few moments both Master Morya and K.H. appeared most distinctly, and spoke clearly in natural voices."

The Colonel asked the Masters if Annie Besant had been deluded, as she feared, about her occult work with C.W.L. The reply was most emphatic; there had been no delusion whatever, both she and Mr. Leadbeater had worked together on the higher planes under the Masters' instructions. What then about Leadbeater's teachings on sex? The Masters made it plain that they did not agree with such teachings. But they pointed out that if they were to wait for perfect human instruments before giving out some of the esoteric knowledge, no such knowledge would ever be given out.

"H.S.O.: 'Has he (C.W.L.) been wronged?'

"Master M.: 'Yes, but only in so far as the matter was made generally public.'

"H.S.O.: 'I am so sorry, Master. What can I do about it?'

"Master M.: 'Write and tell him that you regret the sorrow that has been brought upon him by the matter being made public. . . .' "

The Masters then went on to say that an article must be published for members of the Society, explaining fully that, as it was impossible for the Mahatmas to find perfect instruments to do their work, they took the best available ones whose karma permitted it. Also it must be made quite clear that the Masters were still behind and supporting the Society—and that they had worked through both Mrs. Besant and Mr. Leadbeater, precisely as these two had believed.

Marie Russak ventured to tell the Masters that she felt Mr. Leadbeater would do anything, make any sacrifice, for the Society, and asked if something could be done to help reinstate him.

The Master M. replied: "He will be put to the test;" then added in a kindly tone: "He has been a light in the Society."

The Mahatma K.H. gave Marie some personal advice regarding her occult work, then at the close of the interview, both Masters held up their hands in blessing, and disappeared.

During the next two days a letter to C. W. Leadbeater and the explanatory article were written, the Colonel dictating them to Marie Russak. "He had nearly finished the article and was especially anxious to end it with a strong appeal to the members. He lay for a few minutes in deep thought, and then said [to himself], 'How *shall* I end it?'

" '*I* will end it,' was heard in a deep voice, and there once again stood the Master Morya."

The Master dictated the last paragraph of the article—a fairly long paragraph—ending with the words: "Should any event bring forth seeming injustice, have faith in the Law that never fails to adjust matters. Cease rushing headlong into strife, or taking part in dissensions! Hold together in brotherly love, since you are part of the Great Universal Self. Are you not striving against yourselves! Are not your brother's sins your own? Peace! Trust in us."

The article appeared in *The Theosophist* of February 1907 under the title: *A Recent Conversation with the Mahatmas.* It must have been a shock to many people. The Colonel's letter to C.W.L. was approved by Master M., and was sent to console the exiled priest, who eventually returned to become one of the leaders of the Society.

Now the Colonel's mind was at ease on the two major questions, and his health seemed to improve. He was overjoyed about the many visits from the Great Ones, saying that it was like the old days in New York when the Theosophical movement was being launched.

At a subsequent Mahatma visit, when Henry was expressing his regrets about the many unfortunate conflicts and crises in the Society, the Master K.H. consoled him by remarking that periodically "the true soil must be turned to the sun," and therefore these disturbances were essential to real progress.

But as he lay on his sick-bed in those last days, Henry sometimes wondered what he had really achieved since walking away from his law practice, clubs, companions, and the pleasures that men hold dear.

One biographical sketch of the Colonel in the American *National Cyclopaedia* says: "The Hindu Revival in India was largely due to the initiative of the Society, and particularly to the public addresses of Col. Olcott. . ." Regarding the spread of the Society, it says: "From 1875 to 1906 he issued nearly 1,000 charters to Theosophical lodges all over the world, the majority grouped in eleven territorial Sections, and the remainder scattered over countries in which the lodges were not sufficiently numerous to form a Section."

But the real harvest from the pioneer work done by the Colonel and H.P.B. was not easy to assess three decades after the work began. The ideas sown took time to fructify in men's minds. Eventually the plants grew and began to flower, refreshing the climate of thought in many places, inspiring individuals, creating new organizations based on the concept of human brotherhood. Yet many who cull the flowers today have no idea who turned the first sod a hundred years ago.

As the hourglass of his life was running out, Henry felt impelled to put his personal as well as his public affairs in good order. Marie Russak, who wrote accounts of those last days, says that he showed no fear whatever of death, discussing it in a matter-of-fact way, and even speculating about his next incarnation. She gives some revealing anecdotes about the dying President.

For instance, in making sure that all his debts were paid, he sent for a Mohammedan tailor and asked if there was any debt outstanding.

"No," replied the tailor.

"Well," said the Colonel, "I shall not be needing any more coats. There are two left in fair condition; please give them to your son."

Then in thanking him for his good service Henry gave him a little present of money "because his wife was an expectant mother." The tailor's eyes were filled with tears as he withdrew.

This, says Marie Russak, was typical of the loving way he said farewell and blessed all those who had served him. And he was anxious to make peace with every one. "Afraid he might die without asking forgiveness of any people who felt he had injured them, he dictated to me several letters. There were two or three people in Adyar who were not quite happy about certain of his official actions. He sent for them, talked over matters, generously assumed the blame for making them unhappy, and asked their forgiveness."

Toward the end of January Mrs. Besant returned from Benares because the President had taken a turn for the worse. She helped Marie and the professional nurse take care of him. Frequently he asked Little Mother to read to him—especially from Edwin Arnold's *The Song Celestial*. Book Twelve of this was his favorite section, particularly the lines:

Krishna: But if thy thought
Droops from such height, if thou be'st weak to set
Body and soul upon Me constantly,
Despair not! Give me lower service; seek
To reach Me, worshipping with steadfast will;
And if thou canst not worship steadfastly,
Work for Me, toil in works pleasing to Me!
For he that laboreth right for love of Me
Shall finally attain! But if in this
Thy faint heart fails, bring Me thy failure; find
Refuge in Me! Let fruits of labour go,
Renouncing hope for Me, with lowliest heart,
So shalt thou come: for, though to know is more
Than diligence, yet worship better is
Than knowing, and renouncing better still.
Near to renunciation—very near—
Dwelleth Eternal Peace!

With these words of understanding, love, and mercy from the lips of the Krishna Avatar, the old man felt that even he might finally attain the great Enlightenment.

One day something strange and very moving happened in Marie Russak's presence. She describes it thus:

"As he was resting in a reclining chair by the window . . . I heard him give a short, quick gasp. I turned to see what had caused it. He had half risen and as he extended his arms, he cried, 'Old Horse!'"

Marie herself had clairvoyant power and she says that she saw H.P.B. there, and also Damodar—both in astral form.

On February 3 the Mahatmas paid one more visit to their old servant—the last during his conscious life on earth. The President's diary entry, in the handwriting of his honorary secretary, reads: "The Masters, all four, came this a.m., and told Col. his work was over. They thanked him for his loyalty and work in their interests. He was overcome with joyful emotion, jumped from his bed and prostrated himself at their feet." Mrs. Besant as well as Marie Russak seems to have been present on this occasion.

The diarist does not say who the four Masters were. Doubtless two were the Mahatmas M. and K.H., and a third was probably Master Serapis who came on an earlier visit during this period, and who had been one of the Colonel's first Teachers.

A few years later, replying to a query from author Alvin Boyd Kuhn, Marie Russak (then Marie Hotchener) wrote in connection with this event of February 3, 1907: "There was no possibility of hallucination for too many things occurred physically which could be proven. I did some writing even, and did two or three other things I was told to do, and besides the whole visit of the Masters to Colonel Olcott was to help him and to better the future of the Society. I also saw Master lift Colonel from the floor where he had prostrated himself at His feet, and put him on the bed as though the Colonel was a baby. Master Morya did it, who is seven feet tall. When the doctor came a few minutes later (after the Masters had gone) he scolded the nurse and myself for the fact that the Colonel had been out of bed—his heart and the condition of his body showed it, and the terrible excitement.

"We were told of things which were afterwards proven, and which none of us knew at the time; whole sentences were quoted from the Master's letters to H.P.B. which none of us had seen, and objects mentioned, the existence of which none of us knew, and many other things. . ."

In the days following this visit the patient began to sink rapidly. He expected to die on the 7th of the month in accordance with his fateful number. But he lingered on while his powerful vitality slowly ebbed away. Most of the time he was in a coma, or seemingly back in the past—aboard some ship or with friends in some far land.

At seven o'clock on the morning of February 17 the nurse called Annie Besant, Marie Russak, and Miss Renda. The end was at hand. Writes Mrs. Besant: "We sat quietly beside him, an occasional long breath being taken, till 7:15 a.m. A slight shiver ran through the body two minutes later, and he was gone. The three Masters to whom he had been nearest during his life, and his old comrade, H.P.B., were there in astral presence, and at 7:27 H.P.B. said: 'The cord is broken.' He was free."

That afternoon the body was carried on its bier to the big hall and placed in a flower-ringed space. On tables near it were the scriptures of the great religions. Over the body were draped the Colonel's national flag and the Buddhist flag which he had inspired.

For the funeral ceremony chosen representatives of various religions grouped themselves on the platform around Mrs. Besant. "The ceremony was opened by the Buddhists—as the Colonel was a professed Buddhist—and they chanted some Pali verses, and one of their number spoke a few words of gratitude for what the Colonel had done for Buddhism. Two Brahmanas followed, chanting some Sanskrit verses, and the Hon'ble Sir S. Subramania Iyer voiced the Hindu love and thanks. Then came a representative Parsi, who chanted from the Zend Avesta, and made a short speech of gratitude for the services rendered to Zoroastrianism by the Colonel. A fine passage from the Book of Wisdom preceded a well-spoken tribute from a Christian." For some reason the representative of Islam failed to arrive.

Finally the new President-elect made an appropriate and touching funeral oration during which she read the Colonel's last message, signed by his own hand, on February 2. These were his words:

> To my beloved brothers in the physical body: I bid you all farewell. In memory of me, carry on the grand work of proclaiming and living the Brotherhood of Religions.
> To my beloved Brothers on the higher planes: I greet and come to you, and implore you to help me to impress all men on earth that "there is no religion higher than Truth," and that in the Brotherhood of Religions lies the peace and progress of humanity.

At the end of the oration Annie Besant turned and addressed the body of the late Colonel: "And now, dear friend, we bear away your body; we bid you not farewell, for you, unborn, undying, perpetual, eternal, there is no such thing as death. We have served your body while we could, tended it, loved it, now we give it back to the elements whence it came. Brave soldier of Truth, striver for Good, we wish you Light and Peace. And by this dead body we pledge you our Faith—I to bear the standard of Theosophy, fallen from this

Olcott Memorial statue at Adyar,
erected on the place where Olcott's body was cremated

cold hand, if the Society confirm the choice you made, along the road as you have borne it; all to serve Theosophy through life to death, as you have served it. So long as this Society endures, through the years of an unmeasured future, so long shall your name live in and with it."

The bier was then borne by the Hindus and Buddhists to a spot on the bank of the river. Here in simple Hindu style they cremated the one who, thirty years earlier, had pioneered cremation in America. Against a background of slender, sun-lit palms, a great concourse of people sat watching the orange-colored flames lick the funeral pyre of one who had been the friend of all.

Early next morning the ashes were collected. Half was put into a casket to be dropped into the holy Ganges near Benares. The other half—at the Colonel's own request—was to be given to the sea, for he had learned to love the great oceans of the world which had so often borne him, and The Theosophical Society standard, to his brothers of every continent.

As the sun rose red over the Bay of Bengal, a small boat moved up the shallow Adyar River, in which fishermen stood in narrowing circles to net their fish. Out onto the pearly sea the boat went, out beyond the white line chalked by the breaking waves, out into the red-gold glory of morning. At last it stopped, and there on the heaving waters were cast the last remains of Henry Steel Olcott.

Appendix A

SOME HISTORICAL DOCUMENTS CONCERNING THE CHARACTER AND LIFE OF COLONEL H. S. OLCOTT

Document No. 1

Extract from a Report to the Secretary of the Navy (U.S.A.) from the Assistant Secretary, dated February 24, 1865. Taken from the Journal of the Senate of the United States entry of March 3, 1865:

"In obedience to your orders, to cause to be investigated the alleged fraudulent transactions of all persons amenable to this department, the services of Colonel H. S. Olcott were temporarily obtained. This Officer is attached to the War Department, is familiar with such investigations, and enjoys in an eminent degree the confidence of that department." . . . . .

Document No. 2

From an Editorial of the *New York Tribune* of September 22, 1871. The *Tribune* was at that time the most influential journal in the United States:

"Col. Henry S. Olcott of this city is not a politician, is a gentleman of unsullied record, widely known, and amply responsible. Chosen by Edwin M. Stanton, receiving the confidence of that incorruptible patriot at the outset and maintaining it through the most trying responsibilities to the very end of the War, gaining such reputation in the discharge of his duties that the Navy Department sought his transfer to their work . . . warmly commended by the Committee [of Congress] on the Conduct of the War, and when at last he insisted on returning to his profession, sent out with the highest commendations from all his superiors, Col. Olcott is a witness whose word nobody will question. . . . ."

Document No. 3

A paper signed by the Washington representatives of the leading journals of the United States, of all the political parties, recommending Col. Olcott to the President of the United States for the vacant office of Assistant Secretary of the Treasury.

Document No. 4

Letter from Mr. Le Grand Lockwood of Messrs. Lockwood and Co. Bankers, New York City, to the Secretary of the Treasury:

"I desire to say that I have known Col. Olcott from boyhood, that he is a gentleman of the highest integrity and of first-class ability. I cannot think of anyone who would be likely to fill the position of Assistant Secretary more creditably than he."

Document No. 5

Extract from a letter to Col. Olcott from Major L. C. Turner, Judge-Advocate of the War Department, of the date October 20, 1865:

"I am informed that you have tendered to the Secretary of War your resignation of the Commission which you have held since 1862. . . . . The responsibilities, difficulties and dangers incident to the faithful and fearless performance of the duties of your position, I have been enabled personally and officially to appreciate: it is my duty as well as my privilege, therefore, to say that the faithful performance of these labours required, in an eminent degree, untiring industry and energy, discreet and prompt action, and *unfaltering courage*. . . . . It is a grateful duty to certify that, during the past three years of turmoil, trouble, and fraud you have been energetic, prompt, honest and, fearless; and therefore, eminently successful. You are entitled to the thanks of all honest, loyal-hearted citizens."

Document No. 6

Extract from a letter to Col. Olcott from the Hon. John Wilson, Third Auditor of the Treasury Department, of date

May 7, 1866:

". . . . . The fidelity and ability with which you have discharged the onerous, responsible, and delicate duties entrusted to you by the Government; and the sterling integrity evinced by you, under all circumstances, are the best guarantees that can be offered to all who may seek your aid in future."

Document No. 7

Letter from the Hon. A. H. Green, Comptroller of the City of New York, to E. Delafield Smith, Esq., Counsel to the Corporation, informing him of Col. Olcott's retention as Attorney for the City Treasury in certain large suits pending. Dated April 16, 1873.

Document No. 8

Extract from letter from George T. Hope, Esq., President of the Continental Fire Insurance Company (the largest in the United States) to Albert Powker, Esq., President of the Boston Board of Underwriters. Dated Sept. 16, 1873:

"His (Col. Olcott's) experience and ability combined with his interest in the substantial welfare of the Companies and the Community, in respect to Fire Insurance, are well known here (at New York) and entitled him to be regarded as a public benefactor."

Document No. 9

Extract from Editorial article in the *Baltimore Underwriter* an influential organ of the American Insurance interest respecting the Official Report of the Second Session of the National Insurance Convention (a Congress of the officials of the several State Governments who by law have Supervision over Insurance Companies):

"No addition to insurance literature more valuable than this compact octavo has yet been published. . . . . Col. Olcott will receive the thanks of the profession as well for the judgement thus exhibited, as for the industry and fidelity to fact with which the entire compilation is marked."

Appendix B

CEYLON COMMEMORATION — AUGUST 12, 1967
THE SIXTIETH ANNIVERSARY OF THE
DEATH OF COLONEL H. S. OLCOTT

The following messages were printed in the *Olcott Commemoration Volume* published in 1967 in Ceylon by the Olcott Commemoration Society and edited by Saddhamangala Karunaratne.

Message from Hon. The Prime Minister of Ceylon

Today, we salute the memory of a man who, born an American, did yeoman service for the cause of Buddhism and Buddhist education in this country.

At a time when Buddhism was on the wane in Ceylon, Colonel Henry Steel Olcott came to Ceylon in May 1880 and awakened its people to fight to regain their Buddhist heritage. He embraced Buddhism, and by the blessing of the Triple Gem succeeded in his campaign to make Wesak an official public holiday. He continued with the assistance of the patriots of the day to establish schools and colleges for the education of Buddhist children. Colonel Olcott can be considered one of the heroes in the struggle for our independence and a pioneer of the present religious, national and cultural revival. Colonel Olcott's visit to this country is a landmark in the history of Buddhism in Ceylon.

Colonel Olcott contributed much toward world peace by enriching the moral and spiritual character of men everywhere. He devoted his early life to the service of his mother country. He was an agriculturalist and encouraged farmers to cultivate new crops by applying scientific methods. He introduced sorghum—an Asian crop—to America.

When hunger stalks the world today, Colonel Olcott's life and message has great significance. He was one of those who worked with a far-sighted vision, to keep the world from starvation.

The fitting way to honour his memory is to continue to work for the ideals and principles he stood for.

Sgd. Dudley Senanayake,
Prime Minister

Message from Hon. A. Ratnayaka, President of the Senate, Ceylon

It is a blessing to mankind that there appear from time to time men who dedicate themselves completely and unselfishly to the service of all humanity transcending consideration of race, religion and colour. One such man was Col. H. S. Olcott. It was Ceylon's destiny that brought him all the way from the United States of America in 1880. His arrival in Ceylon resulted in the resurgence of a nation, that had been suppressed by foreign domination. The Buddhist revival received an impetus unprecedented in the annals of Ceylon. He inspired men like Anagarika Dharmapala and a host of other leaders who led the freedom movement and thus adorned the pages of Lanka's history.

Colonel Olcott's ambition was to deliver the message of the Buddha to all men throughout the world—the message of universal love and compassion and thus raise all men to the level of Divinity.

Sgd. A. Ratnayaka,
President of the Senate

Message from Hon. I. M. R. A. Iriyagolle, Minister of Education and Cultural Affairs, Ceylon

Sinhala Buddhist Culture was at its lowest ebb in the latter half of the nineteenth century, mainly due to centuries of foreign domination and the resultant cultural decadence.

A hybrid form of Europeanised society was slowly but surely obliterating the Sinhala Buddhist Culture which had withstood for many centuries successive waves of foreign aggression. This cultural decadence was an erosion from within. Hence, its deadly effectiveness. Cherished ideals of traditional Buddhist education were being almost wiped out by repressive legislation enforced by the foreign rulers. The entire nation was of a lethargic frame of mind accepting without question the poverty and ignominy that came in its wake.

It was at this time that Col. Olcott heard of the beautiful Island Home of ours from the reports of the silver tongued oratory of the famous Ven. Migettuwatte Gunananda. He visualised a land where Buddhism in its purest form was preached to counter the proselytizing activities of the Christian missionaries. Having been nurtured in the freedom movement of America, which included freedom of thought, he saw that a visit to Ceylon would enable him to learn more of the ancient wisdom of the East.

Having seen the pathetic plight of the Ceylon Buddhist, Col. Olcott threw in his lot with heart and soul, for the regeneration of Buddhists of Ceylon. He was the pioneer of a national system of Education in this country. By the time he died there were 3 big Colleges and 205 schools which belonged to the Buddhists. This revival which benefited thousands of Buddhist children was begun in 1880 after the formation of the Buddhist Theosophical Society with the collaboration of Madame H. P. Blavatsky and a few others. The Headquarters of the Theosophical Society which was first established in New York in 1875 was moved to Madras in 1882. The years that followed saw the expansion of the activities of this society all over the world from America to Japan.

Col. Olcott designed the six-coloured Buddhist Flag which is now the international emblem of the Buddhists. He was instrumental in having the Wesak Day declared as a statutory holiday for the first time under British rule in Ceylon in 1885.

Today we commemorate the death of this noble man who passed away peacefully at the ripe old age of 75 years, on

February 17th, 1907 leaving behind a name that shall not wither by the passage of time.

"*Rupan Jirati Maccanam, Namagottam Na Jirati*"
"The form of Man withers, but his name endures"
—Lord Buddha.

Sgd. I. M. R. A. Iriyagolle,
*Minister of Education and
Cultural Affairs*

Message from His Excellency Cecil B. Lyon, Ambassador of the United States to Ceylon

I have much pleasure in associating myself on behalf of my country and the American people with the Colonel Olcott Day Commemorations which are being held throughout Ceylon. During each of the sixty years which have passed since my countryman's death, Colonel Henry Steele Olcott has grown in stature and significance.

In Ceylon he is thought of almost entirely in connection with Buddhism. But he was a man of many parts and there is another facet to the man which I believe is less known here, which I think it would be of interest to recall today when Ceylon is engaged in a serious drive to improve its agricultural production. I refer to Colonel Olcott, the agriculturist.

Colonel Olcott was only twenty-three when his success in the model farm of scientific agriculture, near Newark, New Jersey, led the Greek Government to offer him the Chair of Agriculture in the University of Athens. He chose not to accept the offer, preferring to remain in his own land and to devote himself to its welfare. During this period he founded, with Mr. Vail of New Jersey, "The Westchester Farm School," near Mount Vernon, New York, a school regarded in the United States as one of the pioneers of the present system of national agricultural education. He interested himself in the cultivation of sorghum, just brought to the United States, and produced his first book, *Sorgho and Imphee, the Chinese and African Sugarcanes*, which ran through seven editions and was placed by the State of Illinois in its school libraries. This book brought him the offer of the Directorship of the Agricultural Bureau at Washington, an offer which he also declined.

In 1858 Mr. Olcott paid his first visit to Europe, still interested in the improvement of agriculture. His report of what he saw was published in *Appleton's American Encyclopedia*. Recognized as an expert, he became the American correspondent of the Mark Lane Express (London), Associate Agricultural Editor of the famous *New York Tribune,* and published two more books on agriculture.

Colonel Olcott, in a speech in Bombay in March 1879, also stressed the possibilities of agricultural development in India, citing its natural resources, forests and other products that could be turned into national wealth. He cited the experience of the United States which in two centuries and a half had transformed our country from a "howling wilderness into a scene of busy prosperity."

Let us trust that Ceylon's efforts along similar lines will meet with similar success.

Sgd. His Excellency Cecil B. Lyon,
Ambassador of the United States
to Ceylon

Appendix C

HOROSCOPE OF HENRY STEEL OLCOTT
By Ralph Emerson Kraum

Born: August 2, 1832, 11:20 A.M.
Orange, New Jersey (Lat. 41°, Long. 74°)

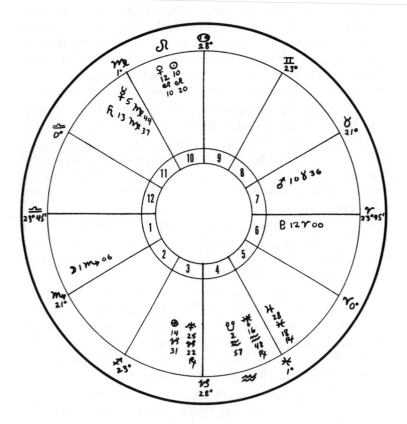

Copied from *World Theosophy*, edited by Marie R. Hotchener, September, 1932, Vol. II, No. 9, p. 716.

In order to make the following interpretation of the horoscope of H. S. Olcott more intelligible to the general reader,
we shall list the four major elements which go to determine
the type of the individual described by a horoscope: (1) The
twelve signs of the zodiac; (2) the twelve houses or divisions
of the horoscope; (3) the planets; (4) the angles or aspects
between the planets. Each of these elements has an influence
upon the other three, and their individual influences must
be blended in order to arrive at a decision.

In the Colonel's horoscope we find the Sun, representing
the Soul Qualities or Life Force, in Leo, the sign of leadership, which in turn falls in the tenth house. This house of
the horoscope indicates the individual's place in society and
his standing before the world, as well as his honor, ambition
and vocation. Synthesized, this combination would indicate
a great leader with force and determination, widely known
and much esteemed, yet of an unselfish, loving disposition.

The mental planet, Mercury, is in the sign of Discrimina-
tion, Virgo, which would indicate a critical, active and com-
prehensive mind; a student of science and philosophy capable of turning knowledge to practical purpose. The
presence of Saturn also in the sign of Virgo would emphasize
the tendency toward a deep and capable intellect fit to deal
with profound subjects.

Both Mercury and Saturn being in the eleventh house of
friendship, hopes and aspiration, would indicate his attraction to people of philosophical nature, would indicate a great
unselfish love for all he contacted.

The Moon, representing the personality, in the sign of the
secret forces of nature, Scorpio, would stimulate an interest
in occultism, and the Moon's good aspect to Mercury would
aid mental perception, giving a quick and alert wit. The
joint influence of the Moon in Scorpio and the Sun in Leo
would indicate much ability as a magnetic healer.

As to the adverse aspects present in the Colonel's horoscope, we may say that while such aspects create great difficulties to be overcome, to an advanced soul they offer
resistance against which the Ego may strengthen itself and
ultimately develop into perfection.

The Colonel's horoscope is, on the whole, a very powerful one, there being four planets essentially dignified: The Sun, Mercury, Uranus and Jupiter. Uranus, the planet of altruism is in good aspect to the ascendant and located in the sign Aquarius, symbolic of The New Man. . . .

—*World Theosophy*, September, 1932

Appendix D

H. S. OLCOTT'S WORKS

The Descendants of Thomas Olcott, (the edition of 1874 prepared by H. S. Olcott).

Sorgho and Imphee: The Chinese and African Sugar Canes. A treatise upon their Origin, Varieties and Culture, 1857. (This work went to seven editions.)

People from the Other World, 1875.

Human Spirits and Elementaries, 1875.

Eastern Magic and Western Spiritualism, 1875.

Inaugural Address of the President of the Theosophical Society, delivered at Mott Memorial Hall in the city of New York at the first regular meeting of the Society, November 17, 1875.

The Joint Labours of the Arya Samaj and its American sister, The Theosophical Society, 1879.

Spiritualism and Theosophy, 1880.

India: Past, Present and Future, 1880.

Buddhist Catechism. This work first published in Sinhalese in 1881, has gone to a large number of editions. It is used as a text-book in Buddhist Schools. Its English edition is now the 45th. It has been translated into French, German, Swedish, Russian, Bulgarian, Spanish, Burmese and Tamil, and several other languages, making 15 foreign translations in 1889.

The Common Foundation of All Religions, 1882.

The Spirit of Zoroastrianism, 1882.

A Collection of Lectures on Theosophy and Archaic Religions (delivered in India and Ceylon), 1883.

The Government and the Buddhists of Ceylon, 1884.

Theosophy, Religion and Occult Science, 1885.

The Peril of Indian Youth, 1885.

Psychometry and Thought Transference, 1886.

The Hindu Dwaita Catechism. P. Sreenivasa Row and H. S. Olcott, 1886.

The Golden Rules of Buddhism, 1887.

Posthumous Humanity, a Story of Phantoms (translated from the
French of Adolphe d'Assier), 1887.

An Epitome of Aryan Morals, 1887.

The Vampire, 1891.

Asceticism, 1892.

The Kinship between Hinduism and Buddhism. H. S. Olcott
and H. Dharmapala, 1893.

T.S. Solidarity and Ideals, 1894.

Old Diary Leaves, 1st Series (1875-78), 1895.

Old Diary Leaves, 2nd Series (1878-83), 1900.

Old Diary Leaves, 3rd Series (1883-87), 1904.

Old Diary Leaves, 4th Series (1887-92), 1931.

Old Diary Leaves, 5th Series (1893-96), 1932.

Old Diary Leaves, 6th Series (1896-98), 1935.

A Historical Retrospect from 1875. (Extract from the 21st
Anniversary Address of the President-Founder of the Society.)

The Count Saint-Germain and H.P.B.—Two Messengers of the
White Lodge, 1905.

Address of the President-Founder at the Third International
Congress of the European Section of the Theosophical Society,
1906.

The Life of the Buddha and Its Lessons, 1912.

Appendix E

TRAVELS OF COLONEL OLCOTT

THE following record is only of Colonel Olcott's travels out of India. His home was at the Theosophical Headquarters in India, and therefore on dates not mentioned in the record he was in India. The record of his tours in India alone would fill many pages, and is not here given.

1878	Dec.	17.	Leaves New York for England with H. P. B.
1879	Jan.	3.	Arrives in London.
		18.	Sails from Liverpool for India.
	Feb.	16.	Arrives in Bombay.
1880	May	7.	Sails for Ceylon with H. P. B.
	July	24.	Returns to Bombay.
1881	April	23.	Sails for Ceylon.
	Oct.	21.	Goes from Colombo to Tinnevelly.
		28.	Returns to Colombo.
	Dec.	17.	Returns to Bombay.
1882	July	15.	Sails for Ceylon.
	Nov.	4.	Returns to Bombay.
	Dec.	19.	*The Founders establish the Theosophical Headquarters at Adyar.*
1883	June	27.	Leaves for Ceylon.
	July	16.	Arrives in Tuticorin.
	Sept.	23.	Returns to Adyar.
1884	Jan.	21.	Leaves for Ceylon.
	Feb.	13.	Returns to Adyar.
		20.	Sails for Marseille from Bombay.
	Mar.	12.	Arrives in Marseille. Visits Nice and Paris.
	Apl.	5.	Leaves for London.
	July	23.	Leaves for Germany. Visits Elberfeld, Dresden, Bayreuth, München, Stuttgart, Heidelberg, and Kreuznach.

1884	Oct.	3.	Leaves for London.
		20.	Sails for India from Marseille.
	Nov.	15.	Returns to Adyar.
	Dec.	1.	Sails for Ceylon.
		17.	Meets H. P. B., C. W. Leadbeater, and Mr. and Mrs. A. J. Cooper-Oakley in Colombo.
		21.	Returns to Adyar with H.P.B. and party.
1885	Jan.	14.	Sails for Burma with C. W. Leadbeater.
		28.	Recalled because of H.P.B.'s illness; sails from Rangoon.
	Feb.	5.	Returns to Adyar.
		11.	Sails again for Rangoon.
	Mar.	19.	Returns to Adyar.
1886	Jan.	27.	Sails for Ceylon.
	May	4.	Returns to Adyar.
1887	Jan.	21.	Sails for Ceylon.
	Feb.	24.	Arrives in Bombay. Touring in India till Oct. 10.
	Oct.	10.	Returns to Adyar.
1888	Aug.	7.	Sails from Bombay for Europe. Arrives in London. Visits Paris, London, Oxford, Liverpool, Glasgow, Cambridge.
	Oct.	22.	Leaves for Bologna.
		28.	Sails from Naples for Bombay.
	Nov.	10.	Arrives in Bombay.
		15.	Returns to Adyar.
1889	Jan.	10.	Sails for Japan, calling at Colombo, Singapore, Saigon, Hongkong and Shanghai.
	Feb.	9.	Arrives in Japan.
	May	28.	Sails for India.
	June	18.	Arrives in Ceylon.
	July	8.	Sails for India.
		11.	Returns to Adyar.
	Aug.	8.	Sails for Europe.
	Sep.	1.	Arrives in Marseille. Visits Paris, lectures in England, Wales, Ireland and Scotland.
	Dec.	28.	Sails from Marseille for Colombo.
1890	Jan.	16.	Arrives in Colombo.
	Feb.	5.	Returns to Adyar.
	Oct.	12.	Sails for Ceylon.
		28.	Arrives in Tuticorin.
	Nov.	10.	Returns to Adyar.

1891 Jan. 21. Arrives in Burma.
    Feb. 7. In Burma.
        16. Sails for Ceylon and Australia.
        18. Arrives in Colombo. Tour in Ceylon.
    Mar. 3. Sails from Colombo for Australia.
        19. Arrives in Melbourne.
        23. Arrives in Sydney.
        27. Arrives in Brisbane.
        30. Arrives in Toowoomba.
    May 3. Arrives in Sydney.
        10. Entry in Diary: "This a.m. I feel as though H. P. B. were *dead*: the 3d. warning . . . *Cablegram, H.P.B. dead.*"
        12. Leaves for Melbourne.
        22. Leaves for Adelaide.
        27. Sails for Colombo.

    June 10. Arrives in Colombo.
        15. Sails for Europe.
    July 4. Arrives in London. Tours in England, and the Continent visiting Paris, Nancy, Stockholm, Copenhagen, Kiel, Hamburg, Bremen, Osnabruck and Flushing.
    Sept. 16. Sails from Liverpool for New York.
        28. Takes train from New York to California.
    Oct. 8. Sails from San Francisco for Japan.
    Nov. 1. Arrives in Japan.
        10. Sails for Colombo. During his stay in Japan, the "Buddhist Platform" is signed by Japanese Sects.
        29. Arrives in Colombo.
    Dec. 13. Returns to Adyar.

1892 Oct. 27. Sails from Calcutta for Chittagong and Burma.
    Nov. 27. Returns to Adyar.

1893 April 7. Sails for Rangoon.
        15. Arrives in Calcutta.
        23. Returns to Adyar.
    Oct. 28. Sails for Colombo.
    Nov. 9. Meets Mrs. Besant and Countess Wachtmeister.
        16. Arrives in Tuticorin with Mrs. Besant. "Annie stepped ashore at Tuticorin at 10.24'. 10″ a.m."
    Dec. 20. Returns to Adyar.

1894 May 14. Leaves for Ceylon.
          16. Arrives in Colombo.
          24. Sails for Europe.
    June 11. Arrives in Marseille.
          12. Arrives in Paris.
          14. Arrives in London.
          20. Leaves for Berlin.
          23. Arrives in Berlin.
    July 4. Leaves for London. Arrives in London.
          30. Starts on tour of English Branches.
    Aug. 10. Returns to London.
          24. Sails for India.
    Sep. 15. Arrives in Bombay.
          19. Returns to Adyar.
1895 May 5. Leaves for Bombay.
          10. Sails for Marseille.
          30. Arrives in Marseille. Leaves for Madrid.
    June 1. Arrives in Madrid.
          4. Leaves for Paris.
          5. At Zumarraga, owing to landslip.
          8. Arrives in Paris.
          20. Leaves London for Amsterdam.
          24. Returns to London.
    July 20. Leaves for Paris.
    Aug. 12. Leaves for Brussels.
          17. Leaves for Antwerp.
          21. Leaves for Homburg Bad.
          24. Leaves for Berlin.
    Sep. 2. Leaves for Amsterdam.
          6. Leaves for London.
    Oct. 8. Leaves for Paris.
          11. Leaves for Marseille.
          12. Sails for Bombay.
    Nov. 1. Arrives in Bombay.
          6. Returns to Adyar.
1896 Apr. 10. Leaves for Bombay.
          30. Sails for Colombo.
    May 3. Arrives in Colombo.
          25. Sails for Europe.
    June 12. Arrives in Marseille.
          19. Arrives in Paris.
    July 1. Arrives in London.
    Aug. 14. Leaves for Paris.

1896 Sept.	3.	Returns to England.
	19.	Leaves for Amsterdam.
	22.	Leaves for Paris.
	26.	Leaves for Marseille.
	27.	Sails for India.
Oct.	14.	Arrives in Colombo.
	18.	Returns to Adyar.
1897 Mar.	24.	Sails for Ceylon.
May	3.	Leaves for Tuticorin.
	5.	Returns to Adyar.
	14.	Leaves for Colombo.
	16.	Arrives in Colombo.
	18.	Sails for Townsville.
	26.	Arrives in Batavia.
	28.	Arrives in Samarang.
	29.	Arrives in Soerabaya.
June	9.	Arrives in Townsville.
	13.	Arrives in Rockhampton.
	22.	Arrives in Maryborough.
	24.	Arrives in Bundaberg.
	28.	Arrives in Maryborough.
July	2.	Arrives in Brisbane.
	15.	Arrives in Sydney.
	21.	Arrives in Melbourne.
Aug.	9.	Sails for Hobart, Tasmania.
	20.	Sails for Dunedin, New Zealand.
	25.	Arrives in Dunedin.
Sep.	4.	Arrives in Christchurch.
	12.	Arrives in Wellington.
	18.	Arrives in Pahiatua.
	21.	Arrives in Woodville.
	23.	Arrives in Wellington.
	25.	Arrives in Nelson.
	29.	Arrives in Auckland.
Oct.	12.	Sails for Sydney.
	17.	Arrives in Sydney.
	22.	Arrives in Bathurst.
	24.	Arrives in Rockleigh.
	26.	Arrives in Sydney.
Nov.	1.	Arrives in Melbourne.
	2.	Arrives in Adelaide.
	10.	Sails from Port Adelaide.
	24.	Arrives in Colombo.

1897 Dec.	2.	Sails for Madras.
	5.	Returns to Adyar.
1898 July	1.	Leaves for Colombo, on business of Panchama Buddhists.
	3.	Arrives in Colombo.
	8.	Leaves Colombo.
	10.	Returns to Adyar.
1899 Jan.	5.	Sails for Burma, with Mrs. Besant.
	9.	Arrives in Rangoon.
Feb.	1.	Returns to Adyar.
May	17.	Leaves for Ceylon.
	19.	Arrives in Ceylon.
June	13.	Leaves for Tuticorin.
	15.	Returns to Adyar.
Aug.	5.	Sails for Ceylon.
	8.	Arrives in Colombo.
Oct.	12.	Sails for Madras.
	15.	Returns to Adyar.
1900 Feb.	11.	Leaves for Ceylon.
	13.	Arrives in Colombo.
	20.	Sails from Colombo.
Mar.	6.	Arrives in Naples.
	7.	Arrives in Rome.
	14.	Arrives in Florence.
	20.	Arrives in Milan.
	28.	Arrives in Nice.
Apr.	1.	Arrives in Toulon.
	4.	Arrives in Marseille.
	7.	Arrives in Grenoble.
	10.	Arrives in Lyon.
	13.	Arrives in Paris.
	15.	Arrives in London.
	17.	Arrives in Edinburgh.
	19.	Arrives in Glasgow.
	20.	From this date till 27th, lectures in Bradford, Harrogate, Manchester, Liverpool, Sheffield, Birmingham.
	30.	Leaves for Brussels.
May	5.	Arrives in Antwerp.
	7.	Back in Brussels.
	10.	Arrives in Copenhagen.
	12.	Arrives in Göteborg.

1900 May 15. Arrives in Christiania.
    19. Arrives in Stockholm.
    24. Arrives in Lulea.
    27. Arrives in Stockholm.
    28. Arrives in Lund.
    30. Leaves for Hamburg.
June 1. Arrives in Amsterdam.
    7. Arrives at the Hague.
    8. Returns to Amsterdam.
   11. Leaves for Hanover.
   13. Arrives in Leipzig.
   18. Arrives in Amsterdam.
   20. Arrives in Paris.
July 4. Arrives in London. Lectures in England till 30th.
   31. Arrives in Paris.
Aug. 10. Arrives in London.
   13. Sails for India.
Sep. 7. Arrives in Colombo.
   12. Returns to Adyar.
1901 Jan. 7. Leaves for Ceylon.
   9. Arrives in Colombo.
   11. Sails from Colombo for Honolulu via Singapore, Shanghai, Nagasaki.
Feb. 13. Arrives in Honolulu.
   19. Sails for San Francisco.
   25. Arrives in San Francisco.
Mar. 20. Arrives in Los Angeles. Begins a tour of American Branches visiting: San Diego, Portland, Tacoma, Seattle, Vancouver, Butte, Sheridan, Denver, Lincoln, Minneapolis, St. Paul, Freeport, Streator, Muskegon, Saginaw, Toledo, Cleveland, Dayton, Washington, Philadelphia.
May 25. Arrives in Chicago.
June 14. Leaves Chicago to continue tour to Freeport, Streator, Muskegon, Saginaw, Lansing, Toledo, Cleveland, Dayton, Washington D. C., Philadelphia, Ridgewood, N. J.
July 27. Sails for Liverpool from Philadelphia.
Aug. 8. Arrives in Liverpool.
   12. Leaves for Rotterdam.
   14. Arrives in Bale.

1901	Aug.	17.	Arrives at the Hague.
		19.	Arrives in London.
		22.	Sails for Buenos Aires.
	Sep.	15.	Arrives in Buenos Aires.
		26.	Sails for England.
	Oct.	19.	Arrives in London.
		22.	Arrives at the Hague.
		24.	Arrives in Amsterdam.
		27.	Leaves for Genoa, to sail for India.
	Nov.	15.	Arrives in Colombo.
		19.	Arrives in Tuticorin.
		21.	Returns to Adyar.
1902	Oct.	27.	Sails for Ceylon.
		30.	Arrives in Colombo.
	Nov.	5.	Sails for Madras.
		8.	Returns to Adyar.
1903	Mar.	3.	Leaves for Europe on business of S. de la Fuente legacy.
		5.	Arrives in Colombo.
		7.	Sails for Marseille.
		23.	Arrives in Paris.
	June	7.	Arrives in Geneva.
		13.	Arrives in Amsterdam.
	July	2.	Arrives in London.
		11.	Arrives in Paris.
		30.	Arrives at the Hague.
	Aug.	28.	Arrives in Paris.
	Sep.	4.	Arrives in London.
		19.	Sails for New York.
		26.	Sails for Cuba.
		30.	Arrives in Havana.
	Oct.	24.	Sails for New York.
		27.	Arrives in New York.
		28.	Sails for Liverpool.
	Nov.	5.	Arrives in London.
		8.	Arrives in Paris.
		14.	Arrives in Marseille.
		15.	Sails for Colombo.
	Dec.	2.	Arrives in Colombo.
		5.	Returns to Adyar.
1904	Aug.	29.	Leaves for Colombo.
	Sep.	1.	Arrives in Colombo.

1904 Sep.	18.	Leaves for Madras.
	21.	Returns to Adyar.
1906 Mar.	15.	Leaves for Ceylon.
	17.	Arrives in Colombo.
	25.	Sails for Europe.
Apr.	16.	Arrives in London. Visits English and Scotch Branches.
May	17.	Arrives in Paris.
July	1.	Arrives in London.
	13.	Arrives in Brussels.
	17.	Arrives in Amsterdam.
Aug.	16.	Arrives in Liverpool.
	17.	Leaves for Boston.
	25.	Arrives in Boston.
Sep.	4.	Arrives in Toledo.
	9.	Arrives in Chicago.
	20.	Arrives in New York.
	25.	Sails for Genoa.
Oct.	3.	Accident on board the steamer: falls down a flight of fourteen steps.
	9.	Arrives in Genoa. Taken to hospital.
Nov.	7.	Sails for Colombo.
	24.	Arrives in Colombo.
	25.	Taken to Nursing Home, very ill with heart disease.
Dec.	8.	Sails for Madras.
	11.	Returns to Adyar.
	31.	Colonel Olcott carried downstairs from his room to read his Inaugural Address.
1907 Feb.	17.	H. S. Olcott passed away at 7:17 a.m.

Appendix F

LETTER FROM COLONEL H. S. OLCOTT—1894

In the archives at the Headquarters of The Theosophical Society in America is a unique collection of letters with photographs and brief autobiographies of many of the pioneer workers and leaders of The Theosophical Society, collected by Mrs. Sarah D. Cape at the end of the last century. Included in this collection is the following letter, written to Mrs. Cape by the President-Founder, Colonel H. S. Olcott, in his own handwriting.

Adyar, Madras
27 September 1894

My dear Madam

My Theosophical history is so nearly identical with that of the Theosophical Society, that I hardly know how to separate the two. From early manhood—say from the year 1852—I had felt an absorbing interest in the study of Practical Psychology as the master, if not the sole, Key to the mysteries of Man. I had devoted much time and my best thought to experimentation as well as to reading the best authors on the subject. I had developed clairvoyance in my first Mesmeric subject and cured my second of an inflammatory rheumatism at a single sitting. For twenty-two years, then, before meeting Helena Petrovna Blavatsky, I had been travelling the path now called Theosophical. My meeting with her, however, converted hypothesis into certainty as to the nature of 'Soul' and 'Spirit,' and that of the Elemental and other "viewless races of the air" and other kingdoms, and their relationship to humanity. First by her testimony, and next through her instrumentality, I came to know of the existence of 'Mahatmas,' the nature of their exalted 'powers,'

...scots, I took advantage of a private gathering of friends at Mme. Blavatsky's rooms in the year 1875, at New York, to propose the formation of a society for carrying on this work. This organization was decided upon, and became the Theosophical Society in due course. You ask me what work I have been engaged in. I reply that I have given my whole time during the past nineteen years to begetting, nourishing, directing and expanding the Society, until its Branches cover almost the whole earth and its objects and trials have been made known to most all nations. The strength of the Society has been derived from the Masters & Companions who stand behind us, its stupendous force is due to the willing cooperation of many humble folk workers in many lands.

H. S. Olcott, P.T.S.

Facsimile of letter (slightly reduced) written by H. S. Olcott in 1894 and the system of training by which they may be evolved. Believing that the spread of such knowledge by, among other things, the vulgarisation of the contents of Oriental Literature, would be of infinite service to this generation of irreligious, or half religious, or atheistical people, and in this epoch of decaying faiths and warring moribund sects, I took advantage of a private gathering of friends at Mme. Blavatsky's rooms in the year 1875, at New York, to propose the formation of a society for carrying on this work. This organisation was decided upon, and became the Theosophical Society in due course. You ask me what work I have been engaged in. I reply that I have given my whole time during the past nineteen years to begetting, nourishing, directing and expanding the Society, until its Branches cover almost the whole Earth and its objects and ideals have been made known to nearly all nations. The strength of the Society has been derived from the Masters of Compassion, who stand behind us, its stupendous growth is due to the willing co-operation of many unselfish workers in many lands.

H. S. Olcott, P.T.S.

INDEX

Adyar, T.S. headquarters at, 167;
Library, 224-25; picture,
226, 284
Alcock, Dr. John, 1
Appu, Cornelius, 154-55
Arnold, Sir Edwin, 146, 185
Arya Samaj, 95-96, 97, 105, 204
Aurobindo, Sri, 214

Babalu, 215
Bates, Rosa, 100, 103, 120-21
Beard, George, 36
Besant, Annie, 238, 248, 257;
lecture in India, 259-60; on
Judge's supposed fraud, 262-63,
267; accusations against, 269-70,
270-71; in Australia and New
Zealand, 270; forms American
branches, 278; on the C.W.L.
scandal, 290; Acting-President,
304; and Esoteric Section, 305;
at H.S.O.'s death, 309, 310, 311,
312-14; picture, 260, 290
Betanelly, Michael C., 52, 53
Bigandet, Father, 142
Blavatsky, H.P., meets H.S.O., 5, 26;
at the Eddy's, 32; investigates
"Katie King", 42-3; teaches
H.S.O., 46-48; background, 48-
49; marriage to Betanelly, 52-53;
and John King, 56-57; on
seances, 58-59; attacked by

Spiritualists, 59-60; as
conversationalist, 62; writes
Isis Unveiled, 69-72; over-
shadowed by Adepts, 70-71; portraits, phenomenally produced,
79-80; amusing tales, 87; departs
for India, 100-1; suspected as
spy, 109, 122, 218; phenomena,
115-18; temper, 115-16;
becomes Buddhist, 135; in
Ceylon, 137; in London, 183-84;
and the Coulomb affair, 190-
202; leaves India for Europe,
203; and Hodgson report, 221;
defends H.S.O., 227; founds
magazine, 228; criticizes H.S.O.,
230; to head the T.S. in occult
matters, 232; heads Esoteric
Section, 235; break with H.S.O.,
240, 242; and T. Subba Row, 242,
244; dies, 247; ashes of, 248-49;
statue of, 286-87; picture, 25, 234,
286. *See also* Materializations;
Phenomena; Society for
Psychical Research
Blavatsky Lodge, 228
Blavatsky, Nikifor V., 49, 270
Booth, John Wilkes, 18, 19
Brotherhood of Luxor, 47
Brotherhood, 223; the, xi-xii, 46,
47, 49, 119; of adepts, 45-46;
Universal, 222

QUEST BOOKS
are published by
The Theosophical Society in America,
Wheaton, Illinois 60189-0270,
a branch of a world organization
dedicated to the promotion of brotherhood and
the encouragement of the study of religion,
philosophy, and science, to the end that man may
better understand himself and his place in
the universe. The Society stands for complete
freedom of individual search and belief.
In the Classics Series well-known
theosophical works are made
available in popular editions.